WATKINS GLEN

1948–1952

The Definitive Illustrated History

By
PHILIPPE DEFECHEREUX

FOREWORD BY
CAMERON ARGETSINGER

ISBN 0-929758-17-X

Cover Design: Llew Kinst, Cupertino, CA
Interior Design: Ruth Kemnitz, Indianapolis, IN

Published by Beeman Jorgensen, Inc.
7510 Allisonville Road, Suite 117, Indianapolis, IN 46250

Printed and bound in the United States of America

CONTENTS

To Alexandre and Olivia

ACKNOWLEDGEMENTS

The author's greatest satisfaction in writing this book was to get to know a large number of fascinating and generous people with so much to tell and so much to share. Without them, this volume would be thin indeed.

At the beginning there were friends **Eric Davison** and **Harold Lance**. They contributed a majority of the remarkable color photographs contained in this book and helped identify every car in them. They they cheered us on tirelessly while independently proofing every page of the manuscript. **Bill Green**, Watkins Glen international historian, contributed a hand-written compilation of all entries for the 13 races, much information and memories, as well as several critical photos. **Harry Newton**, gentleman and author, offered a tough but very positive critique of the entire manuscript as it developed; he also diplomatically helped smooth out the style in key places. **Bill Milliken**, still managing his own company, provided precious technical assistance and shared some indelible experiences which enrich the story greatly. **John Fitch**, always the most pleasant gentleman, provided some invaluable perspective and contributed many personal memories, most funny and all too real. **Phil Walters**, **Fred Wacker**, **Denver Cornett** and **Haig Ksaiyan** also shared personal anecdotes and gave me direct feedback that make the book better. **Richard Faust**, of Columbia University, was a patient and terrific coach about the finest points of English grammar, composition and punctuation.

The **Argetsinger** family, particularly Cameron, Jean and their eldest son, J.C., were simply wonderful taking me through the old course, opening their archives and even their house when needed. They also provided essential perspective and an enormous amount of historical details. **Edward F. Ulmann**, reached only towards the end, spontaneously contributed photos, documents and memories about his father and was a hoot to deal with by E-Mail. **Jean-Paul Delsaux**, motorsport historian from Brussels, friend and author of several superb books, volunteered many contemporary photos of the European racing scene and offered precious guidance. Finally, **Bruce and Genia Wennerstrom**, through the Madison Avenue Sports Car Racing & Chowder Society, generously provided the forum of the Club's monthly luncheon to preview the book and attract many new helpful contacts, among whom **Jack Middleton** of University of Hartford was most diligent.

We are very grateful to these wonderful people and the many others who were so helpful in this great and worthwhile endeavor.

FOREWORD

Philippe H. Defechereux has written a unique history of the early years of racing at Watkins Glen with a backdrop of world events, international racing venues and motor racing politics as influences on this rural upstate village which embraced an exciting, little known sport in 1948.

At the time the sport of road racing was as foreign as the Russian alphabet to most Americans, who associated racing with oval track events. There were, however, a dedicated core of sports car enthusiasts, who wanted a place to race their sports cars. Philippe sets the scene at the beginning of his book with a run down of the glory days of Formula 1 racing in Europe.

America was ready. I believe that had I not organized the first post war road race at Watkins Glen in 1948, someone else would have done it very shortly but at some other place. I chose the original 6.6 mile Watkins Glen circuit through the streets and around the Glen, with European circuits in mind. When the European drivers arrived on the scene in 1961 for the U.S. Grand Prix they were thrilled with the original course, which they compared to the Nurburgring. They called it a circuit for brave men.

Philippe's interviews with men who were there 50 years ago gives an authenticity to the history. Their opinions and viewpoints may stir up more than memories. He has certainly captured the behind the scenes emotions of the times.

It was a happy circumstance for the racing world when Philippe discovered the wonderful unpublished pictures of the early days and was motivated to write this history.

Cameron Argetsinger

Watkins Glen, October, 1948. The 2.4 liter Healey Westland owned by Joseph B. Ferguson in front of the Mobil station along Franklin Street.

Introduction

War As The High-Furnace Of Prosperity

Europe saw the end of the Second World War on May 9, 1945, but the United States had to fight on for another four months in the Pacific before it could still its guns. Only after Japan formally capitulated to General Douglas MacArthur in the Bay of Tokyo on September 2, 1945, was the country at peace again. The "boys" were coming home thereafter, and war-time austerity measures were beginning to disappear. Passenger car production, which had been stopped in February, 1942, eight weeks after Pearl Harbor, was allowed to restart in mid-1945. As the year 1946 began, few Americans knew what to expect on the economic front, especially in view of the rapid disarmament soon promoted by the Truman administration.

What actually happened was an unprecedented boom which benefited nearly the entire population of the United States. In sharp contrast with Europe at the time, America not only had been spared from the scars of war, but also was blessed with plentiful abundance in food, textiles and raw materials. The American economy would reap its highest dividends in the industrial sector for having spawned "the arsenal of democracy." New mass-production techniques that had delivered, for example, a ship a day, and management concepts developed for the war machine, led

> "We raced because of the passion in us. Everyday people say that a race car driver, knowing the risks, is a madman. They are not toally wrong, except that the risks are, deep down, calculated. Still, our passion always made us forget the risks."
>
> Luigi Villoresi

within a short time to a fantastic rise in both productivity and new products to satisfy a pent-up consumer demand.

The first electronic devices and other novel technologies spurred a spiral of innovations. The country's factories, teeming with newly trained segments of the population, especially women, soon created a cornucopia of new and better products at affordable prices. Consumers responded by plunging into a vast shopping spree. One cycle fed the other and soon America was super rich.

In these early stages of the post-war era, though, car production was stymied by serious bottlenecks. Between early 1942 and mid-1945, all automobile assembly lines had been turned into weapons factories. During that period of time, for instance, Ford built nearly 60,000 Pratt & Whitney radial aircraft engines at its main Rouge plant and over 8,600 B-24 Liberator long-range bombers at Willow Run; G.M.'s Oldsmobile produced 48 million artillery shells, Buick 1,000 aircraft engines a month; Studebaker built over 200,000 army trucks and amphibious craft; Willys-Overland 380,000 Jeeps; and Hudson manufactured hundreds of thousands of components for P-38 Lightning fighters and B-26 Marauder bombers.

Converting all of these plants to civilian use all at once after the Japanese surrender, let alone introducing new car designs, was simply impossible. So after four years during which no civilian car production was allowed, it took a while for Detroit to catch up with the fast-growing appetite of Americans for new automobiles. Even though many "independents," such as Nash, Kaiser-Fraser, Packard, and Crosley, stood eager to fill the vacuum, satisfying this enormous demand from domestic plants would take some time.

To make things worse, bitter strikes severely affected Ford and G.M. in 1946, limiting total production to just a little over two million cars, or probably about half the market's actual need. Imports from Europe, whose impoverished car industry was famished for dollars, thus became a big lure for entrepreneurial dealers. Since European car makers would happily divert some of their meager output to America, there was an ideal opportunity for bringing supply and demand somewhat in better balance. Though no one foresaw the long term consequences on either side, America gladly opened its doors wide to European car imports. Of course, this "invasion" did not happen overnight, and before it fully developed, America would renew its ties with its own motorsports tradition: oval racing.

Convalescing Oval

The Indianapolis facilities had deteriorated greatly during the war years. By mid-1945, in fact, local real estate interests were looking at the racing site as a potentially highly profitable housing development area. Thus, the 30th edition of America's most famous car race, and all subsequent 500s, came close to never happening. Thankfully, a passionate individual took up the cause. American racing champion Wilbur Shaw, winner in 1937, 1939 and 1940, led a tenacious effort to save the Indianapolis track. He inspired Anton (Tony) Hulman, an extremely wealthy area businessman, to refurbish the facilities. Wilbur Shaw was made President and General Manager of the track, a position of high influence in American car racing, and he immediately set out to pursue his goal of re-establishing the Indy 500 as a premier event.

The first post-war Indianapolis 500 race was run on Memorial Day, 1946, and was won by George Robson in a Thorne Special. Four Maseratis were on the grid, including three private entries and a works 8CTF driven by Italian champion Luigi Villoresi. This strong Maserati presence

TOP RIGHT: Wilbur Shaw, winner of the Indianapolis 500 in 1937, 1939 and 1940. He is seen here in the Maserati 8CLT "Boyle Special" with which he won both the 1939 and 1940 events. This is the official photo for 1940.

BOTTOM RIGHT: George Robson and his "Thorne Special," winners of the first post World War II Indianapolis 500 (1946) in victory lane. Note the milk bottle, the Borg-Warner Trophy and the WIBC microphone.

undoubtedly was due to the fact that Wilbur Shaw had won his 1939 and 1940 victories at the wheel of a Maserati 8CTF Special. Between 1940 and 1946, Indy racers had not evolved technologically, and therefore the 8CTF remained a very good bet for ambitious drivers.

Indeed in the 1946 race, Villoresi was in fourth place with a shot at the lead in the 31st lap when a magneto problem caused him considerable delay. He still finished seventh. Two other Maseratis survived the ordeal to finish an impressive third and fourth. This was a good European showing, fueling hopes that Maserati and other famous continental makes might come back in large numbers. More significantly, this first post-war race at Indianapolis had proved a success with the American public. The Indy 500 was back on the world calendar of motorsports.

The Changes of 1947

In the early months of the following year — 1947 — three unrelated events marked the beginning of momentous changes that would transform America's automobile culture. In January, Kjell Qvale, Norwegian émigré and import car dealer in Alameda County, California, took delivery of his first six MG TC sports cars, shipped all the way from Britain by the Nuffield Organization, British distributors for the Morris, MG and Wolseley marques. Until he first

TOP RIGHT: Haig Ksayian at Watkins Glen, 1948, sitting in Briggs Cunningham's super-charged MG TC. A perfect picture of the "car that helped bring road racing to America."

BOTTOM LEFT: Bred to win – The Mercedes-Benz 60 and Belgium's Camille Jenatzy, winners of the 1903 Gordon Bennett Trophy. The race was held near Athy, Ireland, and this was the German marque's first international victory. Jenatzy, nicknamed the "Red Devil" because of his fiery red hair, won the 327 mile event averaging 49.2 mph. In 1899, Jenatzy had become the first man to break the 100 kph (62.14 mph) barrier in an automobile: an electric car of his own making called *"La Jamais Contente."*

beheld an MG — probably a TA, predecessor and near-twin to the TC — while on the road during a trip to New Orleans in 1946, Qvale knew nothing about the tiny eye-catching roadster. It was love at first sight, and soon he was West Coast representative for the British car company, adding his force to J. S. Inskip on the East Coast in New York. While seemingly insignificant, these six diminutive cars would become fertile seeds for a revolution in American motorsports.

On April 7, 1947, Henry Ford died at the age of 83. Only six months earlier, he had finally relinquished the presidency of the Ford Motor Company after 46 years at the helm. This man, who did more than anybody to make the automobile accessible to all, had shown little interest in racing after he became a successful automaker. Born on a farm in Michigan, he was first and foremost a tinkerer, then a businessman. He thought of cars as practical objects, as transportation. He thought of the business as a business. Power and thrills for him were in making money.

Henry Ford's attitude stood in complete contrast to the European tradition, which dated back to the early days of the automobile. Armand and André Peugeot, Louis and

Marcel Renault, the Maserati brothers, Charles Stewart Rolls, Walter O. Bentley, and Lionel Martin, founder of Aston Martin, were all constantly racing the cars their companies were building. Automobiles for them were an object of passion, an experience, an exciting way to make a living. For these European pioneers, power and thrill were in speed, competing and winning.

Henry Ford was succeeded by his son, Henry Ford II, at the presidency of the Ford Motor company. At that time, he showed no more interest in racing than his progenitor. Little did he know that just as he was taking on his new duties, a small new Italian manufacturer, in a village near Modena, was preparing the first car bearing his name for its first race. His name was Enzo Ferrari. Within a little over a decade, the wily Italian would have a profound impact on the new president of Ford and his giant corporation. A colossal battle of egos would eventually engulf both men, ending in a magnificent shoot-out at Le Mans in 1966 and 1967.

A few months after Henry Ford II took over from his father, the famous New York Auto Show opened its doors, featuring an international World Premiere: the introduction

The Austin A-40 in 1948 America. Pictured here are Mrs. C.H.A. Davison, Caroline, with twins Mark and Gail, in Detroit.

of the first new post-war British car, the small, bulbous Austin A40. The reason for Austin's choice of New York was simple: the British Labor government was now actively pushing all of the country's major industries to sell overseas under the slogan "Export or Die." The "stick" for this policy was the withholding of key raw materials such as steel and rubber; the "carrot" was of course the hard-currency earnings that the exporting company could earn. Austin had logically chosen the most important auto show of the time, in the world's wealthiest and largest market, for the introduction of their new car. The Austin A40 became a success. In the first year of production, 11,000 A40's were sold across the Atlantic, almost a third of the total produced. Thus, a second British marque was fueling a new trend on American shores.

All of this notwithstanding, when it came to racing, the chasm between the European and American ways remained just as wide as it had been in the 1920s and '30s, but with a difference. Somehow road racing had captured the imagination of a few influential Americans. This had three main causes.

Transatlantic Winds

First, there were several well-publicized pre-war participations at Le Mans, notably Jimmy Murphy's victory in 1921 (French Grand Prix), followed by several good showings in the 24-hour race later in the decade by teams driving cars bearing names such as Chrysler, Duesenberg and Stutz. Second, the 1936 and 1937 Vanderbilt Cup races, held on Long Island, NY, pitting American speedway specials against pure-bred European Grand Prix cars on a road race circuit, received a lot of publicity in the American press. The trouncing American-made racers received both years fired the imagination of many young enthusiasts toward European designs and open-road racing. Third, the appeal of a uniquely European form of automobile, the small sports car, designed and driven mostly for road racing, had struck the fancy of many G.I.s stationed in England or fighting on the continent between 1942 and 1945. The most memorable of those European wonders was the MG T-series, a fact from which Kjell Qvale and others would richly benefit.

Thus, as the post-war boom took hold, car-starved Americans began happily buying sexy imported sports cars from England, Italy and eventually Germany, countries which in turn desperately needed to export them. Living in their isolated world, Detroit's straight-laced, executives could never conceive of investing in the design and production of a sports car, let alone condoning its avowed hedonistic purposes. Therefore, as Detroit's accountants and financiers began investing in the designs of their first post-war models, they ignored sports cars completely. As a result of this blind spot, MGs, Healeys, Jaguars, Triumphs, Porsches and Ferraris gradually became visual magnets in the fashionable East and West Coast neighborhoods of America, as well as in trend-setting Hollywood movies.

These were also the years when road racing in the New World, though merely at an embryonic stage, saw its fate take a sharp upward turn. In 1946, the Sports Car Club of America, or SCCA, created two years earlier primarily to protect classic pre-war American cars from the scrap heap, became the de facto organizing and ruling body of American sports car enthusiasts. Taking over from the now defunct Automobile Racing Club of America (ARCA), the SCCA slowly energized itself to revive the road racing sport in the United States, where stadium-bound oval racing had been the dominant formula for over 30 years.

At first, the SCCA rules followed the ARCA tradition and decreed that road racing in the United States would be for amateurs only: no drivers could be paid for racing. The principles were stated as follows:

No SCCA member who wishes to compete in SCCA events —

1. Shall accept money for appearing in or winning any race or event in the United States.

2. Shall accept wages or other compensation for driving another member's car, or shall make his living as a driver.

3. Shall accept from any local sponsoring body transportation of cars or person, food, lodging or other expenses involved in attending a race or event.

The SCCA thus took its inspiration from the old British clubby attitude ("the right crowd with no crowd-

A 1938 Jaguar SS-100, as drawn by C.H.A. Davison, a Detroit car enthusiast and professional illustrator for the automobile industry. This was his own car which he intended ro race at Watkins Glen.

ing"), instead of the more modern and popular formula of the continental countries. Undoubtedly the result of long-standing Anglo-Saxon kinship, this decision pretty much limited sanctioned American sports car racing early on to the wealthy, and kept many talented dirt and oval-track racers off limits to this new form of motorsports.

Even though this rule seemed to run counter to the American Way ("We the people ..."), it held firm for 12 years and created yet another obstacle across the ocean for European teams, whose top drivers were paid professionals, and therefore were ruled out. Nonetheless, public passion for the sport in the United States was not going to be stopped by short-sighted rules. Especially after an inspired individual born in Ohio, but with deep roots in upstate New York, rose to make a big difference.

Watkins Glen, 1948. The Alfa Romeo 8C-2900 B of Frank Griswold in State Park before the race. Originally built for the 1938 Mille Miglia, the car was powered by a straight-eight super-charged engine delivering 180 hp. Why the racing numbers were painted in pale purple is not known.

chapter one
A Man With a Dream

As post-war affluence spread all over America, the councils of many little towns lost in the vastness of the countryside soon began to wonder about how to channel some of that wealth their way. The village of Watkins Glen, located in the northwest corner of New York state, was one of these. It had a mere 3,000 inhabitants and just three steady sources of income, only one of which had a significant potential for growth. Agriculture and abundant salt deposits nearby provided for a basic level of comfort, but they were about as much developed as nature allowed. Tourism represented both the third opportunity and the challenge.

Watkins Glen is situated in Schuyler County, right at the southern tip of Seneca Lake, the deepest and longest — 35 miles — of the Finger Lakes. Sprawling meadows, thickly wooded hills and trout-rich brooks surround the village and lake for miles on end in all directions, adding their attractiveness to the destination. Last but not least, a most unique and spectacular gorge carved deeply through thick layers of gray shale and featuring grottoes, cascades and swirling pools, cuts deep and jaggedly across two miles of hills due east of the village, ending right at main street, called Franklin Street. Despite such rich tourist treasures, Watkins Glen was on the mind of too few wealthy vacationers in the early post-war years because of its remoteness from major East Coast cities.

"Some people call automobile road racing the greatest sport in the world. One thing is certain ... few passions so quickly separate the men from the boys."

Ken W. Purdy

RIGHT: The famous gorge at Watkins Glen, which cuts right through the village east to west. The gorge is part of the Watkins Glen State Park which opened on July 4, 1863 and is therefore one of the oldest State Parks in America. The native Indians called it "The Devil's Hole."

Luckily both for the village and the future of motorsports in America, that is just when an opportunity presented itself in the person of a bushy-eyebrowed 24-year-old law student with a totally outlandish idea. His name was Cameron R. Argetsinger. Born in Youngstown, Ohio in 1921 and living there, he also had deep roots in Schuyler County. His grandparents lived there and his father owned a summer home by the lake. Argetsinger spent most summers of his youth in and around Watkins Glen.

His father was a successful corporate lawyer for Youngstown Steel & Tube Company. Having cultivated his own passion for fast automobiles, he inspired in his only child an early fondness for automobiles, "My father was a Packard enthusiast, and he sparked my interest in cars," remembers Cameron Argetsinger. As a teenager, Cameron began to follow the major races by avidly reading the *New York Times* then elaborate reports. The 1936 and 1937 Vanderbilt Cup "Grand Prix" races impressed him particularly, especially by the way the famed European marques such as Mercedes and Auto-Union all but wiped out their local, oval-bred competition. A dream was stirring.

TOP RIGHT: Start of the 1937 Vanderbilt Cup in Long Island, New York, which so fascinated young Cameron Argetsinger. The battle would be mainly between the Mercedes-Benz W125s and the Auto-Union C-Types (6.0 liter, 520 hp). The Alfa Romeo 12C-36s were already outclassed, and the American Specials were not even in the game. Rosemeyer won the race in the Auto-Union seen in the middle of the front row.

BOTTOM LEFT: Young Cameron Argetsinger standing by two family Packards: his father's (blue) and his own Darrin.

When Cameron turned 19 in 1940, he received his own Packard 180 Darrin Victoria convertible from his father. In the summer, he took his new car to Watkins Glen and exercised his driving skills by setting time records between the central intersection of Franklin Street and various nearby points, such as the villages of Montour Falls, Burdett and Odessa. Says a friend from those days, "Cameron always bragged nobody ever passed him." More important, the dream was taking shape in his mind.

One year later, in 1941, Argetsinger wed a Youngstown girl, Jean Sause. Children soon followed and, as the war in Europe spread globally, the young father joined the service. After his discharge in 1945, Argetsinger followed in his father's steps by applying to Cornell Law School and pursuing a passion for powerful cars.

Now wishing to own a Duesenberg, his inquiries led him to Russell G. Sceli of Connecticut, the then president of a fledgling SCCA. Through Sceli, Argetsinger found his Duesenberg, but also joined the racing organization. Full membership required the ownership of a true sports car, which the SCCA did not consider the Duesenberg to be. Therefore, he was first accepted as a "subscriber member." At least, he could attend meetings, make important personal contacts, and begin the realization of his dream.

That dream was to organize major road races after the European model, with the start/finish line on the village's main street, directly across from the Court House! "I was

TOP LEFT: Cameron and Jean Argetsinger in 1942, a year after their wedding.

CENTER RIGHT: The "Founding Fathers" of the Watkins Glen Grand Prix, from left to right: Arthur Richards, Cameron Argetsinger, Lester Smalley, Don Brubaker and Leon Grosjean, the Village Chairman. Seated in front is Flossie Smalley.

and eight miles with his ideal "model." Toy cars were placed on the prospective "tracks" to bring more life to his bold idea.

Gorgeous Gorges and Roaring Racers

Once he had a final circuit laid out to his satisfaction, Argetsinger began to invite friends and fellow enthusiasts to enlist their support or hear their objections. Time and again on these occasions, he would pick up his piles of magazines to recreate the race courses on the rug, one issue at a time. Says Jean Argetsinger nowadays with a loving smile, "Once Cameron's friends left the house, the task of clearing the rugs of all those magazines was always left to me." And by now, she had five children!

After the year-end holidays, Argetsinger sold the Duesenberg and bought an MG TC from J. S. Inskip, the

truly thinking of eventually bringing all the great European teams and champions," confides Argetsinger, "and to see Watkins Glen become the first American site to stage major European-style international road races annually, such as a Formula One Grand Prix and a 24-hour endurance event. The steep hills and challenging roads around the village had me convinced we could create a circuit not unlike the famous Nürburgring in the German Eifel mountains. That was my model."

While in Youngstown during the Christmas break of 1947, Argetsinger began to think concretely about turning his idea into reality. Using magazines as "road sections"and a large Persian rug in his family's living room as "land-scape," he traced possible circuits based on the roads radiating from Watkins Glen. Tapping deep into the extensive "racing" experience he gained roaring around the Glen in his Packard, he sought to match the reality of existing geography and a practical circuit length of between four

East Coast Rolls Royce and MG distributor located at 304 E. 64th Street in New York. The MG being an SCCA-approved sports car, the 27-year-old student was accepted as a full member of the club in January of 1948. Having thus taken another step towards the fulfillment of his dream, he decided the time had come to actually implement it.

Clearing The Hurdles

Argetsinger quickly proceeded to lay out his idea on three of Watkins Glen's most influential citizens: Allen D.

Watkins Glen Mayor, Allen D. Erway in 1948.

Erway, the mayor; Donald L. Brubaker, a former lawyer now hotelier and president of the Chamber of Commerce; and Arthur M. Richards, Secretary of the Chamber of Commerce, free-lance journalist plus photographer for the *Elmira Star Gazette*, as well as highly effective public relations man by instinct.

Emphasizing the tourism potential a Grand Prix could have for the community, Argetsinger outlined his plan for the circuit: the start on Franklin Street across from the Court House, then the course over the rolling landscape east of the village, 6.6 miles total, made up of uphill corners, straightaways, tricky bends, a narrow stone bridge and a long, steep downhill curve leading back into Watkins Glen. He proposed early October for the race date, the peri-

od when the foliage turns into wondrous bright hues, providing an extra incentive for tourists and visitors to be there. By the beginning of April, all parties had rallied to his cause and given him the official green light.

Next step would be to obtain the sanction of the SCCA. As in previous years, the club had a cocktail party and dinner meeting planned in Indianapolis in late May on the eve of the 500. Argetsinger knew that no official race could be run in America without the blessing of this new but powerful organization — the SCCA would take care of clearing the AAA Contest Board, the body that then ruled all and every form of motorsport in America. By May of 1948, SCCA membership had grown to over 100, though but a fraction of that number would be present at Indianapolis.

Argetsinger, bespectacled but poised and charismatic, presented the group with a concrete and detailed plan, including the proposed circuit, and pledging the full backing of the most critical Watkins Glen authorities. He secured the Club's enthusiastic support on the spot. Says Argetsinger, "The SCCA was 100 percent behind it. They hadn't sanctioned anything like this. We chose the name "Grand Prix" with malice aforethought. We knew full well what it meant. What a Grand Prix should be. We took a little poetic license." With the SCCA's support formally granted, the ball was now back in the court of Watkins Glen's officials, but of course, still very much on Argetsinger's lap.

The next meeting took place on June 12 at Montour Falls, a village adjacent to Watkins Glen about one mile to the south. The meeting's aim was to gain the final endorsement of all influential or important local people who would be affected, one way or the other, by the novel idea of staging a yearly Grand Prix in their midst. These men and women had a social club in Montour Falls called the "Manufacturers and Merchants Club," or M&M Club. They provided the locale and the stage for that important gathering.

It was a tripartite affair. Present were several men representing the community, four SCCA officials or technical advisers, and, of course, Cameron Argetsinger seconded by his wife Jean. For the community, Brubaker chaired the meeting, flanked by Mayor Erway and Arthur Richards. Representing the SCCA were the Club's director Alec Ulmann and its treasurer Nils Mickelson. They had driven all the way up to Watkins Glen from Connecticut in a 4.25 liter Bentley lent to them by a friend, Briggs Cunningham, for the specific purpose of insuring the success of the meeting. Backing them as technical advisers were two other early SCCA members: William F. Milliken Jr., director of flight research for Cornell Aeronautical Laboratory in Buffalo, New York, and associate Dave Whitcomb. All pre-

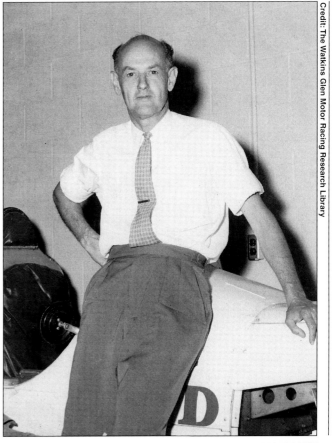

RIGHT: William F. Milliken Jr. with F.W.D. "Butterball" in background, 1948. Milliken would drive his first F.W.D. (a Miller) again at the Goodwood Festival of Speed in 1997.

The Original Meaning of "Grand Prix," and the Generalization of the Term

France ran the first car race ever in 1894. Actually a "concours," it was organized by a Parisian newspaper, *Le Petit Journal*, to determine if that new invention, the "horseless carriage," could now prove at least as practical as the "normal" carriage. The course started in Paris and ended through open roads at Rouen, 78 miles (126 km) later. Of the 21 participants who started, 16 completed the entire course. The prize money of 5,000 Francs was divided equally between a Peugeot and a Panhard-Levassor. A new sport, car racing had been created. Within a few years, it would captivate millions of enthusiasts across Europe.

James Gordon-Bennett, owner of the New York Herald, invented international car racing five years later, in 1899, when he put up the

Gordon-Bennett Trophy. His idea was to have national teams of three cars, representing individual countries, race each other once a year under what turned out to be fairly complicated rules (including combined accumulated times). The winning country would hold the Cup, or International Championship, for the next twelve months. Gordon-Bennett offered the Automobile Club de France (the first such club in the world) the honor of staging the inaugural race, given France's leading role in the early development of the automobile and its infrastructure. So the Gordon-Bennett Trophy was staked in Europe between 1900 and 1905, with France winning four out of six times.

Still, the French resented not having their own event organized according to their own rules and besides, the continental appeal of the Trophy was less than anticipated. The limit of three cars per national team, and the complex rules for eligibility and participation, had left the European public lukewarm at best. The Automobile-Club de France (A.C.F.) soon decided it must take over the matter, since in the eyes of its influential directors, a group of Counts, Barons, Chevaliers and industrialists, it was France's manifest destiny to run the most important motor race in the world. For these men and the supportive French press, this was avowedly as much a matter of retaining leadership in a *bataille industrielle* (industrial battle), as it was a matter of sport.

The way to win the argument, the French began to think, was to organize an annual race that would in every way be bigger than what Gordon-Bennett had created, but also be run under simpler rules of participation. Their first step in raising the stakes pre-emptively was to

offer a much larger purse, one that would be a truly grand prize, or *grand prix* in French. The prix was soon set at an astounding and truly grand amount of Francs that today would correspond to about $750,000. Then the entry rules were simplified, narrowing restrictions merely to a limit on engine capacity and fixed weight.

The French retained the idea of having cars painted by country of origin (blue for France, red for Italy, green for England, white for Germany, etc. ...) but individual cars and drivers were now allowed to represent countries without restricting the number of cars per country — presumably a big advantage for France and its numerous fledgling manufacturers. As an added benefit, the public would find it a lot

9. — Baron de CATERS
(Mercédès) Allemagne

Belgium's wealthy Baron Pierre de Caters at the wheel of the works Mercedes 90 entry in the 1905 Gordon Bennett Trophy held near Clermont-Ferrand, Auvergne, France. He finished 7th.

sent realized that a lot was at stake, not only for Watkins Glen, but also for the future of road racing in America.

Alec Ulmann made a dramatic and eloquent speech, followed by Mickelson, then Argetsinger. The preliminary reception was quite favorable. Everybody then gathered in a large Victorian room for dinner, where the idea was endorsed almost unanimously. The first Watkins Glen Grand Prix for sports cars would be jointly sponsored by the village of Watkins Glen and the SCCA. It was put on the calendar for Saturday October 2 in deference for the

clergy, though that constituency was not directly represented at the meeting. It was simply deemed impractical to get all local churches to reschedule their Sunday masses for the purpose of allowing a series of mid-day car races through the village streets.

Now, it was a matter of clearing all the bureaucratic obstacles and, most important, of getting participants and visitors alike to show up in sufficient numbers to declare the race both a motorsports and popular success.

easier to follow the winning teams' progress, since the cumulative time of team cars would no longer be a central criteria.

On June 25-26, 1906 the world's first Grand Prix took place near Le Mans around a 103 km (64 mi.) closed road circuit. The total distance to be covered was 1,238 km (769 mi.). There were 32 starters and after 12 hours and 14 minutes of racing, a Renault won, followed by a F.I.A.T. The winner's average speed was a remarkable 101.7 kph (63 mph). This performance was helped by an early technical development that proved itself during the race: detachable rims with tires already mounted cut the changing time for fresh rubber from 15 to less than 5 minutes. Most important, the public at large immediately endorsed the new Grand Prix formula as people were captivated by both the size of the purse and the exciting competition between individual cars and drivers representing nations. International Grand Prix racing was firmly established.

In fact, Grand Prix races following the French rules became world famous in the 1920s and 30s. The vast public aware of motorsports knew that "Grand Prix" races represented the top rung of the sport, fielding the fastest, most technologically advanced machines and the world's best drivers. Starting in 1934, as nationalist rivalries intensified across Europe, the annual Grand Prix championship even became an important political arena where a country's pride and industrial prowess were deemed at stake.

Thus, the equivalent of an "arms race" developed between Italy, France and Germany, each country vying to develop ever more powerful racers. The continental public rushed to witness epic races between Italy's Alfa Romeo and Maserati; Germany's Mercedes-Benz and Auto-Union; France's Delahaye, Bugatti and Delage; and England's E.R.A. By 1939, the public had seen 8- and 16-cylinder engines of up to 6.1 liter racing one another, some developing over 640 horsepower! This craving for Grand Prix victories went on until Sunday, September 3, 1939 (Grand Prix of Brno, won by Tazio Nuvolari) when France and Great Britain officially declared war on Hitler's Germany after the Führer refused to pull back from his invasion of Poland begun three days earlier. Shortly after the victory ceremonies, racing came to a screeching halt in Europe for five years.

Racing activities slowly restarted in Europe in 1946-47. It soon became obvious to the A.C.F. that it had committed a mistake early on by not trademarking the words "Grand Prix." For by then, any group of race organizers could call their new event a "Grand Prix" and thereby capture some of the halo of the great races of the 1930s, without fearing a legal challenge. By 1950, the international racing authorities came to their senses and renamed the top motorsports dis-

The cover for the German motorsport magazine Motorschau dated August, 1938. Racing cars and champions were used heavily by the propaganda machines of several nations in the late 1930s.

Felice Nazzaro at the wheel of the works F.I.A.T. (Fabbrica Italiana Automobili Torino) with which he finished first in the 1907 Grand Prix de l'A.C.F. at Dieppe, France. The car had a 16.3 liter engine developing 100 hp! The Italian company was restructured in 1906 to become Fiat Spa.

cipline "Formula One," then trademarked the term. It has been thus ever since.

Key men from both the SCCA and Watkins Glen were appointed to fulfill specific tasks to insure the success of the race. From the SCCA, Argetsinger would be general chairman; Alec Ulmann chief steward; Nils Mickelson starter; and Bill Milliken chairman of the technical committee. Also chosen from the membership ranks were George B. Weaver of Boston as scrutineer; Smith Hempstone Oliver — Curator of the Smithsonian Institution — of Washington D.C., as announcer; and Charles Lytle, as official photographer.

From Watkins Glen, the chief of police, Linwood Miller, and the fire chief, D. B. Stone, were put in charge of insuring maximum safety and maintaining good public order. Leon R. Grosjean, a retired senior executive of the International Salt Company, was named chairman of the local committee. Finally, Lester Smalley, owner of Smalley's Garage on Franklin Street, was appointed pit

Watkins Glen, 1948. George Weaver and his 1936 Grand Prix Maserati V8RI backing up from Smalley's Garage.

chairman. Drawn from a little sleepy town of a mere 3,000 inhabitants located in Upstate New York, these men, along with their SCCA partners, were to turn into leaders who would eventually change the face of international motorsport.

Don Brubaker would play a most important role. Born in 1907, he established a prominent law practice in Altoona, Pennsylvania in the 1930s. After his wife died in childbirth with their fifth child in 1944, he moved to Watkins Glen. Giving up his legal profession, Brubaker built a large tourist lodge on a hill just south of the village. Opened in late 1945, it was named Seneca Lodge. By 1948, Brubaker wielded much influence in and around Watkins Glen.

After the June 12 "M&M Club" meeting, each official quickly proceeded to take on their respective challenge. Among the toughest were getting official clearances for the race from the village itself, plus the nearby towns of Reading and Dix, the county authorities, the New York State Department of Public Works, the State Police and the Finger Lakes State Park Commission. Jerry W. Black, the local Assemblyman, was enlisted to facilitate matters at the State level.

There was another thorny and unusual obstacle to clear. Since the proposed circuit passed through the crossing of a main trunk line from the New York Central Railroad Company, the latter had to be convinced to stop its trains from steaming across the course during the race. Wheelchair-bound but nonetheless very mobile Mayor Erdway managed to convince the company's local manager, Frank Chase, to accomodate the Grand Prix: the schedules of the Central Railroad would be re-arranged on October 2, so that trains would only pass across the course between or after the races!

Meanwhile, Argetsinger and the SCCA spent the summer promoting the Grand Prix and recruiting worthwhile entrants from all over the Eastern half of the country. Famous motorsport artist Peter Helck was persuaded to provide a dedicated painting for the cover of the first race program. It was then decided to organize the day around three events: first, a Concours d'Elégance where stylish automobiles would be displayed for the public; then a

© Harold Lance

13

"Junior Prix" of 4 laps (26.4 miles), actually serving as a qualifying event for the "Grand Prix" itself. The main race would take place in the early afternoon and feature the fastest cars that completed the Junior Prix. Drivers who qualified for the Grand Prix would have to go round the circuit 8 times for a total distance of 52.8 miles. Finally, the field would be divided into four classes based on engine displacement, starting with the biggest engines:

D: Over 4.5 liter (over 274 c.i.)
C: 3 to 4.5 liter (183 to 274 c.i.)
B: 1.5 to 3 liter (91 to 183 c.i.)
A: under 1.5 liter (under 91 c.i.)

A race distance of less than 53 miles was certainly modest by European standards — Italy's Mille Miglia, as the name indicates, ran over 1,000 miles, and the Le Mans 24 Hour contenders of that era had to count on clearing over 2,000 miles to have a chance of winning — but it was still demanding for the expected field of pre-war cars and less than well trained drivers expected to participate in the new upstate New York event. After all, the difference in elevation between Franklin Street and the highest point of the circuit (School House Corner at 2.7 mile mark) was 670 feet, while the twisty, hilly circuit combined a hellish variety of road surfaces such as macadam, oiled gravel, plain dirt and, of course, an actual railroad crossing.

© Harold Lance

SURFACE CONDITIONS

FROM - TO	WIDTH	TYPE	NATURE
0 - 0.06	4 lane	macadam	smooth
0.06 - 1.3	2 "	"	fairly smooth
1.3 - 2.75	2 "	"	patched & somewhat rough
2.75 - 3.3	2 "	oiled gravel	somewhat rough
3.3 - 3.5	narrow 2 "	"	smooth
3.5 - 4.6	1-2 "	dirt*	high camber loose stones
4.6 - 5.9	2 "	concrete	smooth
5.9 - 6.35	2 "	macadam	fairly smooth
6.35 - 6.5	4 "	"	smooth

*Will probably be oiled, too narrow for passing; cars req'd to hold position at moderate pace.

NOTES
1. This map not accurate scale, but all important turns are shown, and mileages are correct.
2. Thickly settled area from 5.8 to 0.4 mile marks.

---- side road

**MAP OF COURSE
GRAND PRIX OF AMERICA
AT
WATKINS GLEN, N.Y.**

SPORTS CAR CLUB OF AMERICA

CIRCUIT LENGTH = 6.5 MILES

TOP RIGHT: Official Map of the Original Watkins Glen Circuit drawn by Bill Milliken at Seneca Lodge

BOTTOM LEFT: Watkins Glen, 1948. George Hendrie's 1928 Alfa Romeo 6C-1750 taking the first turn in the Junior Prix.

Safety First

The SCCA having not expected to stage a road race so quickly, had no formal written rules for racing available. Cameron and Jean Argetsinger enlisted the help of Bill Milliken on this urgent subject. They drove to Buffalo several times to develop those rules and make sure they would be included in the entry blank for all would-be participants. Alec Ulmann was also a key contributor.

Milliken, because of his experience as an enginer and a racing enthusiast himself, proved invaluable. Counseled by fellow Cornell Laboratory specialists, he wrote up the competition rules and safety requirements. Since Cornell had already done some preliminary work on the usefulness of safety belts, their mandatory use was written in the regulations. This was a remarkable world first. Helmets, though, were still qualified as "advisable." Says Milliken, "I was travelling around the country a lot in those days, and time was short to get the entry forms printed at least six weeks ahead of the Grand Prix. I drew the circuit's official map in late July while having breakfast at Seneca Lodge. I wrote most of the racing regulations, as well as the directions to Watkins Glen, while on a train to Dayton, Ohio."

For the circuit, haybales and snow fences were to be positioned appropriately at all corners; "no passing" restrictions imposed on certain sections of the circuit with corresponding signs planted to be clearly visible to drivers; and coordinated radio communications should be established throughout the 6.6 mile course. Argetsinger then worked with the State Police and Fire Department to determine how many emergency vehicles — fire trucks and ambulances — should be available and where they should be positioned. Consulting with Lester Smalley, they agreed that the pit area would be established on the West side of Franklin Street, beginning at the Jefferson Hotel and ending ahead of the finish line. Smalley's garage itself would serve as the technical inspection center.

By mid-September, 35 driving enthusiasts had officially registered qualified cars, which was deemed a good omen. Most of the big-engined cars entered for the first Watkins Glen Grand Prix were of pre-war vintage. That was not too dissimilar from the contemporary European scene, though Italian and British manufacturers were starting to spawn and field new nameplates.

The big difference between the two sides of the Atlantic was in public awareness and interest. While American sports fans were basically unaware of what was about to take place just south of Seneca Lake, an immense European public had again become race-crazy, flocking regularly by the hundreds of thousands to a large number of events which received wide and hyperbolic press coverage, even live national radio coverage in some cases.

A War-Torn Continent Filled with Hope

By the spring of 1948, car racing was back almost in full swing on the continent, with several new designs and makes spurring the excitement of spectators. As Germany lay in ruins and German drivers were banned from racing, Italian makers were feasting on victories with new or significantly updated cars. The ever so conservative French took the rest of the laurels by relying mostly on slightly

Grand Prix du Roussillon near Perpignan, Southern France, 1947. Raymond Sommer at the wheel of a Maserati 4CLT.

improved, big-engined pre-war designs. British makers, most affected by the devastation of war and a dearth of raw materials, were then just beginning to field new designs.

Alfa Romeo and Maserati, the two most famous Italian racing makes of the pre-war era, battled each other constantly in the numerous Grand Prix (single-seater, open-wheel cars) races. Alfa Romeo, with their Tipo 158 "Alfetta," and Maserati, with their 4CLT claimed most of the laurels from 1946 to 1948. These were upgraded pre-war models equipped with two-stage superchargers. Intriguingly, endurance races (for fendered, multi-seat sports cars) saw a third Italian make emerge as a winner almost right out of the gate. Its founder, Enzo Ferrari had been the racing director of the highly successful Alfa Romeo racing team in the 1930s. Spurred by his huge ego and vast ambitions, he had started his own car company late in 1946.

Ferrari's new racers were branded with his own name and the now famous prancing horse emblem. Most impres-

Siverstone, August 1950. Juan Manuel Fangio driving Alfa Romeo's famous Alfetta 158 in the rain at the Daily Express Trophy, in which he finished second.

sive, the Ferraris, powered by an ingenious 1.5 liter V-12 engine, almost immediately proved competitive. By 1948, the Tipo 166, a second-series Ferrari, was already roaring around race circuits. In its first season, this 2.0 liter model won two of the most illustrious and grueling endurance races known in Europe: the Targa Florio in April, the Mille Miglia in May. It completed a hat trick by winning the 12 Hours of Paris at Montlhéry in September. The world began to notice.

British sports car manufacturers were still in the recovery stage in 1948. Aston Martin, recently bought by industrialist David Brown, gave England its only noteworthy victory that year by winning the first post-war 24 Hours of Spa-Francorchamps in July. The winning car was a first and tentative post-war Aston Martin design, with tubular chassis and a 2.0 liter "Meteor" engine. MG's new TC model bowed in 1945, but in reality the TC was a very

modest update of two previous MG models actually conceived and produced from 1936 to 1939: the TA and TB. The success of the MG line of diminutive sports cars in post-war America, and the impact it had on driving enthusiasts, was a reflection of how far ahead in affordable sports car design Britain was, before World War II brought the country's automobile industry to its knees.

In 1948, over thirty international races were staged in eight European countries: Italy, France, Great Britain, Switzerland, Belgium, Holland, Spain, and Sweden, some drawing hundreds of thousands of spectators. Over two million Italians lined up along the frenzied Mille Miglia course, cheering on the heroic drivers. This was remarkable testimony to the sport's renewed vitality, given that the continent was still in a state of widespread destruction and impoverishment, as the Marshall Plan was barely beginning to take effect. But road racing had been a highly popular sport in Europe since the first town-to-town races in the early century. The return to peace in the spring of 1945 unleashed a heated passion that had been held in check for five long years.

As the early autumn of 1948 slowly chilled the air in the northern hemisphere, some of that passion was about to spill across the ocean, towards a quaint little village of upper New York state. Before "his" first Grand Prix even started, Cameron Argetsinger had already accomplished an amazing feat.

Watkins Glen - October 2, 1948

Finally, the Watkins Glen Grand Prix weekend dawned. With the national presidential election just a month away, the tight race between Harry Truman and Thomas E. Dewey barely distracted the local citizens from the amazing hordes of newcomers that had invaded their territory daily for almost a week. The race and concours participants driving proudly around the village streets in their splendid automobiles, added to their wonderment. These precious racers were each entrusted to selected local garages. By race day, over 10,000 visitors and enthusiasts had congregated at Watkins Glen, quadrupling the village's resident population. The police and fire department, plus the local chapters of the Boy Scouts and the American

Legion, were mobilized to help insure that everything would run smoothly.

The first true modern road race in America was about to begin, but the old racing establishment did not think it had a future. Wilbur Shaw, President of the Indianapolis Motor Speedway, predicted it would fail, "Continental people have been brought up on that type of racing, and appreciate the skill required negotiating the difficult turns, no matter how slow the turn might be. This is something I am afraid we will never be able to sell the public in this country." In these words confided to a participant, one could hear still-bitter echoes of Shaw's 1936-37 Vanderbilt Cup experience, where he and his rudimentary American-made "Specials" were whipped two years in a row on the twisty Long Island circuit by Italian- and German-made Grand Prix racers.

Thankfully, neither the spectators nor the participants were in agreement with Shaw. They were thrilled to be where they were, their anticipation running high. On that bright Saturday morning, October 2, 1948, the normally quiet village of Watkins Glen looked transfigured. The downtown streets, decorated with countless fluttering flags, were empty of cars and slowly lining up with files of spectators. Rows of haybales protected all corners that had been designated part of the racing circuit planned earlier by Cameron Argetsinger. The Jefferson Hotel, on the north side of Franklin Street, was filled with guests. A strange mixture of festivity, expectancy and sense of wonderment hung in the air.

As the autumn sun neared its high point above the Glen, fifty race entrants and participants in the Concours d'Elégance displayed their superb automobiles on the State Park grounds, adjacent to Franklin Street. Curious and dazzled spectators came by the hundreds to inspect what a local newspaper man called "the underslung machines."

Shortly before noon, the 23 drivers entered for the Junior Prix began to take their racers to their assigned grid positions on Franklin Street, two abreast. Real racing was about to begin, though there had been no time for any practice on this brand new course. The town and surrounding roads simply could not be closed to normal traffic for more than one day. Thus, the only practice any participant had

TOP RIGHT: Watkins Glen, 1948. The field as seen in the State Park's entrance area from the top of the gorge.

BOTTOM: Watkins Glen, 1948. George Boardman's 1936 Jaguar SS-1 Tourer.

experienced by the time the grid formed was either by speeding from their hometown on the way to Watkins Glen, or by driving around the course in prior days while respecting all road signs and speed limits. Most cars were driven to the race and if possible were expected to be driven back home. Truth be told, several entrants were just there to participate and "animate the landscape," as one put it. George Boardman was one of those; he removed the windshield of his Jaguar SS-1 "to make it appear to be moving more rapidly than I intend to drive it."

Without actual qualifying times to establish grid positions, these were assigned by drawing numbers from a hat — though the most powerful cars, class D, had first draw, then successive classes were drawn in sequence. Forming the front row were Dud C. Wilson and his 1928 Stutz BB

TOP RIGHT: Watkings Glen, 1948. The grid for the Junior Prix, the first race ever held in the village.

Briggs "Swift" Cunningham, Gentleman Driver

Cunningham was typical of the priviledged members of that grid. He was to have a great influence on the evolution of the sport over the next two decades. Known in racing circles as "Mr. C.," Briggs Swift Cunningham II was born of wealth in 1907, in Cincinnati, Ohio. His was a family of successful merchants involved in a diverse array of banking, shipping, and meat packing activities. As Briggs grew up, he experienced a life where yachting, private railroad cars, transatlantic travel and multiple residences in the exclusive resort towns of America were commonplace. Yet he developed a character blending remarkable strength, integrity and dedication to chosen goals.

Despite their wealth and the new century's crush for the automobile, Briggs' parents continued to prefer horses. Nonetheless, Briggs was given his first driving lessons at age 10 in his father's Pierce-Arrow, the family's first automobile, by the family chauffeur. He received his own first car, a Dodge phaeton, at age 16 as a Christmas present. He was given a new car every summer thereafter until he finished prep school. When he started college at Yale in 1927, he bought a brand new Packard 8 and had it transformed into a sleek two-seater speedster. However, having little liking for academe, especially mathematics, Briggs left Yale after two years at age 22, and married Lucie Bedford, a Smith student and avid sailor, in the summer of 1929.

Briggs Swift Cunningham II before his car racing days. Later, he would become the first American sports car team owner and spearhead the early American efforts to win the Le Mans Twenty-Four Hours.

The young couple boarded the German liner Europa soon after their wedding for what would be a nearly year-long honeymoon in Europe. The Cunninghams' first stop was London, and there Briggs ordered a pale yellow and brown Mercedes-Benz SSK for delivery in Paris, the newlywed's next stop. He negotiated a deal with the importer whereby he would rendez-vous with famed Mercedes Grand Prix driver Rudi Caracciola at the Paris *Salon de l'Automobile* and receive the keys of his new car from him in person. The Mercedes would also come with a factory mechanic who would travel with the Cunninghams and take care of the automobile while they toured Europe.

Briggs and Lucie thereafter entered the annual Concours d'Elégance in Cannes where they won a prize. They sojourned in Southern France for the rest of winter, racing their sailboat in a dozen

Two of the greatest German champions of the 1930s: Rudi Caracciola (left) and Bernt Rosemeyer (right) seen here at the Nüburgring. Rosemeyer died in January, 1938, while attempting to break the land speed record for Auto Union on a stretch of Autobahn near Frankfurt. Caracciola had just established the new record for Mercedes-Benz at 430 kph (268 mph).

regattas along the Côte d'Azur. Meanwhile, a mansion was being built for them in Green Farms, Connecticut and was scheduled to be ready upon their return. In the spring, they attended the 1930 Grand Prix de Monaco, the first car race Briggs ever witnessed. Bugattis took the first three places and the event left an indelible memory on Briggs' mind.

When he returned to America, Briggs continued to sharpen his competitive spirit in a series of regattas, as his wife was keen on sail-

Black Hawk Speedster, next to E. Mike Vaughn in his 1938 Lagonda Rapide. Behind them were George B. Weaver in a formidable-looking 1937 Grand Prix Maserati, and Charles S. Addams, wearing a deerstalker hat and sitting in a more patrician-looking 1929 Mercedes-Benz S Tourer.

The third row was made up of Frank T. Griswold in a deceptively elegant 1938 Alfa Romeo 8C 2900 B Berlinetta, and Briggs "Swift" Cunningham in his specially-built "BuMerc," short for Buick-Mercedes. It consisted of a Buick Century chassis and 5.2 liter engine, dressed up in a modified Mercedes SSK body. Heavy but fast, the BuMerc was rumored to be going from 0 to 50 mph in just 7 seconds. Fourth row consisted of George E. Felton in his 1927 OE 30/98 Vauxhall, and Kenneth F. Hill in his specially-built, blue-painted 1947 "Merlin" (Mercury-

Lincoln), a tube of a car with tandem seats and open wheels, dubbed "the Flying Banana" for obvious reasons.

Off They Go!

When the eclectic grid of 23 cars was fully arrayed on the straight, tree-lined main street of Watkins Glen, it was quite a sight to behold. Except for the MG TCs and one or two home-made specials, such as Ken Hill's strange Merlin, these cars had first come out of their respective factories between 10 and 21 year earlier. The scene seemed like a flashback to a local "formule libre" meet in a back province of Europe, perhaps circa 1937, though the differences in body styles, engine types and sizes were enormous. (See chart Page 20.)

ing and his mother opposed car racing. In 1933, Sam and Miles Collier, close friends from wealthy Westchester County north of New York City, with whom Briggs had attended Yale, finally got him hooked on road racing. In those days on the East coast of America, road racing's appeal was limited to a tiny circle of wealthy enthusiasts who more often than not just raced around private estates at speeds rarely exceeding 35 mph.

By 1939, Briggs was addicted enough to commission his own car, an American special. He asked Charles Chayne, chief engineer at Buick, to design a roadster made up mostly of domestic components, but capable of rivaling the famed Mercedes-Benz SS model, which had won many major European road races, including the 1931 Mille Miglia. Chayne picked a Buick Century chassis and engine as the basis for Cunningham's wish, as that model was then one of the fastest stock cars on dirt tracks. He boosted the 5245 cc (320 c.i.) in-line eight engine by increasing its compression ratio to 9.5:1 and replacing its standard camshaft with a racing version; then he repositioned the powerplant further back and lower in the chassis to improve handling.

It was up to Briggs to find a "coach builder," and his friend Byron Jersey of Bridgeport, Connecticut, was in this case the right man to finish the job. Having found the body of a wrecked SSK at Zumbach in New York, Byron Jersey and his men lowered the front sheet metal, including the grille, and adapted it to the Buick underpinnings. They achieved a remarkably balanced aesthetic job for a car with a 105-in.

wheelbase and weighing 2,840 lbs. The silver blue color chosen for its finish even gave it a deceptively gentle look. This centaur of a car quickly became known as the "BuMerc," a name and concept that would make many hairs stand on end in Stuttgart. Though a bit heavy, it was fast, rumored to be capable of going from 0 to 50 mph in just 7 seconds.

The BuMerc was raced only once in October, 1940 at the New York World Fair's Grand Prix. With Briggs' friend Miles Collier at the wheel, the car was second with a shot at the lead when it crashed into a lamp pole three laps from the finish. Shortly thereafter, war in Europe interrupted all further racing in America. Briggs went to flight school and, after being rejected by the U.S. Navy, joined the Civil Air Patrol. He flew his own seaplane off the Florida coast on the lookout for German submarines.

Now, eight years later, there sat Briggs Cunningham at the wheel of the thoroughly refurbished BuMerc on the grid of the qualifying Junior Prix at Watkins Glen, and with a good shot at victory. Though probably the wealthiest of the contestants, Cunningham was in like company. Charles Addams was the famous New Yorker cartoonist whose work would later inspire a movie and one of the country's first popular TV series: The Addams Family. Frank Griswold owned a precision tool company in Wayne, Pennsylvania and also had the Alfa Romeo disributorship for the Northeast. George Weaver, from Boston, was the son of the Chief Engineer for the Indian Motorcycle Company

Watkins Glen, 1948. The famous BuMerc in action, with Briggs Cunningham at the wheel. This turn was known as "Thrill Curve" as it marked the end of the long downhill stretch called "Big Bend" and the return into village streets. The flatiron building at the corner was then owned by Kelly & Son, distributors for Genessee beer.

of Springfield, Massachussetts; he was also one of the founders of A.R.C.A. and a good friend of Briggs Cunningham. Felton was a Colonel in the U.S. Army, and had the title of director of production, National Security Resources Board. Milliken sat about mid-grid in his own Bugatti T-35 A which he had bought for $2,000 from Russ Sceli in late 1946; the French car had been fielded a few times in the A.R.C.A. races. It was definitely an elite field.

Entrant	Car	Engine Type	Displacement	Body Type	(Seats)
Addams	Mercedes-Benz S	Straight-6 superch	6789 cc	Tourer	(4)
Wilson	Stutz BB Black Hawk	Straight-8	4893 cc	Roadster	(2)
Cunningham	BuMerc	Straight-8	5245 cc	Roadster (*)	(2)
Weaver	Maserati V8RI	V-8 superch.	4788 cc	Open-wheeler	(1)
Felton	Vauxhall OE 30/98	Straight-4	4224 cc	Tourer (*)	(4)
Griswold	Alfa Romeo 8C 2900	Straight-8 superch.	2905 cc	Coupe	(2)
Milliken	Bugatti T-35 A	Straight-8	1955 cc	Open-wheeler	(2)
M. Collier	MG TC	Straight-4 superch.	1250 cc	Roadster	(2)

(*) Fenders removed

© Harold Lance

CENTER LEFT: Watkins Glen, 1948. Col. George Felton's Vauxhall OE 30/98 in the paddock. It was nicknamed "Quicksilver."

BOTTOM LEFT: Watkins Glen, 1948, Junior Prix. George Weaver's Maserati V8RI leads Frank Griswold's Alfa Romeo 8C-2900 B at turn one. The BuMerc can be seen in third place. Note the early Fall leaves caught in the Alfa Romeo's radiator grille.

BOTTOM RIGHT: Watkins Glen, 1948. Frank Friswold's Alfa Romeo takes "Thrill Curve."

Despite the diverse nature of its appearance and composition, this grid signified the dawn of modern American sports car racing. At 12:30, SCCA's Nils Mickelson dropped the green flag, hand-sewn by his wife less than a week earlier. A thunderous roar filled Franklin Street as the racers lunged ahead. Milliken best describes what lay ahead for the daredevil contestants, once they left the village streets and turned right then left up Old Corning Hill Road, "Down the long stretch from White House corner, the driver has his hands full as the car takes punishment from the surface roughness and he wrestles with the dips and camber changes of the road. He slows slightly, negotiates the bends, then finally brakes and shifts for Schoolhouse Turn, and literally dives down toward Stone Bridge. Another shift, more heavy braking, and he is past the bridge, and accelerating through the valley. A series of tricky bends finds him approaching Archie Smith's Corner, which must be taken in low gear and at moderate pace, and then a fast bit of gravel leading to the railway crossing. At this point the harder sprung machines aviated for some distance as they took the tracks at unabated speed. Seconds later, with Friar's Bend behind, they may be seen at really high speed on that long sweeping downhill stretch known as Big Bend. Skill and judgment are at a premium, as speed must be reduced for the famous "S" back onto Franklin Street, and then a smooth and glorious run up the home stretch."

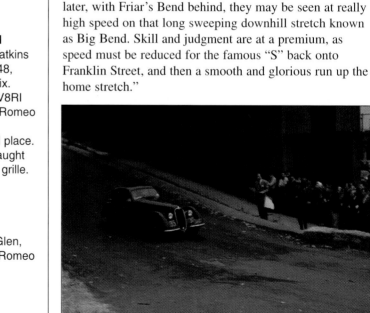

© Harold Lance

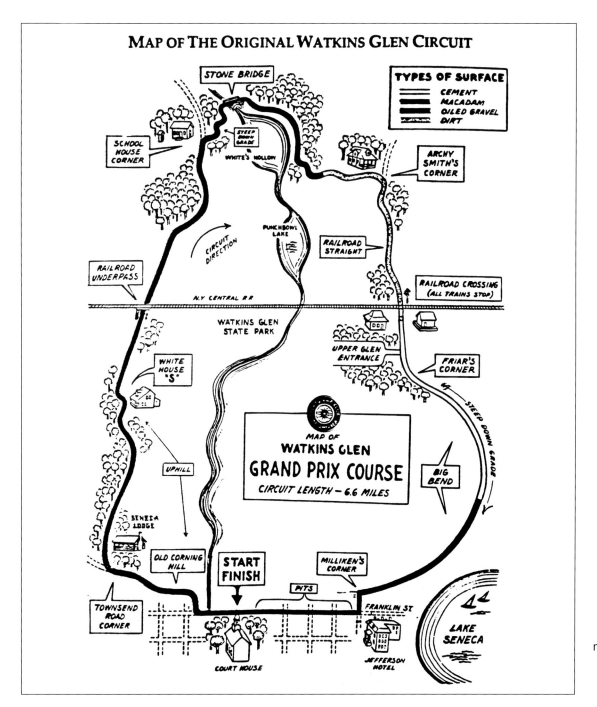

Map of the Original Watkins Glen Circuit
Drawn by Sam Cobean, famed New Yorker magazine cartoonist, and summer resident of Watkins Glen

© Harold Lance

© Harold Lance

© Don O'Reilly

TOP LEFT: Watkins Glen, 1948, Junior Prix. The first turn of the first race in the village streets. Cameron Argetsinger in the red MG TC (number 2) is followed by George Caswell's B.N.C. (number 5), Otto Linton's MG J4 (with the big monicker), and four more TCs: Dean Bedford's (number 3), Denver Cornett's (number 7), Phil Stiles' (number 29) and Bill Gallagher's (number 14). To the left is the tail of Bob Gegen's Bugatti T-38.

CENTER LEFT: Watkins Glen, 1948, Junior Prix. The first turn of the first race in the village streets. I.J. Brundage's 1931 Duesenberg (number 33) leads Sam Collier's supercharged MG TC (number 4), Bill Milliken's Bugatti T-35A (number 21) and Haig Ksayian driving Briggs Cunningham's supercharged MG TC.

BOTTOM LEFT: Watkins Glen, 1948, Junior Prix. The first pass at Stone Bridge, "Poison 'Lil" leads Cunningham's BuMerc and Griswold's Alfa Romeo in a very hot early race.

Seconds after the green flag was dropped the howling pack turned right less than two town blocks past the starting line, then quickly left up Old Corning Hill, then right again around Seneca Lodge to tackle the uphill stretch of road leading to the White House "S" turn. By now the spectators standing along Franklin Street, nostrils still filled with the novel scent of burnt Castor oil, could only hear a muted roar, muffled by the woods and steadily diminishing in the distance. The excitement turned to who would re-appear first at the northern end of Franklin Street in what "experts" had predicted would be about seven minutes.

Less than 6 minutes later, the growing roar of engines was heard again from the other side of town and all heads in the grandstands turned in the direction of the Jefferson, with the lake surface shimmering just beyond. First to appear back into Franklin Street was a red *monoposto* with the menacing black snout: Weaver's Maserati. It crossed the start/finish line 6 minutes and 17.4 seconds after the start, averaging an impressive 63 mph on this first historic lap. Chasing him for the lead was another Italian car, Griswold's blue Alfa Romeo, then the first "American special," Cunningham's BuMerc.

It was little wonder that the Maserati V8RI was in the lead. Not only was Weaver an experienced driver, but his car, nicknamed "Poison Lil," was clearly the most potent entry in the race. Built in 1936 for European Grand Prix races by the Maserati works, it was powered by a 4.8 liter supercharged V-8 racing engine capable of delivering 320 hp at 5300 rpm. In a flat straight, "Poison Lil" was capable of reaching over 140 mph! Weaver's car was chassis number 4504 — one of four such models built. It was first acquired by Weaver in 1947 to compete in road races after it failed to finish in the 1937 Vanderbilt Cup (Mauri Rose at the wheel), then the 1938, 1939 and 1940 Indy 500s.

Griswold's Alfa Romeo Berlinetta was also a strong contender. Built by the Milanese factory in 1938 on a 8C-35 Grand Prix racer chassis, it featured four-wheel independent suspension and was powered by a supercharged 2.9 liter straight-eight engine delivering up to 180 hp. Its top speed was over 130 mph and its handling was superb. A similar car had won the first post-war Mille Miglia in 1947. The long-hooded body, made by Italian coachbuilder

Touring, was also aerodynamically efficient for the times, important in the dive down Big Bend.

In fact, before the second lap was even over, Griswold and his Alfa Romeo were in the lead. Weaver's Maserati, suffering from the only-too-frequent Maserati disease of unreliability, experienced brake failure and the Bostonian had to drop out. That put Cunningham and his BuMerc in the second spot, pursued by Haig Ksayian of Trenton, New Jersey, in a supercharged MG TC lent to him by the man driving the blue car just ahead. Argetsinger, driving a normally-aspirated MG, was enjoying the drive of his life in the middle of the field, just as he had intended when he came up with the whole scheme.

A Bridge Too Fast

The first scary moment of the Junior Prix happened at the northern edge of the circuit, just about that moment. Denver B. Cornett Jr., of Louisville, Kentucky, then only 22 and driving another "standard" MG TC, tells the story, "I entered Stone Bridge too fast and drifted out of control exiting the bridge. The car fishtailed as I counter-steered, then plunged off the road to the right into the boulder-strewn riverbed below. The MG rolled over two and a half

TOP RIGHT: Watkins Glen, 1948, Junior Prix. Bill Milliken taking the first turn in his Bugatti T-35A, coming off tree-lined Franklin Street. The white "steeple" is actually the Courthouse. The start/finish line is straight in front of that building.

CENTER LEFT: Watkins Glen, 1948, Junior Prix. Haig Ksayian racing the supercharged MG TC lent him two hours before by Briggs Cunningham. Ksayian, who had never driven an MG before, finished third in both races. He is having fun!

times before reaching the bottom. I felt as if that happened in slow motion. My seat belt kept me in the seat while I used my arms and hands as sort of a roll bar. When the rolling stopped, I was upside down with my face just level with the dashboard. I heard the gas pump still working, so I turned off the ignition key, and began to wonder how I would get out of this fix. Then I started hearing voices of approaching spectators. As they got closer, someone said: 'I wonder if he's dead?' Upon which I answered, 'Why don't you (expletives deleted) turn the car and find out?' This they did, and we all found out I was totally unscathed. As to my car, aside from numerous minor dents and two broken wire wheels, it was still race-worthy!"

By now, the running order was well established for the final two laps: in front were Griswold, Cunningham and Ksayian, followed by Milliken in his Bugatti, then Felton in his antique-looking though superbly prepared Vauxhall nicknamed "Quicksilver." The Collier brothers ran in close formation behind Felton in their own supercharged MG's, displaying masterful driving. Then, at the bottom of Big Bend, entering the so-called "Thrill Curve" leading back to Franklin Street, the Vauxhall suddenly went into a spin as

First Grand Prix

The boys were at last separated from the men shortly before 3 p.m. The Grand Prix grid of 15 cars began to form along Franklin Street, two abreast again, for the big race. This time, the top two D-Class Junior Prix finishers were in the front row: Cunningham in his BuMerc and Vaughn in his Lagonda (even though he had only finished twelfth overall). Behind them were Weaver's Maserati next to Griswold's Alfa Romeo followed by a gaggle of MGs.

© Harold Lance

Credit: Charles A. Lytle Jr.

CENTER LEFT: Watkins Glen, 1948. Mike Vaughn's Lagonda Rapide Tourer. Built in 1938, this car had a 4451cc straight four engine. Vaughn finished 12th in the Junior Prix and retired in the Grand Prix.

BOTTOM LEFT: Watkins Glen, 1948. The Grand Prix grid on Franklin Street.

TOP RIGHT: Watkins Glen, 1948. Frank Griswold's Alfa Romeo comes off the small stretch of Fourth Street which connects the end of "Big Bend" with Franklin Street.

© Harold Lance

As the clock struck 3 pm, Mickelson dropped the green flag again. Amidst the deafening thunder of over one thousand horsepower suddenly turned lose, Griswold and his Alfa Romeo rushed into the lead, followed by Weaver and Cunningham. The racing machines quickly sped up towards White House Corner, providing a vivid contrast to the normally peaceful background of the surrounding woods. The crowd obviously delighted in this thrilling blend of screaming exhausts and speeding machines driven by men who seemed larger-than-life.

First to reappear at the northern end of Franklin Street was Griswold and his Alfa Romeo. The Pennsylvanian cut the start/finish line 6:14.6 minutes after the green flag dropped, an impressive 3 seconds faster than in his first Junior Prix lap. Weaver's Maserati passed by the Court House seven seconds later, in hot pursuit of the Alfa. Cunningham, Ksayian and Vaughn followed within 30 seconds.

For a while, Weaver valiantly tried to catch the Alfa Romeo. Then on lap 4, his Maserati expired once again, handing the second position, and the chase, to Cunningham, who was pursued by the drivers of three supercharged MG TC's: Ksayian, then Sam and Miles Collier.

The Collier brothers, veterans of the 1939 edition of the Le Mans 24 Hours, were aiming at winning class B in which they raced as their 1250 cc MG engines were super-charged, or "blown" as they said in those days. But their

© Harold Lance

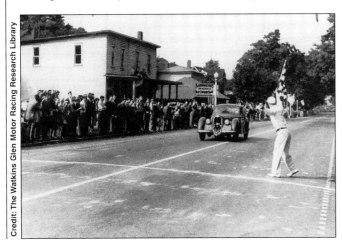

TOP LEFT: Watkins Glen, 1948. Sam and Miles Collier coming down Steuben Street (end of "Big Bend"). The two brothers were well prepared and ran their race together, but were nonetheless beaten by Haig Ksayian.

BOTTOM LEFT: Watkins Glen, 1948. Frank Griswold gets the checkered flag waved by Nils Mickelson on Franklin Street. The crowds would grow tremendously in the following years.

best friend Briggs had his MG superbly prepared by Alfred Momo, who worked for J. S. Inskip. By lending that car to Ksayian for the race, Cunningham had sprung a surprise on the Colliers. Ksayian proved unbeatable, even after the experienced siblings raised their racing rev-limit to 5,500 rpms, or 500 rpms higher than they had originally planned, in the middle of the race.

Gradually, as several more cars dropped out — Felton's Vauxhall, Vaughn's Lagonda, George Boardman's Jaguar SS-1, then Wilson's Stutz — the race stabilized and the suspense became focused on the duel between the two leading drivers: Griswold and Cunningham. At the completion of the fifth lap, with three laps to go, Cunningham was trailing Griswold by 51 seconds. At the next pass in front of the Court House, the gap had dropped to 29 seconds, then a lap later, to a mere 4 seconds! The crowd went wild.

But with the BuMerc now highly visible in his rearview mirror, Griswold stepped on it. Making the most of his own experience and the Alfa Romeo's superb handling, he took almost every corner faster than he previously had, eventually crossing the finish line ahead of Cunningham by 11 seconds. In so doing, he established the lap record for the day in 5:46.1 minutes, averaging 68.5 mph. His total time for the 52.8 miles of the race was 49:41 minutes, for an overall average of 63.7 mph. Behind Cunningham's BuMerc, only eight more cars were able to finish; all MG's! The order was Ksayian, Sam Collier, Miles Collier, Phil Stiles, a brave Denver Cornett, followed by Bill Gallagher, then a very happy Cameron Argetsinger in 9th place. Dean Bedford finished 10th and was the last classified entrant.

After the race, Ksayian went to see Cunningham and thank the generous patron for loaning him the MG. Then the New Jersey engineer added, "I hope you did not mind my getting close behind you a few times during the Grand Prix." Answered Cunningham, "Not at all. I was aware of where you were at all times, and I was not going to let my own car pass me!"

Happy Aftermath

Everybody involved or present, including the local press, considered the day a wonderful success. Bob Gegen, whose Bugatti Type 38 did not even complete the Junior Prix, wrote to the organizers that "The race was the best sport ever; and I hope to participate again, but not in a Bugatti. No sir! I know when to stop pushing my luck." Denver Cornett, though a little humbled, wrote, "I did enjoy myself very much and plan to do it again next year. I think the spirit of cooperation was wonderful, and also the sportsmanlike attitude shown by all throughout the race weekend." Bill Gallagher effused, "... it was the grandest affair I have ever attended from every standpoint. The organization deserves every praise in handling it as it did." It did not take long for the Watkins Glen authorities to decide to have a repeat in 1949. The SCCA directors them-

© Harold Lance

selves had caught a glimpse of a bright new future. American car racing would never be the same again.

Ironically, almost no one in Europe had any idea that this race was even taking place or that it would, in a relatively short time, have an effect on them. In fact, on the very same day across the Atlantic, the attention of car enthusiasts was focused on the British Grand Prix run at Silverstone. A former wartime airfield with X-shaped runways, Silverstone, near Northampton, had become England's second new racing circuit after Goodwood. The 1948 British Grand Prix was its inaugural event and marked the return of Britain as host to international motor racing. Villoresi won the Grand Prix in a Maserati, confirming one more time the domination of the Italian automobile makers in these early post-war years.

There was only one more noteworthy international racing event in 1948 after that: the Paris *Coupe du Salon*, run the following Sunday, October 10, on the famous Montlhéry track near the French capital. In the preliminary sports car race run over a distance of only 150 km (93.2 mi), the opposition to a swarm of large French cars was mostly Italian and relatively weak. Three 3-liter Delages swept the podium, followed by a 4.5 liter Talbot. The Grand Prix for Formula cars was won by French champion Louis Rosier in a new Talbot T26 C (also powered by a 4.5 liter engine), once more against a thin Italian presence.

Less than a month later, America re-elected Harry Truman to the Presidency, by a narrow margin. His victory promised the continuation of both the Marshall Plan and the wave of prosperity and rapid evolution which was sweeping the country. The move to suburbia, and all its attendant societal changes, was underway. America remained fundamentally conservative, though, and the landscape would be reshaped faster than its people's world view. The automobile would be a key agent of that transformation and the European imports would help diversify choices and open up attitudes in a mighty way.

What Did It All Mean?

Though few realized it at the time, the foremost importance of the first Watkins Glen Grand Prix was the fact that this official race, sanctioned and supported by the SCCA, established a firm beachhead for sports car racing on the North American continent. Slowly but surely, this would lead to two momentous consequences:

- The authority and influence of the SCCA grew and spread quickly to the entire United States. In 1949, a second New York State village organized a road race: Bridgehampton on Long Island. Then in 1950, five more major sites appeared on the enthusiast's schedule: Palm Beach and Sebring in Florida in the east, Elkhart Lake in the midwest, plus Palm Springs and Pebble Beach in California (though the former was under the authority of the California Sports Car Club, or Cal Club). By 1951, road racing, though still small, was in full swing across the continent, and there was a strong American participation at the Le Mans 24 Hours.

- The gauntlet for road racing supremacy had been thrown between European and American car makers. Shortly after the end of World War I, oval racing became the dominant formula in the United States, while Grand Prix racing on road circuits prevailed in Europe. The two cultures, widely different, remained essentially apart for decades, and are in fact still so to this day. Sports car racing would become the bridge between the two continents.

The SCCA's success encouraged American teams, with Briggs Cunningham in the lead, to compete in Europe's major endurance races. After that, little by little, European teams and champions started taking their American cousins seriously. The Twelve Hours of Sebring became the first link between the two worlds. By 1953, Sebring was officially put on the calendar of the "World Endurance Championship" series.

To an observer with a perfect crystal ball, the first Watkins Glen Grand Prix could also have brought several insights which actually took decades to penetrate the tradition-bound minds of both Detroit and Europe.

- On challenging road circuits, raw horsepower hooked to a rudimentary chassis is far from a sure bet against a combination of a smaller but high-revving engine mounted on a more sophisticated chassis. The Americans would take 18 years to absorb that lesson fully, until the Ford GT-40 finally beat Ferrari at Le Mans in 1966 by combining the best of both worlds: raw horsepower (7.0 liter engines) and a sophisticated chassis (first designed by England's Lola, then refined by Ford engineers).

- Reliability proved to be even more important than technological sophistication. The advanced, stunningly powerful 90 degree V-8 supercharged engine of Weaver's Maserati did him little good as the rest of his car could not last around the Watkins Glen track under race conditions for more than 30 miles. The Europeans, particularly the Italians (except Ferrari), the British and the French, would also take almost two decades to learn that lesson. From the get go, the American V-8 was reliable.

- Technological innovations, such as four-wheel independent suspensions, high-rev engines, and aerodynamic improvements, should be adopted and perfected quickly. It would take everybody about the same period of time to let that seemingly obvious truth sink in. In the early 1960's, Jim Hall and Chaparral in the field of aerodynamics, then Ford and its GT-40 a few years later in the realm of the scientific approach, would do much bring that change about.

- Inspired safety measures save lives without impeding good driving. Denver Cornett and Bill Milliken accidentally demonstrated that truth on October 2, 1948 at Watkins Glen. Yet it would take over a decade, and

Watkins Glen, 1948, Junior Prix. Dud Wilson's Stutz BB Blackhawk (number 32) leads Charles Addams' 1929 Mercedes-Benz S (number 1) while Griswold's Alfa Romeo is about to lap them.

many lives, for elementary safety measures to become mandatory. In 1948 alone, three drivers died while racing in major events, including Italian champion Achille Varzi, when he crashed his Alfa Romeo on a wet road on June 30 during a time trial session for the Grand Prix of Bern in Switzerland.

All those lessons could have been obvious to a keen observer the day after the 1948 Grand Prix at Watkins Glen. It is, of course, easier to make that comment almost 50 years after the event. Nonetheless, they were all there to be learned. Cameron Argetsinger had not dreamed up the American Grand Prix concept just to have fun driving his MG around his favorite summer resort at high speeds made legal for one special afternoon; he did blaze a very big trail.

One more lesson became evident four decades later: while the cars that first raced at the Glen could have been bought for a pittance in 1948-50, they would appreciate dramatically in value over time. In 1995, the Auction House Brooks Europe put up for sale the ex-Charles Addams Mercedes-Benz S the cartoonist raced at the Glen in 1948. It quickly sold for £471,000, or over $765,000 at today's exchange rate.

Watkins Glen, 1949 - Miles Collier on his way to Grand Prix victory in "Ardent Alligator," a Riley Brooklands re-engined with a Mercury V-8. The car is now owned by Pete McManus of Thornton, PA.

chapter two

Europe's New Marques Make Their Mark

Lift And Drag

While the Watkins Glen organizers and the SCCA were beginning to plan their second run for mid-September, 1949, the world around them was changing fast. Breakthrough inventions dreamed up in the steaming cauldron of World War II were beginning to have an impact on daily life.

In aviation, the science of aerodynamics was fast developing from a "black art" to a critical science. The practical development of the jet engine, achieved during World War II by Germany and England, had effectively doubled the maximum possible speed of airplanes, from 300 to 600 mph. But in 1945, no airframe existed that could both sustain the continuous shock waves generated by near-sonic flight and create the efficient, controllable lift needed for safe long range flight. The promise of affordable non-stop transatlantic travel was at hand, but first a problem demanding a conceptual breakthrough, then affirmed by long hours of wind-tunnel testing, needed to be solved. This was done by an exceptional team of engineers working for the Boeing Company in Seattle, Washington.

On February 8, 1949, a large experimental six-engined American jet bomber, the Boeing XB-47, set a world record by flying non-stop from the West Coast to the East Coast of America in 3 hours and 46 minutes, averaging a

"Until I was twenty-one, I was equally interested in speed boats, aircrafts and automobiles. ... More than anything, I was intrigued by the finesse that was needed to control a fast moving car and fast boats and planes."

George C. Rand

stunning 607.2 mph. What made this speed possible, besides jet power, was a large-span thick wing, swept at a steep 35 degrees, and carrying the engines in suspended pods underneath. The revolutionary swept-wing-and-jet-pods design was the key that permitted such a revolutionary breakthrough in aviation.

Racing car designers were slowly beginning to face a similar challenge, though in specific speed ranges and circumstances that were obviously quite different. Before World War II, car engines with high horsepower output could only be made in small batches by special technicians; they were extermely expensive. The 6.8 liter straight-six engine of the Mercedes S (220 hp) or the 2.9 liter straight-eight of Griswold's Alfa Romeo (also 220 hp), both supercharged, are relevant examples.

By 1948, stock engines saw their specific power output increase considerably, due the availability of higher octane no-knock gasoline, leading in turn to reliable higher compression ratios. An output of 200 hp from a minimally race-tuned stock engine, say from a rumored new General Motors V-8, was definitely on the horizon. Therefore the maximum possible speed of everyday racing cars would soon be greatly augmented to about 150 mph. So a new question for race car designers would soon become: how to reduce drag and keep the car on the road, while maintaining cooling efficiency for both engines and brakes. Could the example of the industry serve as a conceptual guide?

This cross-fertilization almost happened but the opportunity, in the end, was missed. In the post-war years, there were few professional contacts between the aircraft industry and the automobile industry. There were, of course, many former fighter pilots who were now racing cars in both Europe and America; very few of them, however, were engineers. Then there were rare aeronautic engineers who liked to race, such as Bill Milliken. But their racing skills and machinery in those days were such that concentrating on how not to get off the road in a fast turn paid much higher dividends than thinking up and designing more efficient aerodynamic shapes.

In Modena, Coventry, Paris or Detroit, stylists and coachbuilders would continue to rely mostly on guts and aesthetic feel when drawing new body shapes for race cars. Bill Milliken would eventually be involved with a radical

TOP RIGHT: Lea-Francis at Watkins Glen - 1948. Owners of European-made cars were predominant at the Glen in the early years.

BOTTOM: 1938 Talbot-Lago SS "Goutte d'Eau" owned by Russell G. Sceli, then President of SCCA, at State Park, Watkins Glen, 1948. The car did not start. The splendid body is by Figoni and Falaschi. The engine was 3996cc straight-six.

cross-cultural effort between aeronautic and automobile engineers, which would lead to a revolution in racing aerodynamics: Jim Hall's Chaparral and Chevrolet engineers. That desert bird and its stunning wing, however, were nowhere near Milliken's visible horizon in 1949.

America Becomes Fin Land

The automobile industry still generated many happy developments in 1949. All of America's manufacturers produced their first genuinely new designs since 1941. Compared to pre-war models, all cars became lower and wider, with the fenders fairing into the doors. The 1949 Ford Custom was the most innovative in this new styling direction: its front fenders, doors and rear fenders formed a continuous, elegant, uninterrupted shape. It was the shape of things to come. At Cadillac, the small fins perched atop the rear fenders which the marque's stylists had introduced a year earlier were perpetuated on the 1949 models. Cadillac's embryonic fins would have an enormous and diversified effect throughout the world over the following fifteen years, though they would eventually prove an evolutionary dead end.

These new 1949 designs were markedly better cars. All gave up solid front axles for independent front suspen-

sions and offered more room and better accomodations inside. Oldsmobile and Cadillac also introduced the first new post-war engine design: the valve-in-head, high compression V-8. At 331 cubic inches (5.4 liter), the Cadillac version developed 160 hp thanks to a compression ratio of 7.25:1, plus "slipper pistons" allowing shorter connecting rods, which in turn lead to a reduction in the block's size and weight. The brand new G.M. V-8 engine, evolved in different versions, would soon be turned into a potent racing powerplant.

Kick-Off In The Southern Hemisphere

The 1949 international racing season started in January in Argentina. Not only were President Juan Perón and his wife Evita genuine racing enthusiasts, but they clearly understood that sponsoring a widely popular sport officially could only enhance their public image. Thus, they made sure that every year, during the winter lull of the European season, Argentina would stage several major races with sufficient prize moneys to attract most of the top European teams. Early in 1949, no less than four Grand Prix's were staged in or near Buenos Aires between January 30 and February 27. Italian *monopostos* won all four races. The

TOP RIGHT: Europe's lust for car racing runs deep. Three Soap Box racers, parents, spectators and Gendarme in Belgium in 1949. This photo was taken in Verviers, the author's hometown situated between Liège and Spa-Francorchamps.

BOTTOM LEFT: French champion Jean-Pierre Wimille aboard a Gordini 7GC T15 at the 1947 Grand Prix du Roussillon in France.

fourth victory was claimed by local champion Juan Manuel Fangio driving a Maserati 4CLT/48 of the Automovil Club Argentino, a racing team subsidised by the Perón regime. Within a year, Fangio's name would be known throughout Europe.

A great tragedy also marked that long racing festival. During the first qualifying session on February 28, French champion and hero Jean-Pierre Wimille lost his life in an unexplained crash at the wheel of his Gordini 10 GC. Such was his popularity in France that he was given a state funeral in Paris on March 3, which was carried live on national radio and followed by millions.

American Racing Gains An Ocean Front

The rest of the 1949 season was centered on Europe and dominated by Ferrari (see pages 34-35). In America, the first Watkins Glen Grand Prix had stirred the imagination of racing enthusiasts across the country, but other venues for such events were hard to find in those pioneer-

Credit: Jean-Paul Delsaux Collection

Credit: Jean-Paul Delsaux Collection

ing days. During the first part of 1949, a few minor rallys and hillclimbs were planned or held in various places, none of significance. It seemed that eager enthusiasts would have to wait until the second Grand Prix of Watkins Glen in the fall to run in their next real race. Until, that is, another entrepreneurial enthusiast, inspired by Cameron Argetsinger, took it upon himself to organize a summer race in Bridgehampton, New York.

Bridgehampton is one of several lovely towns jointly called "the Hamptons," located near or along the shores of the Atlantic about 100 miles east of New York City. In the 1930s and 40s, they were manicured little communities surrounded by farmland, dotted with splendid mansions and clapboard houses, lined with trimmed hedges and white picket fences. They were the summer refuge of the New York rich. They were a perfect setting for a car race of gentlemen drivers. In fact, the Hamptons were a natural choice for another reason—the first Vanderbilt Cup races

Red Tide Rising:

Ferrari's 1949 Conquest of Europe And Arrival In America

The big 1949 opener for the sports car racing season was the Targa Florio on March 20th. The famous endurance race, inaugurated in 1906, consisted in a mad dash of several hundred miles over, down and around the scrappy hills of northern Sicily. The 1949 event, the 33rd Targa and second post-war edition was combined with the Giro di Sicilia (Tour of Sicily) as the traditional Madonie course was not yet repaired from damage sustained during the war. Two Ferraris were entered, both equipped with the new version of the V-12, increased to 2.0 liter. Only one of those two cars finished, but it won the race in a little over twelve hours, driven by Biondetti-Benedetti. The fact that the opposition was not exactly overwhelming allowed skeptics to call Ferrari lucky. Enzo Ferrari knew better.

In fact, the Ferrari factory was well prepared for a smashing 1949 season. It had now developed six different and much improved models on its basic chassis/V-12 design: four pure racing versions and two "street" versions for non-racing customers. Even the latter were planned with racing in mind. Enzo Ferrari knew that only by building and selling such road cars to wealthy customers at a significant profit could he hope to keep financing his racing activities for the long term. In addition, Carrozzeria Touring, the illustrious Milanese coachbuilders, had developed for him a completely original super-light spyder and coupe body design for the 1949 model year. The spyder came out first and was displayed in public at the Turin Auto Show on September 14, 1948. It was so stunning and different, a renowned Italian journalist had to find a new designation to describe it; he came

up with the word *barchetta* (row boat). The name stuck. So did the bright red color (vermillon) selected by Touring to showcase the bold Ferrari spirit.

The next opportunity to test Ferrari's racing mettle was an endurance event even more grueling than the Targa Florio: the astonishing Mille Miglia, inaugurated in 1927. The Mille challenged drivers and cars alike to complete of one thousand miles on public roads from Brescia (east of Milan) to Rome and back, twice crossing the

The Touring-bodied Ferrari 166 MM of Luigi Chinetti, winner of the 1949 Twenty-Four Hours of Spa-Francorchamps. Here, the Touring body is still intact. Chinetti would end up hitting a fence to avoid a wild spectator, but the can-do-driver Lucas would still manage to win.

Apennine mountain range, and running through cobblestoned town streets, narrow village roads, mountain hairpins, rough railroad crossings, long, dark tunnels and even past some of Rome's most famous monuments and sidewalks overflowing with thousands of crazed spectators. It was called "the race of 10,000 corners," and demanded unfathomable endurance and skill from the drivers who hoped to win. These were expected to race for over 12 hours at maximum speed to complete the circuit. There were no rest stops other than for refueling

and tire changes.

An early Ferrari 166 had won the 1948 Mille Miglia, allowing the then one-year-old marque to begin establishing an international reputation. Ferrari named its new *barchetta* the Ferrari 166 Mille Miglia in celebration of that critical victory. A year later, a stunning

Luigi Chinetti congratulated by officials and spectators after winning the 1950 Twelve-Hours of Paris (Montlhéry).

nine Tipo 166's were entered for the new edition of the Mille: three works cars and six similar private entries, two with highly skilled drivers. The main competition was expected to come from Alfa Romeo and Maserati, with two other new Italian marques considered possible dark horses: O.S.C.A. and Cisitalia. But there was no stopping the red machines from Maranello. The Ferrari of Biondetti-Salani won the race, followed by teammates Bonetto-Carpani. A potent Alfa-Romeo Coupe, a direct descendant of the model with which George Griswold won the first Watkins Glen races, came in third, 44 minutes behind were staged there between 1904 and 1910. Meant to offer an American version to international road racing teams, they had been watched by the best of New York's society.

Early in 1949, one Bruce Stevenson, a former B-25 Mitchell bomber pilot otherwise best described as the Cameron Argetsinger of Bridgehampton, made plans to make his favorite summer resort the second road race venue on the East Coast of America. He had heard of the first Watkins Glen Grand Prix, its success and the

enormous goodwill it had generated in the local community. Like Argetsinger, he owned an MG TC; like Argetsinger, he knew a lot of influential people; like Argetsinger, he wished to benefit the village where he spent most summers.

the winner.

The rest of 1949 became a succession of Ferrari triumphs. Before the second Watkins Glen Grand Prix took place, Ferraris racked up eight additional sports car race victories. On May 26, Italian champion Luigi Villoresi won the Grand Prix of Luxemburg; three days later at Monza, Bruno Sterzi won the three-hour Coppa Intereuropa; on June 19, Roberto Vallone won the Grand Prix of Naples. Next came the most stunning victories, at Le Mans on June 26 and at Spa-Francorchamps on July 10. In both cases, the opposition was strong, especially from French and British teams. The French aligned a number of potent 4.5 liter Talbots and Delahayes and 3.0 liter Delages, while the British fielded a squadron of Aston Martins, plus Bentleys, Frazer Nashes and Healeys.

In both cases, a little red *barchetta*, powered by its two-liter V-12 engine, crossed the finish line ahead of all other finishers. In both cases, Luigi Chinetti was the racing director and principal driver for the winning car; he beat the greatest odds and helped turn the daring concept of a small-displacement V-12 into a winning bet for Enzo Ferrari. Three more Ferrari sports car victories were recorded in 1949: Vallone won both the Tour of Umbria, on June 29, and the Dolomite Cup, on July 17; Franco Cornacchia won at the Senigallia Circuit on August 21. Finally, to crown a truly extraordinary year, Alberto Ascari loosened the grip Maserati had held on the 1949 *monoposto* championship, in the one-year absence of Alfa Romeo participation: he won three major races with the Ferrari 125/F1, including, the Grand Prix of Italy at Monza on September 11, six days before the second Watkins Glen.

Enzo Ferrari was becoming famous worldwide, and god-like in

Italy, a mere two and one half years after the first Ferrari prototype took its first test drive down the small country roads of Emilia Romana, just south of Modena.

American Beachheads

All of this, of course, did not go without notice in North America. Tommy Lee, Cadillac distributor for the West Coast, owner of radio and TV stations in Los Angeles, playboy and collector of unusual cars, was the first American to order a Ferrari. At the Turin Auto Show in September of 1948, the first 166 Touring *barchetta* built, the first Ferrari designed both for normal street use, as well as racing was displayed. It was chassis number 002 M. Tommy Lee placed the order, though he had no intention of racing the car. He was, first and foremost, a playboy. His business manager, Willey Brown, was interested in racing; he would soon send one of Tommy Lee's cars to race at Watkins Glen, an Alfa Romeo.

More significant was the second American order: it came from Briggs Cunningham to friend Luigi Chinetti who had by then become de facto Ferrari importer for the United States. The car, a 166 Spyder Corsa with cycle-fenders, was chassis number 016-I. Chinetti had broken three world speed records at the Montlhéry Autodrome with this car on November 3, 1948. Cunningham ordered it the following spring and the red car reached the Eastern United States in early June of 1949.

Cunningham's first Ferrari sat on a wheelbase of a mere 98.4 inches, weighting just 1,764 pounds without its driver on board. When it was first seen in the United States, Americans marvelled at a design so far removed from the familiar. Not only was the body made of

thin, hand-hammered aluminum sheets, the Ferrari featured vented aluminum drum brakes inside Borrani wire wheels and was powered by an exceptional high-revving two-liter V-12 engine capable of producing 155 hp (almost as much as the new 5.4 liter Cadillac V-8 ...) at 7,000 rpm. Early Ferrari driver Franco Cortese said later, "In America, they went mad when they heard of this small V-12 that could easily rev up to 7,000-8,000 rpm ... Ferrari's success was linked to the twelve-cylinder engine." It did not hurt either that the marque had already racked up several remarkable victories in Europe prior to its first appearance in the United States.

Watkins Glen, 1949 - Briggs Cunningham's Ferrari 166 SC overtakes a field of MGs in the Junior Prix's first turn while Col. George Felton "Quicksilver" Vauxhall looms high behind it. This is the first Ferrari ever to be raced in America, in its second race (its first race was at Bridgehampton three months earlier). The number of spectators lining Franklin Street has visibly grown since the previous year.

In relatively short order Stevenson, aided by Alec Ulmann, secured the backing of the village's council, the local Lions Club and the MG Car Club of America. Next he selected a squarish four-mile course on the flat roads in and around Bridgehampton, which the town approved; set June 11 as the race date, then managed to attract a choice selection of entrants. In organizing this new race, Stevenson was also providing a great rehearsal stage for all the players who would be at Watkins Glen three months later.

On race day, an estimated 15,000 spectators lined the course, among them Cameron and Jean Argetsinger. The

Credit: Earl Gandel Collection

feature race, the 100 miler for the fastest machines was due to start at 3:15 p.m. The biggest attraction was the small red cycle-fendered Ferrari entrusted to George Rand for this event. Rand was another of Cunningham's wealthy New York friends and racing enthusiasts. He had lived and raced in Europe in the mid-1930s and made many friends there in racing circles, particularly in France. After his return to the States in late 1936, he became the New York agent for Bugatti and Maserati with a showroom and garage in Manhattan. He also imported used European Grand Prix cars for resale to his peers. He joined A.R.C.A. in 1936 and, with the Collier brothers, helped the organization develop into a serious racing body, of which he

became its president in 1939. After World War II, Rand became one of the early mainstays of the SCCA and often acted as its race steward.

The Ferrari to be driven by Rand sat on the grid next to more conventional cars. George Huntoon of Miami, Florida, yet another friend of "Mr. C.'s," sat in a supercharged 1935 Alfa Romeo 8C-2600 lent him by father-in-law Sam Bird of New York; Tom L. H. Cole Jr. in a 3.5 liter Jaguar SS-100. "Tommy" Cole was a wealthy young Englishman with considerable charm and talent who claimed both British and American citizenship. Larry Kulok would drive an Allard K1 equipped with a 3.8 liter Ford V-8. After MG and Ferrari, Allard was the third new racing marque from Europe to appear in America.

New Brit

Sidney Allard, a racing enthusiast since the early 1930s, had managed to manufacture a few sports cars of his own before World War II. Having done well financially during the conflict by handling military contracts, he officially founded the Allard Motor Co. Ltd. in 1946. He was able to proceed immediately with the design and production of the Allard K1, a crude but racy two-seater, usually powered by a Ford Flathead V-8. The K1 followed Allard's pre-war philosophy of using a large American block posi-

© Harold Lance

tioned behind the front axle and bolted to a strong chassis. This resulted in a somewhat heavy machine, but one which attracted a sufficient clientele to encourage the British entrepreneur. Americans in particular liked his cars because of their big and familiar engines. There were 11 Allards in the United States as Kulok sat on the grid at Bridgehampton. But his was the first one to be tested in an actual road race in America.

At exactly 3:15 pm, Bruce Stevenson released the eager drivers with a wave of the green flag. Rand shot for-

Credit: John Fitch Collection

ward first as the high-pitched howl of the Ferrari V-12 stunned the crowd. Huntoon and Kulok followed in hot pursuit. The pack of colorful racers zoomed past the lines of haybales and white fences, weaved into and out of the square bends of the picturesque course, producing loud, exciting sounds and generally dazzling the spectators. The Ferrari seemed unbeatable until the 16th lap, when Rand was suddenly forced out by a ruptured oil line. Since Kulok's Allard had also failed, Huntoon and the blue Alfa Romeo grabbed the lead, tailed by Tom Cole's Jaguar and Sam Collier's blown MG. That was the order in which they finished at the end of 25 laps.

Spectators greeted the finishers with cheers and enthusiastic rounds of applause, indicating that America's second road race venue was now also on the map. While a modest beginning, it was a outstanding one. If victory had escaped Ferrari, the bright red car from Maranello certainly had cre-

John Fitch in his first racing car: an MG TC seen here at Bridgehampton in 1949.

ated a lasting impression. Also noticed was the fact that no American-made cars were present on the circuit.

Back To Watkins Glen

With Bridgehampton successfully inaugurated, all eyes in the still small but fast growing community of road racing enthusiasts turned to Watkins Glen. They knew the second edition of the Grand Prix would be even more spectacular than the first. Indeed, the organizing committee had been doing everything possible to achieve that goal. Because the first Glen event had been such a success, Cameron Argetsinger and his associates decided early on not to tinker much with their winning formula. The race day schedule would again start with the Concours d'Elégance at 10:00 am, it would then be followed by the four-lap junior event now called Seneca Cup at noon, then by the Grand Prix at 1:30 pm.

The organizers made only four major changes: they moved up the race date to September 17 — higher probability of good weather; lengthened the Grand Prix distance from 8 to 15 laps, or to 99 miles — more demanding and slightly closer to the European tradition; required at least one pit stop to take on a minimum of one gallon of fuel as a test of pit crew capability; and finally, they modified the engine displacement class definitions as follows:

Class A:	**Up to 1100 cc**	
Class B:	**1101 cc to 1500 cc**	**(and supercharged Class A)**
Class C:	**1501 cc to 2000 cc**	**(and supercharged Class B)**
Class D:	**Over 2001 cc**	**(and supercharged Class C)**

The latter three measures were intentional steps gradually to make the Watkins Glen Grand Prix an official international event where famous drivers and teams from all over the world would come to compete. Alec Ulmann, Chairman of Activities for the 1949 Grand Prix, said so in unmistakable terms in an article printed in the 1949 race program and titled, *The International Aspects Of Road Racing*.

"The Sports Car Club of America has, in the interest of furthering international racing in this country, moulded its Road Racing regulations to the international usage, and has worked hand in hand with the AAA Contest Board, as a result of which this race of today has received their official sanction.

It takes a year to place an event on the international calendar of the FIA. If this most hospitable community of Watkins Glen, and our Club do elect to make the 1950 race an invitation event known the world over, we can do so now via the good offices of the Contest Board of the AAA. Just imagine what it would mean to see several teams from overseas in our midst, bringing to the shores of beautiful lake Seneca the atmosphere of Le Mans, The Grand Prix of Monaco, or the excitement of Shelsley Walsh."

In fact, Argetsinger had made sure to register "his" Grand Prix event with the FIA that summer, with the AAA serving as middleman. The FIA had responded favorably and would grant its stamp of approval in 1950 provided the 1949 race ran smoothly.

The New Grid

Thanks to the publicity generated by the 1948 race and the more recent Bridgehampton event, the entrants' list almost doubled from the previous year, to 58 drivers. Many of the inaugural race participants, having had so much fun at the first Glen, came back for more. A few chose to drive the very same car they had raced the year before, such as George Weaver (Maserati V8RI), Sam Collier (MG TC

TOP RIGHT: Watkins Glen, 1949 - Col. George Felton at speed in his Vauxhall OE 30/98 just past Seneca Lodge.

BOTTOM LEFT: Watkins Glen, 1949. James Melton, opera star and vintage car collector, leads the parade in his Mercedes-Benz 540K before the Seneca Cup.

Supercharged), Denver Cornett (MG TC), George Felton (Vauxhall 30/98), George Hendrie (Alfa Romeo 1750 cc), I. J. Brundage (Duesenberg) and Kenneth Hill (Merlin).

Several other "veterans" chose to switch mounts. Cunningham decided to drive his new tiny marvel, the Ferrari 166 SC, and lent his big BuMerc to another friend, George Roberts. Miles Collier opted for a 1929 Riley Brooklands he and his brother had owned since 1934, and refurbished just prior to the war with a Mercury 3.9 liter flathead engine and drivetrain. The tuned powerplant could deliver up to 175 hp. The Colliers, being from the Everglades in Florida, dubbed their unusual hybrid "Ardent Alligator." Miles Collier had raced it at Bridgehampton and though he did not finish there, he thought the potent Riley might be just the right car to win the Watkins Glen Grand Prix.

As to Cameron Argetsinger, he borrowed Milliken's Bugatti T-35 A of 1948 fame and chose to race it, hoping the French car would give him a better chance at an overall win. Milliken himself would drive a pure Indy racer, a four-wheel-drive 1932 F.W.D.-Miller powered by a 4.2 liter engine. He had actually intended to race that car in the 1948 Grand Prix, but was unable to do so and thus had driven the Bugatti instead.

Milliken's car had been built by Miller on request from the F.W.D. company of Clintonville, Wisconsin. The three letters stand for Four-Wheel-Drive, the company having been in the business of building trucks with such transmissions since World War I. In the early 1930s, F.W.D. decided to have its core design tested under racing condi-

tions. Thus, Harry Miller built two Indy racers featuring the integral transmission system, which consisted of three differentials: two standard units for the front and rear axles, then middle unit that could be locked or unlocked from the cockpit. The cars were raced several times at the Indy 500. Mauri Rose obtained the best result, finishing third in 1940. During the war years, the cars were returned to the F.W.D. company.

In 1948, Bill Milliken started looking for a car that might give him a good shot at winning the famous Pikes Peak hillclimb. He had raced the Bugatti there the previous year and now thought a four-wheel-drive racer would be better, but he knew of no such car. Good friend Hemp Oliver told him of the F.W.D. Company. After contacting the president, Walter A. Olen, Milliken was allowed to borrow and race one of the two Indy cars, both of which F.W.D. had kept. He ran it first at Pikes Peak on Labor Day, where the transmission broke. Unable to have it fixed in time, he drove his Bugatti instead a month later at the first Watkins Glen event. Now, with a year passed, he was ready and anxious to test his integral-transmission racer around the hills of Watkins Glen.

Impressive Newcomers

The 1949 field also saw significant number of interesting newcomers, both drivers and cars. Two H.R.G.s, powered by a 1498 cc Singer engine, were entered by Tom

TOP LEFT: Watkins Glen, 1948 - George Boardman (with hat), wife (behind him) and friends.

TOP RIGHT: Watkins Glen, 1949 - Tom Cole in his H.R.G. "hitting the haybales" backwards. He would recover.

CENTER RIGHT: Watkins Glen, 1949 - Zora Arkus-Duntov at speed in his Ford-powered Allard J2 "Ardun." Though the racing number looks like a "4", it is actually a "34" with the "3" painted hastily in front of the "4" before the race (visible on the hood).

Cole and Peter Iselin, both from New York. H.R.G. was a small, specialized British marque founded in 1935 by three enthusiasts, Halford, Robins and Godfrey. The marque's name stood for their initials. Though produced in 1949, these two sports cars had a pronounced "square" 1930s look. Of British origin too were three Allards J2s, the new lighweight and much more competitive model replacing the K1. These J2s were still powered by the same Ford 3.8 liter V-8 as the K1, but three of the V-8s at the Glen would have an advantage: a modified overhead-valve head designed to improve performance significantly.

That mechanical marvel was called the "Ardun," short for Arkus-Duntov, the surname of an extraordinary man.

Zachary "Zora" Arkus-Duntov was born in Brussels of Russian parents in 1909, then brought up in St. Petersburg and Berlin. He earned a German degree in mechanical engineering in 1934 and started racing motorcycles, then cars. He moved to Paris In 1938, where, a year later he married a Follies Bergères dancer named Elfi Wolff. After the war, Arkus-Duntov emigrated to the United States with his brother Yura and, of course, Elfi. The brothers soon founded an engineering firm whose most popular product quickly became the modified Ford V-8 head.

Arkus-Duntov would drive an "Allard Ardun" at the Glen. A gentleman by the name of Corwith Hamill would drive a J2 with the regular flathead, and Larry Kulok would try to improve on his Bridgehampton result with his K1. Paul J. Timmins of Boston entered an "Ardun Special," a modified midget racer powered by a 4.2 liter Ford V-8 capped with the Ardun head. George Huntoon came with the blue supercharged 8C-2600 Alfa with which he had won the Bridgehampton event. Mal Ord of Los Angeles, racing mechanic for Tommy Lee, would drive a yellow and tan 1938 Alfa Romeo 8C-2900 Mille Miglia racer; the car's sweeping front fenders being removed to shed unecessary weight. Eclectism was definitely part of the standard racing menu in those early days.

BOTTOM LEFT: Watkins Glen, 1949 - Anthony Pompeo taking the first turn in his Fiat 1100 Mille Miglia Coupe.

BOTTOM RIGHT: Watkins Glen, 1949 - Logan Hill taking the first turn in his Cisitalia Coupe.

Italian Outsiders

Besides Alfa Romeo, Maserati and Ferrari, two more Italian marques would be represented in the field. Antonio Pompeo of New York and Richard Haynes of Detroit each entered 1100 cc Fiat coupes with the hope of at least winning class A. Based on the 508 model originally introduced in 1934, the two Fiats were thoroughly revamped 1948 models, with new aerodynamic bodywork, strengthened chassis and an updated four-cylinder engine capable of delivering 51 hp at 5200 rpm. Top speed was 93 mph. Pompeo's version was called 508 C Mille Miglia because of the numerous class victories the earlier versions had gained in the famous endurance race during the 1930's. Haynes' Fiat was a 1100 S with slightly different bodywork.

Their main competitor would be another new Italian marque, Cisitalia. It was the brainchild of industrialist and racing enthusiast Piero Dusio, who had made a fortune during World War II by making boots for the Italian army. The name Cisitalia, invented by him, was a contraction of his car company's corporate name: Consorzio Industriale Sportivo Italia. Dusio's idea was that if you could use as a building base the key components of a small, cheap mass-produced car, such a the Fiat 508; then give it a lighter,

more rigid chassis and wrap it in a "racy, sporty body;" you could sell the new package as an elegant sportster at a much higher price than the cost of the original components.

Cisitalias used an innovative super-light "spaceframe" chassis to which mostly Fiat components were added, then the structure was clothed in shapely Italian coachworks. Cisitalias had become famous in 1947 when Tazio Nuvolari, against all odds, almost won the first pre-war Mille Miglia by outracing a herd of much more powerful cars. He finished second. Joseph B. Ferguson Jr. of Bridgehampton, New York and Logan Hill of Riverside, Connecticut, were among the first American Cisitalia owners. They were looking forward to racing their pretty Italian sports coupes at the Glen. Perry Boswell of Upper Malboro, Maryland, entered a similar car, though his was equipped with a 1478 cc Offenhauser engine, and therefore would compete in Class B against the MGs and the two H.R.G.s.

Happy New Faces

Then there were a few colorful characters new to the Glen who entered car makes which had already been seen racing near the south shore of Seneca Lake. Charles Moran Jr. came to drive a yellow 1929 Bugatti T-35 A. Born in the early century, Moran was married to a DuPont, lived in Westchester county north of New York, and was the head of a Wall Street firm called Francis I DuPont & Company. While still a student at Columbia University, he travelled twice to France where he raced in two 24-hour endurance events: the 1928 Bol' d'Or and the 1929 Le Mans — the latter in a 5.3 liter eight-cylinder DuPont. In the 1930s, Moran became a key member of A.R.C.A. and a very close and dear friend to Briggs Cunningham.

Dave Garroway of Chicago was another personality, being America's first successful talk show host on the new medium called television. His show *Garroway at Large* where he sometimes had as sidekick a chimpanzee named J. Fred Muggs made him extremely popular. Like many of his famous successors, he loved expensive high-performance cars and raced them. For the Glen, he entered an impeccable-looking Jaguar SS-100 graced with distinguished pale yellow paint and brown upholstery made of genuine alligator skin.

TOP RIGHT: Watkins Glen, 1949 - Dave Garroway, America's first TV talk show host, racing his immaculate Jaguar SS-100 at the Glen on his way to the "White House Esses" before the railroad underpass.

BOTTOM RIGHT: Watkins Glen, 1949 - The railroad crossing, situated just before "Big Bend," was often taken at full speed and acted as a "take-off ramp." Here is Tom Cole in his H.R.G. in mid-flight just past the railroad tracks. Suspension gear and chassis took a real beating. So did the driver's body.

Also from Chicago, and son of a man who was developing a profitable business in the automotive tooling industry with a company named Ammco, Fred G. Wacker Jr. entered a regular MG TC. So did Bridgehampton's Bruce Stevenson for the Seneca Cup, though he would drive an Indy-type Offenhauser special for the Grand Prix. John Bentley, New York correspondent for *The Autocar* and famous journalist would compete in Class C with his supercharged MG TC. John Cooper Fitch, also a former fighter pilot and currently a 32-year-old MG dealer from White Plains, New York would also be there with his MG TC. Fitch had raced for the first time at Bridgehampton,

shortly thereafter married Elizabeth Huntley, an attractive young woman he had known for awhile and who served there as his pit crew. They were now honeymooning, not totally by coincidence, in the eastern Finger Lakes region, with the MG as their means of transportation.

With such quality and diversity of participants, Argetsinger and the Watkins Glen Race committee were more than pleased. After Labor Day weekend, their anticipation grew by the day.

Watkins Glen, September 17, 1949

As the year before, the participants and some of the spectators started arriving a few days before the "Grand Prix." Each driver and car was assigned to a specific garage in or near the village. As dawn broke on Saturday, September 17, a bright sunny day was undoubtedly in the offing. For the second time in a row, the organizers had great luck with the weather.

An estimated 15,000 spectators had descended on the village and its environs, about fifty percent more than the previous year (*).

The villagers and neighboring farmers were in an effervescent mood. Not only was their hometown receiving publicity on a near-national scale, but, as they had learned in one Saturday the previous year, they could charge $1.00 for every parking space on their property they could make available to those eager out-of-towners. Having fun while making money was honoring one of the best of all American traditions.

At 10 am, the Concours d'Elegance quietly opened the day's activities. The participating cars were organized in five classes ranging from Modern (1949-50 model years) to Classic (1937-40) and Veteran (1927 and older). Almost all of the pre-war cars exuded might and power tamed under elegant shapes. Be it the Mercedes-Benz 540K of opera star James Melton, the blue Lagonda Rapide of Henry Stevens, the black Duesenberg J Phaeton of Arthur J. Hoe,

---

(*) *The November, 1949 issue of* Motor Trend *estimated the crowd at 100,000 and that number has often been reprinted ever since. Dispassionate people who were there and the Watkins Glen Chamber of Commerce use 15,000 as a much more accurate number.*

Watkins Glen, 1949 - A Lagonda Rapide exhibited at the Concours d'Elégance takes the parade lap.

or the Bentley of James Wheaton, these were splendid automobiles to behold. But dazzling as they might be, they were beauties of the past. What got the crowd of on-lookers most excited were the newest cars entered in the Concours, those pointing to the future.

New Cat From England

Most stunning among these was the brand new Jaguar XK-120 roadster. Among the very few in America, two were at the Glen, brought by New York Jaguar importer Max Hoffman's first XK-120 buyers: Chicagoan James Kimberly, whose grandfather had founded the Kimberly-Clark company, in a white rendition; and Austin James, in a silvery blue version. The XK-120 was brand new. Jaguar Cars Ltd of Coventry had previewed the new model with great acclaim at the London Motor Show the previous October. The final design was now in production and Hoffman had been quick to grab two from the factory to showcase in America. The Austrian emigré had open his first "Foreign Car Showroom" on Park Avenue in New York in 1947. He had since used hard work and great talent to prosper by importing exotic cars from Britain, France and Italy.

The XK-120 was an open two-seater powered by a new 3442 cc six-cylinder engine developing 160 hp at 5400 rpm. It was a magnificent machine, with a low, tapered body sensuously accentuated by the curves of long,

TOP LEFT: Watkins Glen, 1949 - One of the first Jaguar XK-120s seen in America, both of which were imported by Max Hoffman and present at the 1949 Watkins Glen Grand Prix weekend. The other was purchased by Jim Kimberly and won the Class 1 prize at the Concours d'Elégance.

TOP RIGHT: Watkins Glen, 1949 - The gorgeous Fiat 1100 Special bodied by Paul Farago of Detroit, Michigan. It won the Class 2 prize at the Concours d'Elégance.

streamlined fenders. It looked futuristic, yet was an entirely practical sports car. Wrote British journalist Alan Clark in a later dispatch from the United States about the reaction of early American owners, "Clark Gable has already had three. Another owner described it to your correspondent as 'the car which rings all the bells.' And so it does. Everything about the Jaguar is just dead right, from the name on. ... Certainly, it would be very difficult to see how this car could be improved."

The XK-120 had already proven how potent a pool of racing genes it had inherited from its predecessors. An early XK-120 had broken all existing records for standard production cars on May 30, 1949, by averaging 132.6 mph (213.4 kph) over two runs on a flat, straight stretch of expressway at Jabbeke in Belgium — the nearest speed course Europe had to Bonneville in those days. On August 20, three XK-120s were entered at a one-hour production car race at Silverstone against a highly competitive group of Healey's, Frazer Nashes and Allard J2s. The brand new Jaguars, in the hands of works drivers Leslie Johnson and Peter Walker, beat all opposition, finishing first and second. The British press went wild, and the word about the new Jag spread fast and wide.

Other intriguing newcomers at the Watkins Glen Concours d'Elegance were a Standard-Triumph 1800 Roadster, two Fiat 1100s with special coach work and a very unusual Morgan Three-Wheeler painted bright red.

Top prizes for the first three classes were awarded to Jim Kimberly for his new Jaguar (Class 1); Paul Farago, a Detroit foreign car garage owner, for a navy blue Fiat 1100 roadster he himself had designed and built (Class 2); and Dave Garroway for his impeccable pale yellow Jaguar SS-100 (Class 3).

First Seneca Cup

Once the concours prizes were awarded, owners and officials boarded the participating automobiles. Led by Melton's Mercedes-Benz 540K sporting two red signal flags high on either side of its windshield, and following the school marching band and the festive music it played, they formed a single line and proceeded down Franklin Street. The parade around the village staged by these mighty modern-day charriots brought awe to the sun-drenched crowd and delight to the hearts of enthusiasts.

Now the sun was nearing its high point over the Finger Lakes for this mid-September day. As the circuit was cleared, the 34 Seneca Cup participants began to line up their racers along Franklin Street. This time, instead of forming a grid of side-by-side rows along the axis of the street, the cars were lined up at a 45 degree angle against the left-side curb, one next to the other, about six feet apart. Before the start, the drivers would stand by the right-side curb, exactly across from their machines. Once the green flag was dropped, they would dash across the street, get or jump inside, turn on the engine, fasten their seat belt,

TOP LEFT: Watkins Glen, 1949, Junior Prix. The "Flying Banana" or Merlin Special (Mercury-Lincoln) of Kenneth Hill, repainted red since 1948. Taking the inside track are Tony Pompeo's Fiat 1100 Mille Miglia and Logan Hill's Cisitalia.

INSET LEFT: Watkins Glen, 1949 - The first turn for the Junior Prix. Dave Garroway's Jaguar SS-100 leads E.R. Ogilvie's white MG TC (number 38), Leyland Pfund's Ford Special (nearly hidden), two more MG TCs (including Sam Collier's supercharged version (number 5), and Dud Wilson's Mercedes-Benz S (number 9).

TOP RIGHT: Watkins Glen, 1949 - John Bentley's supercharged MG TC (number 14) leads Tony Pompeo's unique red BMW 328 Coupe driven by Bob Grier (number 25).

CENTER RIGHT: Watkins Glen, 1949 - George Hendrie's doorless ("to save weight") Alfa Romeo 6C-1750 dices in turn one with Richard Hayne's Fiat 1100 S (number 32) and Joseph Ferguson's Cisitalia (number 53).

release the handbrake, engage first gear and get underway as fast as they could, all the while avoiding possible faster starters rushing on from down the grid. This was called a "Le Mans" start as it had been inaugurated by the famous French 24-Hour race long before World War II. This choice of start for the Seneca Cup was yet another effort on the part of the Watkins Glen organizers to make their event as close in both form and spirit to Europe's most prestigious sports car race.

When, almost exactly at noon, Nils Mickelson dropped the green flag, 32 cars managed to get off in good order, with Weaver taking the lead followed by the Collier brothers. One car was briefly left behind, as its driver struggled to get the engine going: George Huntoon's blue Alfa Romeo of Bridgehampton fame.

When the racket returned to Franklin Street, Weaver was in the lead, almost 24 seconds ahead of Miles Collier — driving a supercharged MG TC, pursued by his brother, Sam, who crossed the line 13 seconds later. Next came Garroway's Jaguar immediately followed by Cunningham's tiny Ferrari, showing a handicap of 48.4 seconds on the leader. But at the end of lap 2, Cunningham had moved to

second spot and gained 18.4 seconds on Weaver. It almost seemed like an Italian race; two red cars battling for the lead and fighting for the reputation of two competing marques: Ferrari and Maserati! The Collier brothers and their supercharged MGs followed Cunningham in close formation, while Cole's H.R.G. moved to fifth less than half a minute behind them.

When the leading cars reappeared onto Franklin Street to complete the third of four laps, the Seneca Cup had turned into a suspenseful drama. Weaver was still in the lead, but Cunningham's Ferrari had cut the Bostonian's advantage by another 8 seconds, to just 22.4 seconds. Behind them, Miles Collier was nowhere to be seen, while brother Sam now held third place 10 seconds behind the

Ferrari. Cole had moved up to fourth but Roberts and the famous BuMerc, which had completed first lap in 12th position, were now charging mightily and up to fifth place, a mere 8.3 seconds behind Cole's H.R.G. How would it all end?

Roberts made a superb effort in the fourth and final lap, establishing the lap record for the race in 5:42.1, thus averaging 69.44 mph. But Sam Collier and Cunningham managed to stay ahead of him. Though the Ferrari regained another 8.7 seconds on the leader in the final lap when Weaver hit the haybales in Milliken's Corner, the red wonder from Maranello had had too slow a start to have a chance to win over the short distance of 26.4 miles. Weaver won by 13.7 seconds, giving the Maserati its first road course victory on American soil. The winner's total time was 23:52.9, or an overall average of 66.33 mph. This was almost 2 mph faster than Griswold's Seneca Cup winning Alfa Romeo in 1948.

Grand Prix Time

The thrill experienced by spectators, drivers and officials alike was obvious. There was little time to calm down, so the adrenaline kept flowing. Indeed, the 44 cars which were going to race in the Grand Prix soon filled Franklin Street with great ruckus and pungent smells. Many of the Seneca Cup drivers would simply drive the same car for the Grand Prix, such as Cunningham, Roberts, Cole, Felton and Sam Collier. Others had saved their mounts for the big race: Milliken and his F.W.D.-Miller, Argetsinger and Charles Moran with their Bugatti T-35 As, Arkus-Duntov and Kulok and their "Ardun-Ford" Allard J2s, John Bentley and his supercharged MG TC. Finally, two men changed cars for the Grand Prix: Miles Collier switched from the MG to his much more powerful Mercury Riley Special. Bruce Stevenson switched to an Offenhauser Special. Clearly, things were getting serious.

For one man, though, things were getting bleak instead. Weaver had felt the brakes on his Maserati failing once more the moment he had crossed the finish line to take the Seneca Cup's checkered flag. With less than one hour before the Grand Prix, his crew did not have enough time to fix the trouble. When the announcement of

Watkins Glen, 1949 - The Grand Prix Grid. Front row is occupied by George Huntoon in Alfa Romeo 8C-2600 Monza and Kenneth Hill's Merlin Special. Behind them are Mal Ord in a supercharged Alfa Romeo 8C-2900 B and Bill Milliken in the Miller F.W.D. Mal Ord's Alfa Romeo was entered by Willett H. Brown but actually owned by his business partner Tommy Lee. Phil Hill would buy the car in 1951 and drive it to several victories.

Weaver's misfortune was made public over the loudspeakers, most spectators felt a tinge of disappointment, but not for long. There were enough formidable machines in the field to make for a highly exciting race.

As in 1948, grid positions were drawn from a hat and by class, with Class D drawn first, then successive classes in descending order. The luck of the draw put an unlikely pair of drivers on the front row. On the right side side — equivalent to the pole position — was George Huntoon in the blown 8C-2600 Alfa Romeo, sitting next to Ken Hill's "Flying Banana," repainted red since the first Grand Prix. The second row was occupied by Mel Ord in the two-tone Alfa Romeo, flanked on the left by Milliken in his white F.W.D.-Miller. Behind them was an even less likely pair of cars: Felton's massive silver Vauxhall sat next to Paul Timmins' midget-like "Ardun Special." In the fourth row were Roberts in the BuMerc next to Kulok's Allard K1. Cunningham's Ferrari, classified in Class D because of its V-12 but having an unlucky draw, sat in 6th row next to Miles Collier's Ford-Riley. The 22 pairs of competitors filled Franklin Street over several blocks.

At 1:25 pm, all engines were running, filling the village with swirling wafts of blue fumes and a loud rumble of excitement. Following Milliken's safety instructions, 16 volunteer wireless radio operators from the region, located at strategic points around the circuit, were on alert ready to report any danger or accident. Six freight trains were held up at the railroad crossing, waiting for the end of the Grand Prix before proceeding across state route 409, the flat stretch leading to Friar's Corner and Big Bend. The likely winner of this Grand Prix, according to the experts of the day, would be among the following participants:

Entrant	Car	Engine Type	Displacement	Estimated. hp @ rpm
Roberts	BuMerc	Straight-8	5245 cc	175 hp @ 4000 rpm
Cunningham	Ferrari 166 SC	V-12	1995 cc	150 hp @ 7000 rpm
M. Collier	Ford-Riley	V-8	3916 cc	175 hp @ ? rpm
Felton	Vauxhall OE 30/98	Straight-4	4224 cc	120 hp @ 3500 rpm
Milliken	F.W.D.-Miller	Straight-4	4199 cc	225 hp @ 6500 rpm
Timmins	Ardun-Ford	V-8	4195 cc	175 hp @ 5200 rpm
Arkus-Duntov	Allard J2 (Ardun)	V-8	4195 cc	175 hp @ 5200 rpm
Garroway	Jaguar SS-100	Straight-6	3485 cc	125 hp @ 4500 rpm

Green Flag Down

At 1:30 sharp, with Wilbur Shaw standing by as honorary starter, Mickelson dropped the green flag and the second Watkins Glen Grand Prix was underway. Huntoon was off first and led the pack up Old Corning Hill. Soon, however, the experienced drivers with the most competitive cars caught up with him. Roberts, making the most of the BuMerc's fantastic acceleration, was the first to pass the

BOTTOM LEFT: Watkins Glen, 1949 - Briggs Cunningham's Ferrari 166 SC leading Bill Milliken's Miller 4WD towards the railroad underpass.

BOTTOM RIGHT: Watkins Glen, 1949 - The railroad underpass, midway through a long straight. Dave Garroway's Janguar SS-100 about to be lapped by Miles Collier's "Ardent Alligator."

blue Alfa Romeo, while Cunningham and Sam Collier extricated themselves quickly from their less-than-advantageous grid positions, catching up with Milliken, Timmins and Felton before the first crossing of the railroad tracks. Miles Collier in his "Ardent Alligator," having suffered a bad start, trailed in 17th position.

When the lead group reappeared on Franklin Street, the BuMerc was ahead, crossing the line in 6:02.1, followed by Huntoon 6 seconds behind, Cunningham 20 seconds behind, then Milliken and Sam Collier a few car lengths behind the Ferrari. Miles Collier had moved up to the 14th spot, but was almost a full minute astern of the leader.

In the second lap, Huntoon spun and had to stop for repairs, which put him in the last spot only a short while after he had led the start. Roberts, taking skilfull advantage of the BuMerc's tremendous power, consolidated his lead while Cunningham, now second, was pleased no longer to see anybody in his rear-view mirror. Milliken was still third, but already trailing the Ferrari by over 30 seconds. Less than a quarter mile behind the white Miller, however, there was intense action, some already visible in Milliken's rearview mirror. Miles Collier, irked by his bad start, had turned his frustration into extra speed and moved his Ford-Riley all the way up to fourth, only a few car lengths behind the Miller.

Even more surprising, young Tom Cole had succeeded in moving his 1.5 liter H.R.G. from 12th in the first lap to

5th, only 13 seconds behind the Ardent Alligator. Felton was 6th and John Fitch an excellent 7th in his home-tuned TC. Sam Collier dropped to 41st place as he became one of the first contestants to make the mandatory pit stop on the left side of Franklin Street — costing from 45 to 120 seconds depending on the efficiency of the specific crew. While the two leaders had established their respective positions firmly over the first two laps, the situation behind them was highly fluid, and the required pit stops were just beginning to scramble the positions of the leading contenders.

Indeed, at the end of the third lap, Milliken had dropped to fifth, having been passed by a roaring Miles Collier, then an amazing Tom Cole. The four-wheel-drive Miller was torquey and fast — up to 130 mph — but its three-speed gearing, designed for oval racing, was quite a burden on a course requiring frequent shifting. Behind Milliken, John Fitch had moved ahead of Felton. Official times at the start/finish line were recorded as follows (after 3 laps):

1. G. Roberts	BuMerc	17:29.7
2. B. Cunningham	Ferrari	0:23.9 behind
3. M. Collier	Ford-Riley	0:51.8 behind
4. T. Cole	H.R.G.	1:13.6 behind
5. W. Milliken	F.W.D.	1:30.0 behind
6. J. Fitch	MG TC	1:51.6 behind

At the back of the pack, Sam Collier was beginning to move up through the field after refueling, finishing third lap in 39th place, but only 5:05.0 behind Roberts. Huntoon was still last, a staggering 23 minutes behind the leader. Six cars were already out of commission, including Argetsinger's Bugatti, Ord's Alfa Romeo and Timmins' Ardun-Ford. With so many cars dropping out after only one fifth of the Grand Prix's 15 laps, the event was turning into a race by attrition.

One lap later, the top six positions remained unchanged, although Roberts increased his advantage over the Ferrari by nearly another 5 seconds. In fifth place, Milliken seemed in a bit of trouble, as he completed fourth lap 2:03.7 behind Roberts, and Fitch was fast catching up on him. In fact, the Miller's ignition system was beginning

to act up, cutting off the engine every now and then. Garroway and his Jaguar SS-100 were now occupying 7th place; an impressive performance, having moved up from 12th. Sam Collier continued his catch-up race, moving up seven positions to 32nd.

This overall situation remained fairly stable until the 6th lap when Cunningham narrowed the gap between himself and Roberts to 21.5 seconds; Fitch passed Milliken to gain 5th position; and five more cars dropped out, including the Allards of Arkus-Duntov and Kulok. On the next lap, Milliken experienced mechanical trouble and would lose almost 30 minutes in his pit, restarting in last position 3 minutes behind Huntoon. Meanwhile, Sam Collier had moved all the way up to 16th. Was his very early pit stop going to prove crucial?

On lap 8, Sam Collier and his MG gained another seven positions, crossing the finish line in 9th spot. But the action was all at the front. Cunningham was now putting the pressure on Roberts and the two leading cars roared down Franklin Street practically wheel to wheel. Soon after the right turn into the hills toward White House Corner, the more agile Ferrari passed the huge blue four-wheeled centaur and took the lead. Immediately notified by the public announcement system, the happy crowd applauded. A Ferrari was leading a race for the first time at Watkins Glen. The top seven drivers, none of whom had yet pitted, completed that historic 9th lap in the following order:

1. B. Cunningham	Ferrari	52:06.7
2. G. Roberts	BuMerc	0:07.8 behind
3. M. Collier	Ford-Riley	0:49.3 behind
4. T. Cole	H.R.G.	1:51.5 behind
5. J. Fitch	MG TC.	4:09.6 behind
6. G. Felton	Vauxhall	5:37.3 behind
7. F. Wacker	MG TC Sup.	5:53.3 behind

The only major contender who had already pitted was Sam Collier. His MG TC was now in 8th place, about 6:25.0 behind Cunningham. On lap 10, the situation stabilized somewhat, though Cunningham increased his lead to 11 seconds and lapped fifth placed John Fitch. Sam Collier moved up to 7th only 10 seconds behind Felton and 6:23.0 behind the leader. Then on the next lap his seemingly bril-

enough relevant cars and enough eager spectators to turn road racing into a successful sport in the United States.

- A big part of that enthusiasm came from men who had experienced high flows of adrenaline during the war years while flying the latest airplanes or riding the latest tank into battle. These men were looking for a peacetime outlet which would keep providing them with high levels of excitement and controlled danger. Fitch and Stevenson, for instance, had flown missions in combat planes during the war.

Here is how Bill Milliken expressed his related experience, "I worked as an engineer for Boeing during the war. I had some pretty exciting moments, including being aboard the first prototype of the B-29 on its maiden flight. In the beginning of 1946, as I was staying in New York for a meeting at the Lexington hotel, I saw my first MG, a pre-war TB, parked just in front of the hotel as I walked outside one day. It was love at first sight; I had never seen anything like it. I stood there for quite a while, waiting for its owner to show up. When he finally did, I approached him and he soon agreed to let me buy the car for $1,500. A day later, I drove the MG all the way back home to Buffalo. The old excitement was back!" There was a big reservoir of such men in America then.

- Part of the appeal of road racing stemmed from the obvious rivalry between the sophisticated European production sports cars and the potent but rough-hewn American specials. Most European sports cars had an almost genetic advantage in chassis and suspension designs — European roads were narrow, winding, often poorly paved; indigenous cars required stiff chassis sprung on agile suspensions. American specials had an almost genetic advantage in engine power output — gasoline was cheap in America, roads were mostly straight, the majority of cars were large and heavy; big engines, L-6s, straight 8s, and V-8s, were the norm. Europeans wanted sophistication to prevail; Americans believed first in raw power, especially since new amenities, such as air-conditioning and automatic transmissions, were becoming commonplace. When mixed with national pride and rival class attitudes (the east coast establishment had a much

more European mindset than the Southern California hot-rodders) this rivalry would often become heated and lead to magnificent, and sometimes colorful contests and arguments. This seemed sure to continue for a long time to come.

- Now that the mold had been set in two different places — the waving hills near the Finger Lakes and the flat roads of sandy Long Island — the SCCA and related clubs would have an easier time organizing similar events in varied venues across the country. In fact, the San Francisco MG Club ran its first event on November 20, 1949 on the Buchanan Airfield runways in Concord, situated in Contra Costa County. While the field was small and made up only of MGs, the event meant that Northern California was no longer virgin territory for road racing and the SCCA. The country was now criss-crossed coast-to-coast by enthusiasts preaching the new gospel. In 1950, the SCCA successfully expanded to five new venues in three new states.

- In addition to all this domestic activity, the lure of actually participating in major European road races grew much stronger among several American SCCA members. In fact, around the year-end holidays of 1949, the Collier brothers had pretty much convinced their good friend Briggs Cunningham to stage an all-American effort at Le Mans for the 1950 edition of the famous 24-hour race. "Mr. C." having now gained the experience of fielding a team of three cars — Ferrari, BuMerc, MG TC — at Watkins Glen, had already mastered one of the many essential skills needed to compete sucessfully at Le Mans. He leaned towards going for it; if he did however, he would do it in his customary style and with a winning spirit.

The biggest challenge now facing the SCCA was to attract much more of the attention of the American press, then to convince the European professionals — teams, drivers and ruling authorities alike — to take the tinkering of their American cousins so seriously that they would come and compete in the New World. That would take a lot of doing.

Watkins Glen, 1949. One of the first few Jaguar XK-120s seen in America. Two, imported by Max Hoffman, were present at the 1949 Watkins Glen Grand Prix weekend. This one belonged to Austin James. The other, cream colored, was purchased by Jim Kimberly and won the Class 1 prize at the Concours d'Elegance.

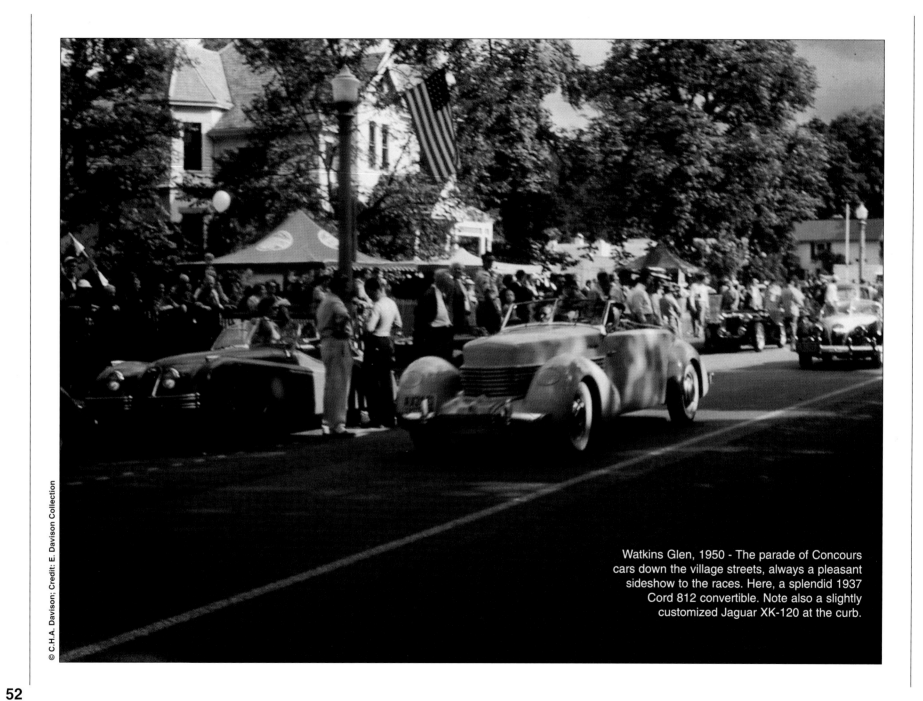

Watkins Glen, 1950 - The parade of Concours cars down the village streets, always a pleasant sideshow to the races. Here, a splendid 1937 Cord 812 convertible. Note also a slightly customized Jaguar XK-120 at the curb.

chapter three
Innocence Lost

Split Asunder

If the formal onset of the cold war can be ascribed to any specific period of time in history, then the ten months that followed the 1949 Grand Prix of Watkins Glen must be among the most pertinent choices. Even before the new year was ushered in, the world had irretrievably split into two deeply antagonistic ideological camps, with nuclear bombs at the ready to prove points. One of the last fateful steps towards a global schism was taken at the beginning of October when China, the world's most populous country, formally proclaimed the People's Republic under Mao Tse-Tung, then allied itself with the Soviet Union. Shortly thereafter, the Kremlin felt secure enough to enforce the effective division of the former Third Reich by setting up the German Democratic Republic with its own government in East Berlin. Because the Federal Republic of Germany in Bonn had elected Konrad Adenauer its first Chancellor a month earlier, there were now two German states, one in each ideological camp.

The fate of German carmakers, former leaders in automotive manufacturing and racing technology, turned mostly on which side of the dividing line their factories had been located before the war. Mercedes-Benz was the luckiest. With most of its production facilities located in Stuttgart not far from the Rhine, the firm's challenge was

"Today, most of our heroes are cultural figures - that is creations of our culture - especially of our entertainment industry. Today rock stars, movie stars and television personalities are all heroes. Yet very few of today's heroes have ever done anything heroic. How many rock stars and athletes have ever risked their lives?"

James Grinnell
(From his book
John Fitch - Racing Through Life)

to dig itself out of the war's rubble and to develop new models despite extremely scarce resources. BMW faced a much tougher task. Though the Bavarian company's original industrial core still existed in Munich, not only was it also in ruins, but much of its design and engineering resources were allocated to Britain as part of war reparations. Worst of all, BMW lost its main manufacturing center which lay in Eisenach just fifteen miles beyond what was soon called the Iron Curtain. Auto-Union fared the worst. Its facilities, concentrated in Chemnitz and Zwickau, were totally inside East Germany, and therefore the company soon ceased to exist. Most of its machine tools were shipped to Russia, along with 17 of the precious pre-war Grand Prix racers designed by Dr. Porsche.

The onset of the Cold War affected France in a much different fashion. The country's natural *gauchisme* found great inspiration in the propaganda war waged by the Soviet Union. The strong influence on public opinion exerted by *les intellectuels*, from Jean-Paul Sartre to André Malraux, also reinforced the socialist and communist parties. The consequences on the domestic automobile industry, which led the world early in the century, were dramatic. At the top end of the spectrum, highly regressive taxes were levied on cars with engines bigger than 2.8 liter, soon making them all but unaffordable. As a result, the few

Credit: Audi Archives

TOP LEFT: The 1937 Eifelrennen at the Nürburgring. Cars number 1 and 4 are examples of the great pre-war Grand Prix Auto-Unions, designed by Dr. Porsche, which were shipped from East Germany to the Soviet Union after World War II. These were Type Cs powered by a 6.1 liter V-16 engine developing 520 hp. Cars number 7 and 8 are Mercedes-Benz W125s.

TOP RIGHT: Roger Barlow's Simca Special at Watkins Glen in 1952. One of the three founders of Cal Club, Barlow was a francophile and owned several prestigious French cars, as well as a showroom on Sunset Boulevard. His Simca is a rare example of an American special of the 1950s based on French mechanicals.

illustrious French manufacturers which had survived the second World War, names such as Delage, Delahaye and Talbot, were gradually driven out of business.

At the low end, the strongly dirigiste government subsidized small inexpensive "popular" cars, such as the Renault 4CV and the Citroën 2CV. While these sold well in their home market, they proved less than practical for both export markets and adaptations for competitive international racing — unlike the Fiat 1100. Simca was a lone exception. Once a source of tremendous prestige for France, the national automobile industry found itself slowly strangled by ideologues. Within a decade, the few surviving French makers would be unable to compete effectively either in major world markets or international racing events. Of the few French cars that participated in the "village streets years" races at Watkins Glen, all were of pre-war vintage, or specials heavily modified by American tinkerers. It would take the French car industry twenty-three years to

produce a competitive car that would win at Watkins Glen: the Matra 670, winner of the six-hour endurance race in 1973.

Leftist propaganda also pushed Great Britain deeper into the illusory utopia of socialism. At the onset of the new decade the Labor Party, led by Clement Atlee and in power since the end of the war, devalued the British pound by 30 percent, formally socialized medical care, and expanded the nationalization of major industries. While the damaging consequences of those decisions on the British automobile industry would not be grasped clearly for a few years, they quickly made life a lot more difficult for small racing entrepreneurs, such as Sydney Allard and Donald Healey.

The outlook was quite different in America where the year 1949 ended on a particularly upbeat note. In November, General Motors publicized a set of financial figures which helped the American public size up the extent of its increasing prosperity. With a press release declaring that "General Motors has always believed in a liberal dividend policy," the world's biggest car company announced that its board had voted to pay its nearly 500,000 shareholders a total of $190 million in dividends on record net profits of $502 million for the first nine months. The majority of American corporations were doing relatively just as well as G.M., and optimism was widespread across the nation.

Nonetheless, the "red scare," fanned by the "loss of China," then the split of Germany, began to creep deeper inside American politics. By the spring of 1950, McCarthyism had become a national malady. The fears it encouraged were fanned mightily at the end of June when communist North Korea declared war on western-backed South Korea and then staged a massive assault southward across the 38th parallel. By Labor Day, three weeks before the third Watkins Glen Grand Prix, hundreds of thousands of American soldiers were committed in the Far East to salvage what appeared to be a desperate military situation. Some automotive plants began to switch back to war production.

Racing Still Thrives

Despite these ominous developments, car racing blossomed further on both sides of the Atlantic during 1950. A favorable stage had been set in 1946 by the Fédération Internationale de l'Automobile (FIA) when it promulgated worldwide regulations for major aspects of the sport. Most important were the decisions affecting Grand Prix racing. Starting with the 1950 season, leading drivers would compete for a newly established Formula 1 World Championship, points for which could be earned in six major European races (*Grandes Epreuves*) plus one American event, the Indianapolis 500. This top championship would be open to both 4.5 liter normally aspirated single-seaters and 1.5 liter supercharged single-seaters. Starting earlier, in 1948, a separate championship would be established for small-displacement cars (under 2.0 liters unsupercharged), formerly known as voiturettes and soon to be called Formula 2. Sports car races kept their existing *ad hoc* regulations within a broad FIA framework.

The world's first Formula 1 championship season began at Silverstone on May 13, 1950, and ended at Monza on September 3, just three weeks before the third Watkins Glen Grand Prix. It was completely dominated by the Alfa Romeo works team, which won all six European events and finished second in four. The first world champion title was in question only between the Milanese team's two top

TOP: The year 1950 saw the official inauguration of the Formula 1 World Driver Championship. The Alfa Romeo works team, driving the superior Alfetta 158, dominated the season. Here, "Nino" Farina is seen leading Juan Manuel Fangio at Spa-Francorchamps in the early stages of the Grand Prix of Belgium on June 18, 1950. Fangio won the race but Farina clinched the first world championship title at Monza on September 3.

MIDDLE: Alberto Ascari in a Formula 2 Ferrari at the Grand Prix de Mons, Belgium on May 14, 1950. The Italian champion won the race in front of three other Ferraris. The real action that weekend, however, was at Silverstone in England for the first Formula 1 Grand Prix ever. Ferrari forfeited the event because it did not have a car ready to compete with the Alfettas.

drivers: Farina and Fangio. Early in the season Fangio seemed well positioned to win but in the end, 'Nino' Farina prevailed. Italy went wild.

Ferrari's best Formula 1 result was second at Monaco in late May. The new Italian marque's tally in 1950 was again the envy of every other car maker, in the sports car formula, even though Maranello's results were slightly less spectacular than in 1949.

Ferrari engineers had developed two larger versions of the V-12 to fit into the successful Carrozzeria Touring bodies (195 S with 2341 cc and 275 S with 3322 cc). However, there would be no official factory team; privateers such as Luigi Chinetti, Lord Selsdon and the Marzotto brothers being entrusted with the task of winning endurance races. Enzo Ferrari soon found out that increasing raw horsepower while leaving racing entirely to private teams had its limitations. The red cars stamped with the prancing horse only won two major such events: the Mille Miglia in April (G. Marzotto - Crossara in Tipo 195 S) and the 12 Hours of Paris in July (Chinetti - Lucas in Tipo 166 MM). Le Mans turned into a disaster as none of the five Ferraris entered finished the race. Enzo Ferrari at least saw the law of numbers begin to work in his favor. There were now over 60 Ferraris of various types riding proud on three continents. Ferrari sports cars earned another five noteworthy race victories during 1950: *Coppa Intereuropa* at Monza in March,

55

Grand Prix du Luxembourg in May, *Coppa della Toscana* in June, *Coppa d'Oro delle Dolomiti* in July, and the Silverstone International Trophy in August.

Still, the competition was assuredly getting fiercer for the seemingly indomitable Italian teams. The British, in particular, were beginning to show results. Jaguar won two major but very different races with their new XK-120 in 1950: the highly challenging five-day *Rallyes des Alpes* in July and the three-hour Tourist Trophy at the rough Dundrod road circuit near Belfast on September 16. The latter marked a very young lad's first international victory, a day short of his 21st birthday. His name was Stirling Moss. Aston Martin won their class (3 liter) at Le Mans and Dundrod, placing well overall whenever they raced their new DB2s.

French makers also showed renewed competitiveness, although theirs was a spottier picture. Talbot did well, not only finishing first and second at Le Mans in June, but also winning the pre-Grand Prix sports car race at Rouen in July. In August, a Peugeot 203 won the first post-war Liège-Rome-Liège, a crushing 5,000 km (3,100 mi.) ordeal across the Alps and back in one single stage. Ecurie Gordini, fielding sleek racers based on Simca components, competed well in the smaller displacement category — up to 1500 cc — but failed to earn major laurels in spite of having Fangio as their lead driver on a few occasions, including Le Mans. No potent new French design was in sight and the new government policies seemed to ensure that none would soon emerge.

BOTTOM LEFT: The Peugeot 203 *Spéciale* of French team Dubois-de Cortanze, winners of the first post-war Liège-Rome-Liège "Marathon de la Route" Rally. The start was given on August 16, 1950 and those who finished returned to Liège on August 20. The winning Peugeot had its original engine enlarged from 1290cc to 1490cc and equipped with a supercharger.

BOTTOM RIGHT: All-Porsche race at the Nürburgring in 1953. The cars on the grid are 1951-1953 356s with between 1100 and 1300 cc engine displacements.

Silver Lining

Italian fans could only wonder where the next threat to their dominance might come from. Could it be from their former nemesis? Germany's western half had just been welcomed back in the international motorsport community. A strong challenge was bound to come from there again one day. The question was how soon. The most fearsome former opponent, Mercedes-Benz, was still reeling from the war and nothing serious from Stuttgart was thought to be on the drawing board. Perhaps Dr. Ferdinand Porsche, the brilliant engineer who had designed Auto-Union's famous rear-engined Grand Prix racers of the 1930s, was to be watched.

Dr. Porsche, his son Ferry and a small cadre of family members and engineers had founded Porsche Konstruktionen GmbH in Gmünd, Austria, in 1946. This group, together with a lean team of craftsmen, were now producing the first car model to carry the name Porsche. Called the 356, the first small two-seater roadster was powered by a slightly modified Volkswagen engine located ahead of the rear axle. The automotive press gave it rave reviews. Nonetheless, the first Porsche's powerplant rated a mere 28 hp, while the company's modest workshop could only hand-produce a handful of cars per year. Italian fans could sleep easy, it seemed.

For the keen observer, though, there were some signs pointing to a possible return of German racing might in the

© Harold Lance

relatively short term. Two new small firms founded by BMW veterans, using proven BMW 328 engine and chassis components, were perpetuating, with limited means, the great German racing tradition. The first company, named Veritas by its three founders, mated pre-war Bavarian mechanicals to an innovative tubular frame chassis and clothed the end-result in a highly aerodynamic, all-enveloping body. Their handsome silver cars allowed former Mercedes team member Karl Kling to win the German sports car championship in both 1949 and 1950. The other new venture was named AFM, which stood for Alex von Falkenhausen, Munich. AFM first set out to build Formula 2 racers, hiring former Auto-Union champion Hans Stück as its main driver. Having shown promising results in 1949, the Munich company aimed for success in Formula 1 during 1950.

The German people's uninterrupted passion for motorsport would prove another mainspring for the renewal of the national automobile industry. After a ten-year twilight, the Nürburgring circuit was officially reopened to car racing for the weekend of August 19 and 20, 1950. Alfred Neubauer, the Mercedes-Benz racing director who had become a living legend in the 1930s, was in charge of the event. A sports car race, then the "Grand Prix of Germany," were the main features on the program. As at Watkins Glen in 1948, the title of Grand Prix was used "with malice aforethought," as Cameron Argetsinger

would have said. The planned main event, to be held over 16 laps, or 227 miles, was for Fomula 2 cars, as no existing German machinery stood a chance within the new Formula 1 regulations.

That Sunday morning, under bright sunshine, more than 400,000 spectators were crowding the fences around the majestic 22.8 km (14.2 mi.) circuit. Most had camped out there since the day before. Not long after dawn, the loudspeakers began blaring martial music. Then, announcers recounted the great German victories of the 1930's. Beer soon began to flow freely. The races proved exciting, with Trintignant's Gordini capturing the sports car race, and Ascari's Ferrari the "Grand Prix." In spite of two fatalities in the junior race and the lack of notable results by any home teams, the first post-war German event held under international scrutiny proved a tremendous success. It became a major morale boost for the German automobile industry.

In fact, the rotund Neubauer made a revealing speech at the awards banquet closing the weekend. After congratulating the French and Italian winners, he declared, "... the great German champions who participated in the races today did not come to win. They all knew beforehand that their machines were not yet competitive, but they raced nonetheless to get their reflexes back in shape." He followed up with a stunning announcement, "... in this way, they will be in great shape for 1953, when we plan to have our new Mercedes-Benz racing car ready. And may I remind you that Hermann Lang still holds the lap record on this track, which he established in 1939 with our super-charged three-liter car at 138.5 kph." German pride was not dead and neither was German industriousness. In fact, the first post-war Mercedes sports car, the 300 SL, would start winning major races one year ahead of Neubauer's boast.

American Wild Fire

In the United States, 1950 was the year of the "Big Bang" for road racing. The spark ignited by Cameron Argetsinger and the SCCA with the 1948 Watkins Glen Grand Prix had ignited fires across the entire nation. The first flash point of the new year was in Florida. Many of the "Eastern Establishment," men who liked to race at the Glen, owned houses both in the Northeast and in Florida where they wintered. A coastal resort in the Sunshine State was therefore a logical outreach for the Connecticut-based club.

Singer Island off Palm Beach Shores became the choice as it featured a new housing development with the roads completed but few structures yet built. Since no racing in the Eastern United States was yet planned for 1950 until Bridgehampton in June, the gentlemen of the SCCA decided that the new year should be kicked off early.

Palm Beach Shores, 1950 - The Fitch Type B, affectionately called the "Fitch Bitch," ready to race. Nearly fifty years later, John Cooper Fitch is still an entrepreneur and passionate innovator.

Credit: John Fitch Collection

Accordingly, they scheduled the Florida race for Tuesday, January 3rd. Their member drivers would not even have to wait for the year's first weekend to race but they would still enjoy a courteous interval for repairing from a possible extended celebration of the passage into a new year. Not surprisingly, the list of entrants for the first Palm Beach Shores Race looked, with few exceptions, like a carbon copy of the 1949 Watkins Glen Grand Prix list of three months earlier.

Though the third day of the new year in South Florida turned out to be affected by inclement weather featuring cool temperatures, wind and even light rain, an estimated 19,000 spectators were crowded on Singer Island before the two-hour show began. They were not disappointed. George Huntoon won a thrilling 105-mile race driving the Duesenberg Special of Ira J. Brundage. He beat Briggs Cunningham in his new Cadillac-powered Healey Silverstone, and George Rand driving the Cunningham Ferrari.

Of note, a factory Jaguar XK-120 came in fourth, at the hands of works driver Leslie Johnson. Sir William Lyons, head of Jaguar Ltd., was quite pleased with the result obtained by his driver in the United States. Great Britain's lofty Royal Automobile Club did not feel the same way. Its board was appalled that one of their "registered" drivers had dared to race in a "non-sanctioned event." They talked about revoking Johnson's licence. Thanks to forceful lobbying by Jaguar, they eventually relented, but a strong message nonetheless had been sent to the talented community of European drivers who could have brought so much to the nascent racing community in America. "The right crowd with no crowding" philosophy hurt on both sides of the ocean.

The West Also Rises

The next official road race in the United States was held three months later on April 16. As in Florida, palm trees graced the landscape, but everything else about the event was quite different. The new site was Palm Springs in Southern California and the organizing body was not the SCCA, but the California Sports Car Club; Cal Club for short. Southern California had none of the three pillars which had allowed the SCCA and its racing activities to spread and blossom so quickly: a pre-war road racing tradition, an establishment of monied aristocrats passionate about racing and a large pool of roadworthy imported sports cars. Nonetheless after the war, southern California being the trend-setting place that it is, caught up quickly with the imported car fashion. That proved a strong enough base to start a local road racing movement. Southern Californians of course approached the sport in their own idiosyncratic way.

Cal Club was founded in 1947 by three enthusiasts: Roger Barlow, John von Neumann and Taylor Lucas. The new Club saw itself as a friendly rival of the SCCA, promoting less stringent qualifying rules for either membership or racing machinery. Hot-rodding was the one racing tradition Southern California had had prior to World War II, and many of the early Cal Club members were former hot-rodders. Bill Stroppe was among the best known and he called himself "one of the backyard guys." Informality and raising hell were always part of their program. Accordingly, blue blood never would be a tacit requirement for belonging to CSCC, nor would one's car need to show, for example, proper door upholstery or an absolutely perfect paint job to be declared raceworthy. Also, if prize money was available, "backyard guys" would feel no shame in accepting it.

John von Neumann racing his MG TC at Torrey Pines in December of 1951. Shortly thereafter, von Neumann became the Porsche distributor for California. Later, von Neumann picked up the Volkswagen franchise as well. His showroom, Competition Motors, was on Sunset Boulevard. He raced and fielded Porsches and Ferraris for a long time.

The California Club had staged several minor events between 1947 and 1949, such as hillclimbs or sprints on private estates or dirt ovals like Carrell Speedway, south of Los Angeles. In retrospect, these were truly rehearsals for bigger and better things. Motivated by the popular successes of the SCCA in the east, Cal Club planned four events for the 1950 season: two road races, at Palm Springs in April and Santa Ana in June, and two hillclimbs. The 52-mile Palm Springs race, held over a 1.5 mile course near the town's airport, was won by Sterling Edwards in his own Ford-powered Edwards Special. The Santa Ana event, run over 44 miles on a Navy Blimp base, was won by Roy Richter (manufacturer of the famous Bell helmets) in a Mercury-powered Allard J2. Two XK-120 Jaguars finished second and third. The second-place finisher, a young Californian whom many thought had good prospects thanks to his performance in an MG at Carrell Speedway in July of 1949. His name was Phil Hill. His car was a brand new black machine just brought from England.

The fact that Cal Club had chosen small airfields with little air traffic as their venue was no accident. The flat surfaces of airfields were a natural choice for Californians at that time. They were readily available and easy to turn into a European-style circuit with curving walls of haybales connecting the natural long straights offered by the main runways. They were easily accessible and made the race itself simple to organize and control — no need to secure approval from countless administrative bodies to stage an event. They also offered plenty of parking space and finally, being flat by nature, they allowed the public who sat in grandstands to view most if not all of the course at all times. The "Nürburgring of America," of course, airport circuits could never pretend to be!

East Meets West

The SCCA, meanwhile, fully intended to be the sole road racing organization in America, with regional chapters eventually covering the entire country. Keeping the sport strictly for well-groomed amateurs remained one of its top priorities. In 1950, capitalizing on its own successes of the previous two years, and benefiting from passionate proselitizing by key members across the country, the young orga-

© Jim Sitz

nization was able to establish strong beachheads in the Midwest and Northern California, first near San Francisco then down to the Monterey peninsula at Pebble Beach. A potential clash with Cal Club was bound to occur at some point, but in these early days, friendly rivalry prevailed.

Following the Palm Beach Shores race in January, the SCCA's next three events were held in the Spring at opposite ends of the country. On May 7, the town of Westhampton, New York, neighbor to Bridgehampton, staged a race called the Long Island Heart Trophy on its Suffolk County airport. Briggs Cunningham earned his first victory there, aboard his Ferrari 166 Spider Corsa beating two Allards to the finish. On May 21, the Club's San Francisco chapter staged its second race on Buchanan Field and this event was won by Sterling Edwards in the same car which had brought him victory at Palm Springs. The east coast members of the SCCA gathered on Long Island again on June 10, a little further east than in May, to race in the second Bridgehampton event. This time, Allard beat the Ferrari and Tom Cole won the laurels, giving the small British manufacturer its first victory in America.

From there, the SCCA jumped straight into the heartland, spurred by the strong leadership of Fred Wacker who had started the Chicago region. The first "ready-made" circuit within driving distance of Chicago that could be both found and secured turned out to be the three-mile test track of the Studebaker Corporation in South Bend, Indiana. The first modern road race in the Midwest was held on June 17. It was won by Kimberly in his Ferrari 166 MM, ahead of Bill Maschinter, a Chicagoan, in an Allard J2 prepared by a young mechanic named Andy Granatelli. Wacker and the other key Chicago members, however, were not satisfied with the South Bend course. Inspired by Cameron Argetsinger's vision, they hoped to find "the Watkins Glen of the Midwest" and vowed to keep on looking.

The last east coast event of the summer was held in Linden, New Jersey, on July 9. Between the fast-expanding SCCA and Cal Club, the racing calendar was already getting crowded. The 30-odd participants in New Jersey were among the familiar faces and cars previously seen at the Glen and along the Florida shores. George Weaver and his beloved Maserati V8RI, George Huntoon and the Blue

Alfa Romeo, Tom Cole and Peter Iselin in their H.R.G.s and Briggs Cunningham with his Ferrari and supercharged MG were all entered. Everyone had great fun once more, especially Larry Kulok who won the race in a Frazer-Nash.

Meanwhile in Chicago, a group of leading members had decided to take a drastic step. Kimberly chartered a single-engined plane, planning to fly over the pastoral countryside north of Milwaukee, Wisconsin, in search of a suitable resort village that would serve their purpose. Kimberly invited along Fred Wacker, Dave Garroway, Karl Brocken and Bayard Sheldon, owner of an MG TC and president of the Harris Bank in Chicago. Soon, they found themselves flying between two large bodies of water about 30 miles apart: Lake Michigan on the right, and Lake Winnebago to the left. Beneath them were the verdant meadows, rectangular fields and sweeping woodlands of Sheboygan county. The glittering surface of many small glacial lakes — Wisconsin has over 8,500 of them — dazzled them occasionally. One in particular drew their attention. The village nearby and surrounding landscape suggested Watkins Glen. They checked the name on the water tower: Elkhart Lake. In no time, they found the airfield at Plymouth, landed, and hooked a ride to City Hall.

Theirs was a perfect choice. Just like Watkins Glen, Elkhart Lake was in search of new ideas to attract more tourism from the major cities within driving range, particularly Chicago and Milwaukee. But the village had little money to invest and faced strong competition from the better-endowed resorts abutting Lake Winnebago, such as Oshkosh and Fond du Lac. By the time the Chicagoans got back to their airplane in the late afternoon they had sealed a deal.

The five enthusiasts first presented their idea to the mayor who then invited the Fire Chief, the Chief of Police, and then a prominent local banker to join the session. Using the experience of Watkins Glen, the Chicagoans did not take long to convince the four local authorities that maybe heaven had brought their village a great if unexpected gift. As the chartered airplane gained altitude and headed south in the dimming sunlight, the five men started talking about all the arrangements they would have to make between their return home and July 23. That was the date which had been agreed to for the first Elkhart Lake Road Race.

The Elkhart Lake Businessmen's Association did its job well. Cliff Tufte, an important local businessman, was made head of racing and took on a very active role. Guided by the SCCA and the experience of Watkins Glen, spurred on by Wacker, Elkhart Lake had everything ready on the eve of the race weekend on July 23. The lack of time had forced the use of a simple rectangular circuit with a mere 3.3 miles and five corners, until a better circuit could be secured. Most important, over 50 qualified participants were in town, eager to open up the Midwest to the new sport. Fittingly, Jim Kimberly won this first race with his Ferrari; Fred Wacker finished second in Kimberly's new Healey Silverstone and a James Feld, driving a Jaguar XK-120 filled the third spot on the rostrum. A crowd of 2,000 spectators witnessed the race. With this event, the SCCA successfuly expanded its frontier to the upper Mississippi River Basin.

As the Labor Day weekend of 1950 passed into history preparations for the third Watkins Glen Grand Prix, scheduled for September 23, were in full swing. By now, bits of the early innocence had begun to vanish for both organizers and lead participants. In just two years, the number of registrants had jumped from 35 to over one hundred; the types of car entered were among the world's best and fastest, many having been raced at Le Mans only three months earlier. The sport itself had become a phenomenon already touching many important parts of the country.

Two major international racing developments which took place in mid-year also had a direct impact on the third Watkins Glen Grand Prix.

Mexican Fever

In early May, Mexico ran its first international road race ever, modeled after the toughest of European endurance events such as the Mille Miglia or Liège-Rome-Liège. The first Carrera Panamericana, running a full 3,453 km (2,146 mi.) across the Sierra Madre ranges from the Texan to the Guatemalan borders of Mexico, was staged over six days from May 5 to May 10. The well-planned

Jim Kimberly taking his own Ferrari 166 MM with which he won at Elkhart Lake through a corner at the first Sebring race, on December 31, 1950. He shared the drive with his mechanic Marshall Lewis. They finished second on the Index of Performance and fourth on distance.

event was open only to "production cars with at least five seats and a closed roof." This was a direct appeal to American stock sedans and coupes being mass-produced north of the border. Bringing in yankee tourists and their hard dollars was one of the key objectives for the Mexican organizers.

The appeal worked as among the 132 qualified cars, all but seven were U.S.-made, including 22 Cadillacs, 17 Buicks, 16 Lincolns, 13 Oldsmobiles, 8 Fords and 4 Chevrolets. Among these, 59 belonged to American entrants, including well-known "backyard guys" Bill France, Joel Thorne, Johnny Mantz, Bill Stroppe and Jack McAfee. No SCCA members, had they even wished to, could participate as the Carrera was not sanctioned by their Club. The fatal clincher was that prize monies would be awarded to the top three teams, the winner being promised over $17,000.

The Mexican organizers were backed directly by their country's president, Miguel Aleman. This helped them to attract a celebrated European team. Alfa Romeo was persuaded to send two of its large 6C-2500 Coupes, famed for their performance in the Targa Florio and the Mille Miglia. The Milanese firm entrusted their cars to champions Piero Taruffi and Felice Bonetto, sending two mechanics along with them. The Alfa Romeo group first sailed to New York where they were met by George Griswold, Alfa Romeo

61

Cunningham's goals for his first Le Mans were to compete honorably and learn as much as possible. He achieved both goals, and even a third one. Both Cadillacs finished and placed favorably. The coupe, driven by the Collier brothers wearing business suits, shirts and ties, finished tenth overall. The "aerodynamic" roadster, driven by Cunningham and Walters, finished 11th. For a first try, this was remarkable, especially in a field from which more than half of the participants dropped out, including all five Ferraris.

Much was learned by the American team: what it takes to last 24 hours in racing conditions, what is needed to win and how tough the competition really is. One of the lessons was that much remained to be discovered about efficient race car aerodynamics: Cunningham's Detroit-made coupe placed better than the Grumman-shaped roadster. "*Le Monstre*" had a top speed of 130 mph, 8 mph fater than the coupe, and a lower center of gravity with a height of only 50" versus 64" for the coupe. This, however, had not been enough of a gain to overcome the 30 minute handicap Cunningham earned early in the race when he went wide in a corner and had to dig himself out of the sand.

Most important for the future of car racing, the thrill and importance of intercontinental competition seized both sides. The French public cheered the American challenge with great enthusiasm. This was more than happenstance. The Cunningham team's brash and winning attitude reminded many of the crews manning the columns of

TOP LEFT: The Cadillac Allard J2 of Robert S. Grier racing at Watkins Glen in September, 1950. Powered by the same basic engine as Cunningham's Cadillacs, the Allard weighed 1,300 lbs. less and therefore had a much more favorable power-to-weight ratio.

TOP RIGHT: New York, September 1950 - Cameron Argetsinger sits in his recently acquired Healey Silverstone. Standing behind the car are, from left to right: Smith Hempstone Oliver, Reg S. Smith, Alec Ulmann, Russell G. Sceli, Nils Mickelson, Miles Collier, George Weaver and Bill Milliken.

American tanks, many powered by Cadillac engines, which had liberated France only six years earlier. The Cunningham crew, in turn, publicized their experience broadly upon their return to America. They vowed to go back a year later with more competitive cars. Alec Ulmann even started thinking about laying the groundwork for America's first 24-hour race in the not-too-distant future.

The first Mexican race and the 1950 edition of Le Mans both helped broaden the horizon of all motorsports enthusiasts around Europe and the Americas. Gradually, European racing teams were beginning to think that North America might be worth more than a passing thought. Little by little, Argetsinger's vision of having the most famous European teams coming to race at Watkins Glen began to look less like a dream and more like a possibility. Both sides also started to look at Le Mans as a terrific battleground to demonstrate that their racing car designs and approach to racing were better than the other's. Jingoism was becoming a potent new ingredient of the international passion for racing.

Watkins Glen: International Ambitions and Local Lore

These influences had direct repercussions on the third Grand Prix of Watkins Glen. When Cunningham and Ulmann returned from France in mid-July, they had visited the FIA people and received confirmation that Watkins Glen had secured the federation's approval for international status. Thus, the Grand Prix event now scheduled for September 23, 1950, would be the first sports car race in America to be sanctioned by the international authorities. The only other American racing events bestowed with that international recognition were the Indianapolis 500 and the Pikes Peak hillclimb.

The Watkins Glen Grand Prix program was also adjusted in three major ways. First, there would now be three races instead of two. The "Glen Trophy" reserved for racing cars under 1500 cc, was inserted between the two existing events. The race schedule, still following a Concours d'Elégance, would unfold as follows between 11 am and the late afternoon:

1. **Seneca Cup**

   Unrestricted formula; flying start after paced lap; 15 laps (99 miles); special fuel authorized.

2. **"Glen Trophy"** (name to be confirmed)

   Limited to Sports Cars up to 1500 cc; Le Mans start; 8 laps (53 miles); regular gasoline required.

3. **Grand Prix**

   Limited to Sports Cars — no displacement limitation; grid start; 15 laps (99 miles); regular gasoline required.

Bill Milliken explained clearly in the 1950 Grand Prix program what the rationale was:

> "Broadly speaking, two general types of cars may compete, namely Sports and Unrestricted cars. Only cars which conform to the Sports Category may race in the main event on today's program. To encourage foreign amateur competition in our events, and parallel competititon by our members in the great foreign classics, the definition of Sports category has been made to conform to the regulations of ... the "F.I.A."

> The "F.I.A." regulations for Sports cars state that at least two seats shall be provided, and that mudguards, lights, self-starter, and a door shall be incorporated, which along with other requirements ensure that the machines are practical roadworthy vehicles suitable for normal sports use as well as racing."

> "The unrestricted category includes all those cars ... which are suitable and safe for competition but do not conform to the strict regulations of the sports category machine. The Seneca Cup race on today's program is for these cars, and here will be found a wide variety of "specials," racing cars, and modified and supertuned sports cars ... this category encourages the enthusiast who would build up or modify an existing machine, and hence gives rise to experiment, and innovation, which in time should result in worthwhile automotive engineering development."

> ... "For fair competition, all cars regardless of category are assigned to a particular engine displacement class, which means that a competitor with a small capacity engine may still be able to win a "class" trophy if he performs creditably against cars of comparable size, and in adition the second race on today's program has been established especially for the small car owners."

The second change was in line with the above paragraph. The engine classes were revised compared to 1949 as follows (as in previous years, adding a supercharger to a car's engine would automatically boost it in the next higher class):

A. Over 8000 cc (488 ci)
B. 5000 cc to 8000 cc (305 - 488 ci)
C. 3000 cc to 5000 cc (183 - 305 cc)
D. 2000 cc to 3000 cc (122 - 183 ci)
E. 1500 cc to 2000 cc (91.5 - 122 ci)
F. 1100 cc to 1500 cc (67.0 - 91.5 ci)
G. 750 cc to 1100 cc (45.7 - 67.0 ci)
H. 500 cc to 750 cc (30.5 - 45.7 ci)
I. 350 cc to 500 cc (21.3 - 30.5 ci)
J. Under 350 cc (under 21.3 ci)

© Harold Lance

Finally, with a view to increasing participation, the MG Car Club and the Motor Sport Club of America, though not affiliated with the SCCA, were invited to select three representatives to participate in the event. Even more open-minded, the top three sports cars drivers finishing the Seneca Cup, be they SCCA members or not, would be invited to participate in the Grand Prix. The intended effect happened: by early September, Watkins Glen had received over one hundred valid applications, and a few more were still expected to trickle in.

What's In A Name?
Cameron Argetsinger then decided that the name for the new race, "The Glen Cup," was a name that might cause confusion with the "Watkins Glen Grand Prix." His choice for a better name settled on a remarkable figure of late 18th century local history, showing that the past can always illuminate the present. The new race would be called the "Queen Catharine Cup."

Catharine was a name that permeated the history of the entire region, way beyond the boundaries of Schuyler County. It belonged to a woman of extraordinary French and Iroquois lineage. Her great-grandfather was Louis Montour, a French officer who, after settling in *La Nouvelle France* in the mid-seventeenth century, married a Huron squaw. The couple had a daughter who, in turn, married an Oneida chief. From that union, Margaret Montour was born and she followed the matriarchal tradition by marrying a Mohawk chief. They had their first child in 1710, whom they named Catharine.

Soon after she came of age, Catharine also followed family tradition by marrying a Seneca chief, named Telenemut. He ruled the village of Shequaga situated about a mile south of the lower bank of Seneca Lake, astride a creek which ended in a spectacular waterfall cascading down the higher lake valley 100 feet below. Catharine and her husband had a fruitful life until Telenemut was killed in battle in 1760. The great-granddaughter of Louis Montour, this "remarkable woman who secured for herself the respect of her people by her fearless and determined character," was then proclaimed Queen Catharine Montour and ruled the village "with power and dignity." Then the American revolution caught up with the Senecas, allied to the British. In 1779, Shequaga was burned to the ground by General Sullivan's soldiers.

Catharine Montour escaped to Canada, where she became an unofficial and respected diplomat, resolving disputes between the English and the Indians. After the American Revolution triumphed, she used her notable negotiating skills to shape and help settle treaties between the Philadelphia Congress and the six nations of the Iroquois Confederacy — to which the Senecas belonged. After she died in 1804, her name was perpetuated in several local sites, including in the towns of Catharine and Montour and in the village of Montour Falls, in the middle of which the Shequaga waterfall thunders. Her name would now be honored once more, but in a modern-day event centered on her ancestral land.

Loud, then Silent Prayers
A serious political firefight which reached all the way down to New York City, did develop in the late summer. By offering a partial embrace to MGCA and MSCA members, the SCCA had not imagined that their act could lead to a dilution of their somewhat explicit, but mostly implicit, elitist philosophy. Yet, when they received an entry form from Alfred E. "Erwin" Goldschmidt, a brash and extremely wealthy New Yorker of Jewish descent whom they knew had excellent driving skills and would come with a potent

Cadillac-powered Allard J2, many hackles were raised. Since Goldschmidt was both an AAA and MSCA member, there was no "neat" way to prevent him from racing. Now the possibility must be faced that if Goldschmidt finished the Seneca Cup in the top three, he would automatically qualify for the Grand Prix. This would set a precedent that many of the SCCA members were not willing to contemplate.

Several key SCCA officials, such as Argetsinger and Miles Collier, did not have any such problems and wished to avoid a bitter controversy. Many heated discussions ensued. The fact that Goldschmidt was known to be a loud and arrogant individual allowed the prejudiced faction to use that reputation in trying to bar his participation. In fact, when Goldschmidt at the time complained to a fellow SCCA member that his being a Jew was the only reason for his problems, Fred Wacker who had overheard him shot back, "Erwin, you think we don't treat you right because you're a Jew. That could not be further from the truth; it's because you're a shit!" In the end and once again, wisdom prevailed. Goldschmidt was allowed to enter the Seneca Cup. The whole affair nonetheless left a pervasive feeling

Watkins Glen, 1950 - A gorgeous Italmeccanica entered in the Concours d'Elégance.

of unease among the SCCA leadership. Many prayed openly that Goldschmidt would not do well enough in the first race to qualify for the Grand Prix.

On on August 30, a more personal yet mournful event touched the founding members of the Watkins Glen races. That day, George F. Boardman died at the age of 54, after a long illness. A banker from Hartford, Connecticut, Boardman had celebrated his 15th wedding anniversary on October 2, 1948, by competing in the very first race held at the Glen in his 1936 Swallow — a black Jaguar SS-1 — and finishing 13th. His wife was an active supporter and had helped him in his duties as the Club's Secretary-Treasurer in 1946 and 1947. An enthusiast since 1929, he told her before he passed away, "My only regret is that the SCCA was not started twenty years earlier." His funeral was broadly attended.

Watkins Glen - Friday September 22, 1950

This time, it looked really big time. Since Wednesday, spectators, participants, mechanics and journalists had been descending in droves on the village of Watkins Glen. All available accomodations within miles were filled to capacity, while many out-of-towners were left with the choice of sleeping in their cars, inside a tent, or even in the fields under the stars. The Jefferson Hotel, locale of choice for a number of participants, was a veritable beehive. Drivers, officials and socialites were seen coming and going almost frantically their movements punctuated only by the slower pace of new arrivals or loud, cheerful greetings. By Friday, Franklin Street was packed with people almost shoulder to shoulder.

All of the available car shops in the vicinity of Watkins Glen, such as the Schuyler Ford Garage, the Gates Pontiac Agency, the Frederick Motor Company (the local Chrysler agency), plus Shannon's Station and Smalley's Amoco Station on Franklin Street, were alive with feverish activity, often late into the night. The *furioso* shriek of an unmuffled exhaust would occasionally shatter the air at unexpected moments. At other times, the low, gut-pounding rumble of a racer wheeling slowly down the street as its driver carefully dodged pedestrians, would thrill onlookers. Lofty spirals of unfamiliar exhaust fumes added to this strange, novel range of sensory stimuli. Even more exciting, however, was the expected quantity and quality of participants. A total of 114 entries had been received by the organizers. No assembly of such first class road racing cars had ever been seen in America.

First, three Ferraris would compete in the Grand Prix: Briggs Cunningham's now well known 166 SC, to be driven by Sam Collier; Jim Kimberly's 166 MM, winner at Elkhart Lake; and William C. Spear's brand new 166 MM. Spear, a Connecticut neighbor of Cunningham, had been at Le Mans in June with the all-American team as pit manager and friendly observer. He had already raced an MG and Jaguar XK-120 in various venues. Now he wanted to go back to racing. Still in the Italian camp, Maserati would be represented once more by "Poison 'Lil," George Weaver wishing to give his potent but temperamental V8RI a third try.

Alfa Romeo was the bet of two drivers: George Huntoon would again drive the blue 8C-2600 roadster, now

BOTTOM LEFT: Watkins Glen, 1950 - John Bishop's striking rendition of George Weaver's Maserati V8RI "airborne" over the railroad crossing while pursued by Bill Milliken in Dr. Scher's Bugtatti T-54. Through the two cars ran in different races, this painting is a superb poetic expression of the intensity racing and competition often took at the Glen.

TOP RIGHT: Watkins Glen, 1950 - The Pery B. Fina-entered Nardi-Danese, powered by a 2.4 liter Alfa Romeo engine, and driven by Jim Pauley in the Grand Prix. They finished a creditable 7th.

called "Old Reliable." The car belonged to his father-in-law, Dr. Samuel Bird. Frank Griswold would entrust his hopes to a supercharged 8C-1500 Type 158, a modified 1949 Grand Prix racer. Both of these cars were entered in the Seneca Cup race. Finally, a Nardi-Danese, the product of a small maker from Turin, was entered by Perry B. Fina of New York for friend Jim Pauley to drive in the Grand Prix. Instead of the usual Fiat engine, Fina had the car equipped with the more powerful 6C-2500 Alfa Romeo powerplant, to reflect the emerging reality of American road racing.

British makes, as expected, were represented in force, constituting by far the majority of entries. A fleet of almost thirty MGs was spread out at the Glen. Most of these were entered in the Queen Catharine Cup race, as the little racer was now recognized as uncompetitive against the new "big guns" fielded in the main events. The much more potent Jaguar model was now replacing the MG in the dreams of ambitious racing enthusiasts. No less than seven Jaguar XK-120s were entered. One would be driven by Dud Wilson, who had finally decided to retire his 1928 Stutz. Another drew particular attention: Logan Hill's was equipped with a Shorrock supercharger, said to add at least 25 percent in power output to the original 3.4 liter Jaguar engine. Finally, two SS-100s were expected to complete the Jaguar entries: Dave Garroway's pale yellow stunner

Charles H.A. Davison, sitting in his Jaguar SS-100 in Ontario, Canada. The car broke down on the way to the Glen and C.H.A. Davison ended up never racing near the southern bank of Seneca Lake. Fortunately, he and son Eric were spectators at the Glen for several years and brought back many precious color photos.

and Charles H. A. Davison's recent acquisition. Davison, an automotive commercial artist, would be driving from Detroit with a contingent of fellow enthusiasts from the home of the "Big Three."

Allard was represented by seven J2s, all but one powered by the increasingly popular Cadillac V-8. The exception was Zora Arkus-Duntov's, equipped with a Ford V-8 with his own OHV "Ardun" head. All "Cad-Allards" were now considered potential winners, especially since one driven by Tom Cole and Sydney Allard himself had finished a remarkable third at Le Mans in June. That very car had been purchased by Bob Grier of New York, and he intended to drive it in the Seneca Cup. The three most likely to vie for victory at the Glen, mostly due to the skill of their drivers, were Tom Cole's roadster; followed by Fred Wacker's highly tuned, black "Eight Ball," equipped with a hydramatic transmission and said to deliver close to 300 hp; then Erwin Goldschmidt's own Cad-Allard. Two Frazer-Nashes, two H.R.G.s and a Jowett Jupiter completed the main British fare, but among these five cars, only Charles Boynton's 1950 Frazer-Nash Le Mans Replica was deemed to have winning potential.

There would be three Healeys in the field. Only two were the genuine British article and one was more akin to an American special. Cameron Argetsinger and Richard K. Wharton of Newport, Rhode Island, both had decided to entrust their hopes for the 1950 Grand Prix to Healey

Silverstones. This latest Healey model was a competitive British sports car typical of the era: a raked, light-weight cigar-shaped body flanked by cycle fenders propped on a sturdy chassis and powered by a tuned stock engine, in this case a four-cylinder Riley displacing 2443 cc and developing over 100 hp. The Silverstone was an excellent mount for advanced enthusiasts, though not powerful enough to win in the stunningly competitive field expected the next day.

Cunningham fielded the third Healey, but his was no run-of-the-mill Silverstone. This was the car which, equipped with a modified V-8 Cadillac, had finished second at Palm Beach Shores in January. The Cunningham team, enlightened by their experience at Le Mans in June, had since boosted the engine's power output considerably by increasing displacement to 6390 cc, or almost a full extra liter! They had also fitted a balanced racing crankshaft and the five-carburetor manifold which had proved itself in France, then installed a DeDion-type rear axle plus 6" x 16" Halibrand magnesium wheels to improve handling performance. Rated at 260 hp at 5000 rpm, the "Healey-Cad" would undoubtedly be the car to beat in both the Seneca Cup and the Grand Prix.

Old France, New Germany

Tellingly, three German racers, all new models, were entered, against four French cars dating from the 1930s. From the Federal Republic of Germany, two Veritas roadsters were entered, confirming previous early signs of a German racing revival. These would be the first two postwar German race cars to do battle in an American road race. Both were powered by the famed BMW six-cylinder two-liter engine, rated at 115 hp. German champion Karl Kling would drive one, entered by Otto Linton, in the Grand Prix. Ralph Knudson would drive the other, previously owned by respected British driver Dennis Poore, in the Seneca Cup.

Upon hearing of the Karl Kling entry, John Fitch was intrigued as Kling was a former Luftwaffe fighter pilot. Fitch recalls, "Having been on the opposite side of the 'recent unplesantness,' I may have been in Kling's gunsights at one time, or he in mine just five years before. Karl

© Harold Lance

may have been the more accurate as I spent the last three months of the war as his guest - a POW in Germany."

Young Kurt Hildebrand, a Chicago Volkswagen enthusiast, registered his own German creation: a "VW Special." This racer would turn out to be the only rear-engined machine and to have the only air-cooled powerplant at the Glen. The low-tub bodywork, painted bright-red, had been created by Hildebrand and bolted to the VW chassis. The owner thought it offered many advantages such as, "a low cost, light-weight though rugged platform, featuring four-wheel independent suspension and a low center of gravity." He had driven the two-seater 700 miles from Chicago to "break it in" properly. These three German cars would certainly be a modest showing for a country that, only ten years earlier, completely and totally dominated the world of auto racing. It was nonetheless a healthy one, fresh, innovative, deploying new thinking on race-proven components.

The French cars were three Bugattis and a gorgeous Talbot Lago Coupé called "Goutte d'Eau" ("water drop"), for its flowing aerodynamic profile penned by Figoni & Falaschi. The Talbot was mostly a gallant entry by James Floria of Milwaukee, Wisconsin. His particular car, though powered by a potent 4.0 liter straight six, was intended by its designers more for touring in comfort than racing to win. Among the three Bugattis, the presence of two of only

TOP LEFT: Watkins Glen, 1950 - Kurt Hildebrand talking to onlookers admiring his rear-engined Volkswagen Special. Nobody then, even Hildebrand himself, could imagine that his basic layout (driver sitting in the middle, ahead of the engine) would become the *only* competitive layout for pure racing cars from the early 1960s onward. Not by coincidence, it was Dr. Porsche who pioneered this concept with the famous pre-war Auto-Unions.

BOTTOM RIGHT: Watkins Glen, 1950 - The 1938 Talbot-Lago "Goutte d'Eau," owned by James D. Floria, parked near the Jefferson Hotel. Floria drove the car in the Grand Prix with racing number 115. He did not finish.

five T. 54s ever built by the Molsheim factory was remarkable in itself. The rare Grand Prix cars, the most powerful ever built by the Bugatti works, were capable of creating a surprise at the Glen. Though very difficult to handle, they could match the modern sports car in overall performance, such had been the competitive intensity of Grand Prix racing in Europe during the 1930s.

The "Type 54" was designed and built in 1932 in a hurried attempt by Bugatti to counter the winning streak of the Alfa Romeo P3, the then all-conquering Grand-Prix machine. Bugatti engineers borrowed the large straight-eight from their famous "Type 50" sports car, boosted its displacement to 4840 cc and installed a supercharger, which gave them a phenomenal — for the day — output of 300 hp at 5600 rpm. The engine was laid on a Type 47 chassis extended to a 9 foot wheelbase, resulting in a machine capable of accelerating fast up to 150 mph, but which was also heavy, hard to handle and exorbitantly expensive to make. A reported ten chassis were assembled, but it seems only five "Type 54" racers were ever completed. One was raced by Louis Chiron at the Grand Prix of Italy at Monza in 1932, where it finished third. Count

© Harold Lance

Stanislas Czaykowski broke a speed record with his own "Type 54" on the Avus circuit in the same year, then was killed two weeks later at Monza when the heavy car left the road and rolled over.

Watkins Glen in 1950 was still not equal to Grand Prix racing at Monza in the 1930s. As Miles Collier had demonstrated the prior year, one could win at the Glen in a V-8 powered 1929 Riley Brooklands. Two wealthy Americans who now found themselves happy owners of the two surviving T-54s decided, independently from one another, to make a bid for victory at Watkins Glen with their prestigious French racers.

A Bugatti Saga

Dr. Samuel Scher, a well-known and wealthy New York plastic surgeon, was the owner of his own vintage car collection numbering about thirty automobiles, including an original T-54 Grand Prix racer he had purchased in Paris from the Bugatti showroom. That car, however, would arrive at Watkins Glen only after a rather bizarre series of adventures, which in turn spurred some highly imaginative modifications. "Doc" Sher had bought the French thoroughbred in 1949, after having been advised of its availability by Luigi Chinetti. Shortly thereafter, he had the precious machine trucked to the port of Le Havre to be loaded on a transport ship.

The blue Grand Prix racer was carefully rolled on its own loading platform, then lifted slowly by a crane under the watch of stevedores. As the whole assembly was hovering mid-point between the dock and the hold floor, a cable snapped. The precious automobile crashed into the bowels of the ship, almost fourty feet below. The damage was severe. Besides cosmetic distress, the Bugatti suffered a badly bent frame, a bent front axle, a cracked oil pan and a broken front wheel. After reviewing his options, "Doc" Scher decided to have the battered thoroughbred transported back to Paris to have it restored by Plisson, the renowned Bugatti repairers.

It took a year of painstaking work, then the Bugatti finally and safely crossed the ocean on the Queen Mary, arriving in New York on May 26, 1950. "Doc" Scher was an impatient and avid enthusiast who, upon hearing in mid-

Watkins Glen, 1950 - Dr. Scher's infamous Bugatti T-54 being driven towards Franklin Street for Bill Milliken to race in the Grand Prix. A General Motors Hydramatic transmission had been fitted between the engine and the driving wheels! Both car and driver would end up upside down in a ditch early in the Grand Prix, fortunately without harm to the driver.

May that the car was finally sailing from France, immediately entered it in the Bridgehampton race scheduled for June 10. Bill Milliken, whom Alec Ulmann had strongly recommended to him, would be his driver and technical expert. Milliken had little time to give the Bugatti the intended thorough check as the unusual car took a week to clear customs. Instead of spending a week at Cornell Laboratory before the Bridgehampton race, the Bugatti spent 30 hours at Dick Simonak, of Patterson, New Jersey, a prime tuning shop. It was found to be in reasonable condition, except for the cast-aluminum gear box housing which, French craftsmen notwithstanding, still showed a hairline crack about four-inch long. After a technical debate, it was agreed that the risk of serious oil leakage, even under racing conditions, was very small.

"Doc" Scher insisted on racing the car anyway, so the Bugatti, with Milliken at the wheel, was tied by a tow line to The Cornell engineer's own Hudson sedan, which one of his mechanics would drive. This strange pair of cars then proceeded to Bridgehampton, a trip of about 150 miles, in rush-hour traffic, first through the Lincoln Tunnel, then across Manhattan, then all the way to Bridgehampton. This was Thursday evening June 8, the day preceeding inspec-

tion and qualifying and a mere 36 hours before the race on Saturday. The Bugatti was prepped by mechanics, then road-tested by Milliken that very Thursday night, then again early on Friday morning, proving a delight to drive. The French car passed techical inspection, and did fine in practice.

In the main main event on Saturday, Milliken started from the third row on the grid, quickly moved up and soon held second position behind Tom Cole's Allard, pushing for the lead. Milliken's attack came to a grinding halt when the Bugatti's gearbox, having lost all its oil despite the earlier diagnosis, seized, then broke completely. Milliken was forced out and "Doc" Scher was crushed. As he himself wrote later in Sports Car, "This was a serious predicament because ... no transmission parts or cases were available, making impossible the restoration of the car to its original state."

Yankee ingenuity was called upon to save the precious French machinery from forced retirement. The Bugatti was trucked to Buffalo and entrusted to the Cornell Aeronautical Laboratory under the supervision of Bill Milliken and his engineers. Since finding a suitable transmission would clearly be the toughest problem to solve, the team started by making the Grand Prix car conform to modern road racing regulations and be practical to race, new pieces were manufactured and fitted. Included were headlights on a custom frame in front of the radiator, front and rear fenders, a spare wheel and spare wheel holder in the tail, a horn, and a airplane-type starter with a 24-volt battery.

Meanwhile, no suitable transmission was being found. Then one day, while eating a quick lunch in the Laboratory's cafetaria, a colleague suggested to Milliken that he investigate General Motors' new Dynaflow automatic transmission. This new torque converter technology, conceived in Detroit for comfortable driving in big American cars, had recently been introduced on top-of-the-line G.M. models. Charles Chayne was the engineer in charge of its development. After leaving the cafeteria, Milliken immediately called Chayne, who himself owned a Bugatti Royal. A quickly assembled work group determined that fitting such a new type of transmission to a 30-

year-old French Grand Prix car might be feasible. However, feasible does not mean easy. To quote "Doc" Scher again, "after thousands of man hours, much mathematical work, a great deal of engineering and mechanical ingenuity," the Dynaflow was succesfully integrated to the drivetrain of the 1932 Bugatti Grand Prix racer!

As a final precaution, before being reassembled, and to avoid any further unhappy surprises, the French wonder was also entirely disassembled, every piece magnafluxed and checked by a stress engineer before all parts, old and new, were reassembled! Then, and only then, was "Doc" Scher able to say, "The car was road-tested and the operation of this [Dynaflow] unit was completely satisfying to the staff of engineers." Bill Milliken would have quite a racer ready for Watkins Glen. Had the Bugatti been given a nickname, "Lafayette, Here We Are" would have been most appropriate.

The other Type 54 owner was D. Cameron Peck, scion of the Bowman Dairy in Illinois and current president of the SCCA. His Bugatti was called a "Le Mans 54," as the original mechanicals had been rebodied in two-seater "roadster" style in 1936 by then owner L. C. Bachelier. The Type 54 was one of the jewels of Peck's vintage collection of over one hundred automobiles and many steam boat racers. For the 1950 Seneca Cup, Peck convinced friend Hal Ullrich to be his driver. The third Bugatti was a more "standard" Type 35 B entered by Arthur W. German of Englewood Cliff, New Jersey.

American Brew

The final and most fascinating contingent of entries was the American specials. It was made up of nearly twenty machines, the largest group outside the MG pack. This grouping was only a fiction of nomenclature of course, as nothing in motorsport better expressed American individuality than these special racers. Each of these cars in fact represented in very unique ways the whims, hopes, particular interests and biases, not to mention financial means, of its specific owner.

John Fitch, for instance, came to Watkins Glen with a car he called the "Fitch Type B," as it was the second special of his creation. Actually a refinement of a prototype —

Credit: John Fitch Collection

"Type A" — he had conceived in 1948, the "Type B" was his attempt to come up with a racer he hoped to put into production and sell for a profit. Fitch followed the school of Sydney Allard and Donald Healey, intending to offer "a sport car of moderate size, combining a high degree of controllability with competition performance. Obviously, a high power-to-weight ratio [is] a perequisite." The business aspect, though, was secondary to Fitch. The MG he had raced the previous year — bought courtesy a G.I. loan! — just could not cut it. He could not afford to buy a competitive car, so he built his own.

The chassis and suspension were essentially Fiat 508 components, including lined drum brakes and an aluminum differential. This he enhanced with a rear anti-roll bar. The engine was a modified Ford 60 Flathead displacing 2262 cc, said to produce 105 hp at 5300 rpm. It was a readily available small V-8 developed in a high-revving racing version for Midget cars. The Fitch Type B body was a Crosley Hot Shot roadster base amply redesigned by Fitch himself. With a dry weight of just 1520 lbs., the "Fitch Bitch," as it was soon universally known in racing circles, could go from 0 to 50 in 6.3 seconds. The ex- P-51 Mustang fighter pilot had entered it for the Grand Prix, he would race a 4.9 liter "Merc-Lagonda" in the Seneca Cup, lent to him by R.

N. Sabourin of Flushing, New York. That car had raced both at Indianapolis in 1946 and at Bridgehampton in 1949.

Paul Farago of Detroit, the man who had won his category in the 1949 Concours d'Elégance, entered the winner of that beauty contest into the Queen Catharine Cup race. Also built on Fiat 508 components, but keeping the original 1089 cc Fiat engine, then graced with Paul Farago's own sweeping roadster body design, there was a car with a chance of winning its class (G) in the junior event. In that same race Phil Stiles, seventh finisher of the 1948 Junior Prix with an MG TC, would compete with his own improvement on an H.R.G. "aerodynamic." He had lightened up the newest factory bodywork by cutting deeply into the fenders and rearranging the headlights. The engine remained the original Singer 1.5 liter straight-four.

Denver Cornett, veteran of the two previous Watkins Glen events, decided to rest his trusted MG for the Seneca Cup. Hoping that a much larger pack of horses would give

Credit: C.H.A. Davison; credit E. Davison Collection

him a better chance to finish in the top positions, he entered an unusual car designated Ford Special despite its more complex origins. It was actually an Indianapolis two-man racer which was raced by Charles Moran at the 500 in the early Thirties. Built unofficially for Moran by DuPont technicians, it featured an aluminum body, hydraulic shock absorbers, Ford wheels and brake drums. It was powered by an engine built by Briggs Weaver — George Weaver's father — based on a Ford Model A four-cylinder OHC fed by a single Winfield carburetor. Cornett heard about the car from Otto Linton, who owned Speedcraft Enterprise, an auto and tuning shop located in Exton, Pennsylvania. The car was owned by a David Felix, and it was for sale. Cornett bought it in August of 1950 and asked Linton to test and tune it.

While giving the car a good run on a road in York, Pennsylvania, Linton blew the old Ford engine. The new owner and his friend made a quick decision to drop a more recent 4.6 liter Ford Flathead V-8 in the engine compartment. Its horsepower was over 160, or more than twice that of Cornett's MG TC.

That power range put him straight in the category of Miles Collier who, having won in 1949 with his bright red "Ardent Alligator," decided to re-enter the Riley-Mercury in the Glen's unlimited event. Brother Sam Collier had won the Mount Equinox hillclimb with that car a few weeks earlier. The Grand Prix race now required participating cars to have headlights, fenders and a spare wheel, as FIA regulations dictated for sports cars. Similarly, but in his case despite lack of previous success, Ken Hill once again entered his Merlin, a.k.a "Flying Banana," in the Seneca Cup.

Also in the category of ancient American iron was a 1936 Ladd equipped with a Ford 3.6 liter V-8 powerplant. Its original owner, John C. Reuter, was a friend of the Colliers and had raced the car in a number of the pre-war ARCA events. Reuter had dubbed it "Old Grey Mare." Its new owner and driver, Robert J. Wilder, kept the name. Two modified Duesenbergs would also compete in the Seneca Cup. One was familiar, being I. J. Brundage's Palm Beach Shores winner to be driven by George Huntoon. For the Glen race, this car had just been refitted with a 5.0 liter Oldsmobile V-8 replacing the less potent Ford Flathead.

The second Duesenberg was a J model with its original 6.9 liter engine capable of delivering 255 hp. It belonged to and would be driven by Arthur J. Hoe of Westport, Connecticut, a man known by the road racing community as "the compleat Duesenberg enthusiast."

Bruce Stevenson would field the Meyer Cadillac, the car with which he had won the New Jersey race in July. Frank Dominianni of New York entered a 1946 "D&D Special" for friend Arthur Dury to race in the Seneca Cup. They did change the engine from the original Ford V-8 to the new Cadillac powerplant. Finally, Sterling Edwards, a man who had raced in Cal Club and California SCCA events, planned to be at Watkins Glen with his Edwards Special. There was no better place to be than a car race for a man wishing to promote the first American-made sports car, a product of his own design.

Dawn

When the sun rose over the Glen early on Saturday morning, a pleasant canopy of blue sky graced the Finger Lakes region. A cool wind gusted occasionally, rocking trees and reminding everybody that this was the second day of Autumn. The people who had toured the circuit, especially race drivers, noticed some significant improvements to the road surface. The jarring macadam formerly patched over the first third of the circuit, from Old Corning Hill to the School House Corner, had been entirely and smoothly resurfaced. Drivers could now run full throttle along the long straight dipping and needling through the railroad underpass. As a result, both the spectacle and the lap times would improve. At the opposite side of the circuit, however, drivers would have to remain extra vigilant as the stretch of road leading from Archie Smith's Corner to the beginning of Big Bend was still plain gravel and dirt.

Of the 114 entries, 73 were validated on Saturday morning. Besides the usual scratches caused by last-minute personal priority changes, the loss of entrants was also accounted for by the recent call of military duty due to the raging Korean war. Finally, the late realization by would-be European participants that no reimbursement of travel expenses, let alone appearance or prize money, were allowed by the SCCA, had the same effect. One of those even sniped, upon hearing of the race distance, that he was not interested in "sprint races." To John Fitch's chagrin, Karl Kling and his Veritas stayed in Germany. Leslie Johnson, British champion, and Le Mans winner, Lord Selsdon, also stayed home.

A few domestic drivers could not start the race from sheer bad luck. Charlie Davison's white SS-100 never made it to the Glen. Charlie spun a rod bearing on a fast stretch of road in Ontario, and had to leave the car in a nearby field under the watch of a few puzzled cows. He and son Eric boarded another car from the Detroit contingent of which the SS-100 was part. Had they not made it to the Glen that weekend, this book would be bereft of a great many historical color shots.

In contrast, Logan Hill and his blown XK-120 made it to Watkins Glen, though the British roadster never appeared on the starting grid either. Its engine blew a piston early on Saturday morning, a damage which could not be repaired in time. Logan Hill had found himself on the wrong side of the compromise competitive racers always face: best performance versus acceptable reliability. While superchargers did boost an engine's power output by 30 percent or more, they also added great stress on pistons, rings and bearings.

Others experienced a different kind of bad luck. Despite their great efforts to the contrary, life occasionally surprised enthusiasts with unplanned weekend priorities more pressing than racing. Arkus-Duntov and Sterling

Watkins Glen, 1950 - Ralph Knudson's Veritas RS at Smalley's garage. The beautiful streamlined body of the German car is evident. Karl Kling, German champion, was expected to drive a factory Veritas, which would have been entered by Otto Linton. SCCA rules convinced the Munich-based company it was not worth the trouble.

Edwards could not be present at Watkins Glen, and neither could some twenty other registered entrants. These unwitting absentees, plus the void in representation from overseas works team and drivers, were clearly regretted. Most people milling about Watkins Glen on that late September weekend felt this was almost made up by the international character and racing patina of the validated entries. After all, with a field of 73 cars, many of world class pedigree, some even coming straight from a successful participation at the latest Le Mans event, it was going to be a splendid day! Where else in America could one witness such a field of high performance sports cars?

Concours d'Elégance

Around nine o'clock, as thousands were finishing breakfast, an unfriendly blanket of gray clouds, pushed by a rising wind, began to slip underneath the bright blue sky. The temperature dipped, sending campers back under their tent to grab sweaters or jackets. The skies then seemed to stabilize, easing weather worries that had suddenly arisen. The first event of the day, the Concours d'Elégance, could proceed as scheduled at ten o'clock.

Participating Concours cars were grouped in three main classes: Veteran (built before 1925), Vintage (1925-1931) and Modern. Each class was sub-divided into "regular type cars" and "sports type cars." A total of 53 automobiles were entered, giving the public the rare spectacle of a vast, moving "Automobile Museum" unlike anything then existing in America. Journalist Jim Christy wrote his impressions in a follow-up article, "[the Concours] is a mouth-watering delight from start to finish. It is by no means limited to cars of American origin. Europe's best will vie with western offerings for the crowd's applause and the favor of the judges. You will see examples of next-to-impossible underslung, the meticulous coachwork of unhurried hand craftsmen, bodies of metal panels formed without benefit of 100-ton hydraulic presses, luxury intended for only the world's wealthiest. Here indeed is motordom at its historical and contemporary loveliest."

Chairman for the Concours was Reginald S. Smith, while the Chief Judge was none other than opera star James Melton. The top prize winners in the Modern cate-

© Harold Lance

gory were a Rolls-Royce Silver Wraith (regular cars, awarded gold bowl) and a Mercedes-Benz 540K (sports cars, awarded silver bowl). In the Vintage category, a 1930 Type L29 Cord Convertible was awarded first prize and a silver bowl; while a 1914 Stutz Bearcat won the gold bowl in the Veteran category. As in previous years, the Concours ended with the cars participating in a festive parade through the village streets. This seemed the perfect warm-up for the races to come.

© Harold Lance

The 1950 Seneca Cup

Countless wristwatches now confirmed that the sun would reach its autumnal zenith in a little more than one turn of the big hand, but no one at Watkins Glen could tell by peering overhead. The cloud cover had become thicker yet; the wind chillier. It felt like rain and though not a single drop had fallen, the dusty asphalt covering most of the circuit was moist from the ambient air. It was that unmistakable moment when the landscape could quickly dim as blinding sheets of rain suddenly drenched everything, or instead slowly brighten and stay dry as a lucky shift blew the darkest clouds overhead towards the horizon. As it happened, the wind stabilized and the uneasy suspense continued.

Then, shortly before 11 am, a roar of thunder boomed inside the valley. Not a bolt from the sky, this was the

MIDDLE LEFT: Watkins Glen, 1950 - The Bugatti T-55 entered by Briggs Cunningham in the Concours d'Elégance. With a blue hood, black fenders and trademark aluminum Bugatti wheel hubs, this was a magnificent automobile based on the T-54 Grand Prix racer. This roadster was powered by a 2270cc dohc straight-eight engine.

RIGHT: Watkins Glen, September 1950 - Cameron Argetsinger drives Cunningham's "Le Monstre" as the pace car for the Seneca Cup. Sitting next to him is his proud father.

sound of over 5,000 horsepower suddenly let loose in the straight and narrow confines of Franklin Street. Twenty two drivers had just fired up their engines, readying their unlimited cars for the warm up lap of the first race. Near Seneca Lodge, in the rolling wooded hills a mile west of the starting line, crowds of excited spectators could hear the distant rumble echoing up from the valley. Their impatience to see the snarling racers increased, athough they knew it would take a few more interminable minutes for it to be satisfied.

Cunningham's otherwordly "Le Monstre" had been given the honor of leading the warm-up lap. Cameron Argetsinger was at the wheel, with his proud and smiling father sitting right next to him. The car's hulking mass was now proceeding slowly over the section of Franklin Street spanning the creek. The slab-shaped Le Mans veteran, sporting its deceiving white color with the dark blue "mohawk" in the center, stood in complete contrast to the herd of aggressively curvaceous racers roaring behind it. The daring prototype which had raced over 1,951 miles in 24 hours at an average of 81.32 mph in the heart of France only three months before, now slowly led the field around the circuit. Some ten minutes later, this "Le Mans finisher" would symbolically cross the finish line ahead of the pack, then continue down Franklin Street past the right turn leading to Old Corning Hill, unleash twenty-one snarling racers, and simply retire. It would never race again. "Le Monstre" was too bulky to even make an attempt at racing

Credit: Richard Irish Collection

on the Watkins Glen circuit, and already too outdated to compete sucessfully in international races.

The warm-up lap continued, with the awesome caravan howling on between the thick patches of waving spectators strung along successive parts of the circuit. After Seneca Lodge, it thundered past those spectators stretched before and after the straight through the railroad underpass, then past the Old School House Corner, then by the Stone Bridge hollow, then around Archie Smith's corner. When the 22 cars rolled by each successive group, the booming snarl hit people in the gut and for them everything else turned instantly and strangely silent. When finally the last stragglers disappeared round the next corner, the gradual return to pastoral quietness was almost a relief. One could catch one's breath, regain composure. Then a moment later, one wished to experience that incredible rush again.

Running Start

The rolling thunder boomed on, all the way round Big Bend, then down Steuben Street, then echoed between the first contiguous and tall buildings of the village at "Milliken's Corner." Just as the eleventh morning hour was about to strike, "Le Monstre" veered back onto Franklin Street. Every human on the village's main straight was standing, head craned northward towards the end of the street, with Seneca Lake in the distance. Argetsinger, his own pulse rate accelerating, crossed each successive intersection preceding the Courthouse at a fast-increasing speed, closely followed by the yet unleashed Seneca Cup contenders. Allards, Healeys, plus "Poison 'Lil" and the "Ardent Alligator" were closest behind, ready to pounce the instant they crossed the start/finish line.

As the church-like steeple of the Courthouse loomed briefly in their left field of vision, the lead drivers might have wondered about the strangeness of the rectangular, sloping rear of the Grumman-modified Cadillac racing ahead of them. They had, however, little time to reflect. Just before crossing the white line, the drivers shifted into third gear nearly in synch, turning up the noise volume to ear-shattering levels, leaving behind a heady mist of exhaust fumes which swirled devilishly upwards. When the main pack roared by the Courthouse, the leaders were

Watkins Glen, September 1950 - Jean Davidson's Allard J2 "tangled with a tree while in the lead in lap one. The tree won." The driver was unhurt.

already downshifting for the first turn, the ninety degree right-hander leading up the first hill. Those with the steeliest nerves took advantage of the hectic slow-down to win a position or two, then everybody wiggled up Old Corning Hill, past Seneca Lodge, and rushed up towards the White House esses.

Ahead of the pack in those early moments was, not so surprisingly, a Cadillac-powered Allard J2. Remarkably, the driver was little-known Jean Davidson of Washington D. C. The young man soon demonstrated what for seasoned European race organizers was a basic rule of the sport, "Nothing will stop an inexperienced driver faster than having a fast car to drive." Perry Boswell described it best in the December, 1950 issue of *Road & Track*, "Davidson had heavy foot trouble and argued with a tree — the tree won and the Allard retired with a heavily dented nose." Luckily, only the driver's pride was wounded. This put the George Weaver and his loyal "Poison 'Lil" in the lead; Erwin Goldschmidt into the second spot, chased by Phil Walters in the formidable Healey Cadillac, followed by Hal Ullrich in Cameron Peck's Bugatti Type 54 roadster.

First Wounds

In the pursuing group, Denver Cornett was roaring up the hill in his new Ford Special, attempting to recoup from an unfavorable grid position due to an unlucky drawing. The 24-year-old Kentucky-native was also tired, as he had driven all the way from Exton, Pennsylvania, to Watkins Glen the day before, in order to break in his new engine. As he crested the hill and faced the tantalizing beginning of the long straight, Cornett decided to capitalize on his car's fantastic acceleration to overtake the car a few hundred feet ahead of him, a Jaguar XK-120. The needle's eye of the railroad underpass was threaded at over 120 mph. At the end of the straight, when the road turns right past an apple orchard, Cornett was right behind the Jaguar. As both cars thundered towards the short, crooked descent toward the Stone Bridge, Cornett attempted a pass on the left. Right at that moment, the Jaguar also moved to the left, and its right rear frame horn got hooked by the Ford's front bumper.

Still going close to 100 mph, Cornett's special was thrown off balance. It slid off the road and hit a telephone pole broadside on the right, an instant after felling a fireman. Miraculously again, Cornett, though terribly shaken, was unhurt. Thanks to the safety belt, he had not been ejected and his head missed the telephone pole by a few inches. The car was completely bent. Ken Purdy, the famous editor of *True Magazine*, was first on the accident spot. He freed Cornett from the wreck and quickly realized that the Kentuckian was more concerned about the fate of the fireman than his own condition. Though the fireman was seriously injured, Ken Purdy, who had witnessed the accident, immediately reassured Cornett that it was not his fault.

For the first time, a serious injury had been sustained at Watkins Glen. Luckily again, as hindsight confirmed the real possibilities for a catastrophe, limited harm was inflicted. Cornett was shaken but unharmed, while his new car was a wreck. The young driver, even after being reassured that the victim's life was not at risk, decided he had had enough for the day.

The opening lap claimed another victim, this one of a mechanical nature. George Huntoon saw his hopes flicker

A representation of Hobart A. H. Cook in his MG TC "in full recovery" during a Seneca Cup race at Watkins Glen.

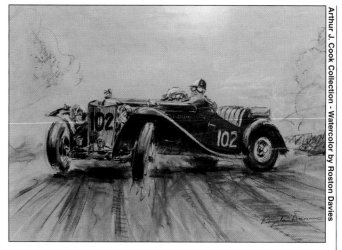

Arthur J. Cook Collection - Watercolor by Roston Davies

as the ignition of the Oldsmobile V-8 recently fitted to his Duesenberg Special began to falter. Before returning even once to Franklin Street, Huntoon had to sideline his potent car. The luckier contenders roared by the Courthouse to start their second lap in tight formation:

End of lap 1:

1. G. Weaver	Maserati V8RI	5:23.6	
2. E. Goldschmidt	Allard J2	0:07.1	behind
3. P. Walters	Healey Cad.	0:16.0	behind
4. H. Ullrich	Bugatti T. 54 LM	0:21.8	behind
5. M. Collier	Riley - Mercury	0:27.1	behind
6. A. J. Hoe	Duesenberg J.	0:29.5	behind

Weaver kept his lead through the second lap, but his two closest pursuers gave him a real chase, steadily narrowing his initial advantage to just a few car lengths. Behind this leading troika, Miles Collier and "Ardent Alligator" began to make their bid, passing Hal Ullrich, moving into fourth and cutting their deficit against Weaver by more than seven seconds. Sixth place was held by Arthur J. Hoe in his de-fendered Duesenberg J. Less fortunate was John Fitch, whose Merc-Lagonda began to break down after holding 9th position in the first lap. Fitch would complete the second lap, but not the third. After only a little more than ten minutes of racing, the black-snouted red Maserati flew across the start/finish line in the lead for the second time, still in the lead but barely ahead of his two Cadillac-powered pursuers.

End of lap 2:

1. G. Weaver	Maserati V8RI	11:01.1
2. E. Goldschmidt	Allard J2	0:01.6 behind
3. P. Walters	Healey Cad.	0:02.3 behind
4. M. Collier	Riley - Mercury	0:41.5 behind
5. H. Ullrich	Bugatti T. 54 LM	0:48.8 behind
6. A. J. Hoe	Duesenberg J.	0:51.4 behind

The third lap soon provided some foretelling drama. The leader, George Weaver, lost control of "Poison 'Lil" when an overexcited spectator ran across the road in front of him. Weaver swerved to avoid the imprudent man, but then slid, tapped a number of haybales, raised a lot of dust, then found himself on the roadside unable to restart. The lead passed briefly to Erwin Goldschmidt but the outsider from New York could not long resist the assaults of Phil Walters' hellishly powerful Healey-Cadillac. Walters passed the Allard before Big Bend and Goldschmidt did not challenge him again. His goal, after all, was to qualify for the main event, not to win the Seneca Cup at all costs.

By the time the leaders were back at the bottom of Steuben Street, Walters held a ten-second lead over Goldschmidt and the Allard driver saw no signs of Miles Collier in his rearview mirror. The "Ardent Alligator," truth be told, was now giving its driver a rough time. Its gearbox

Watkins Glen, September 1950 - Erwin Goldschmidt in the cockpit of his Allard J2 on the grid. The controversy surrounding his entry seems to show on his face.

had locked into third gear, handing Miles Collier a formidable challenge if he was to maintain his position. Collier's best hope was that the ample torque of his Mercury V-8 would make his task somewhat manageable. Behind him, both Ullrich and Hoe were keeping pace in fourth and fifth position, while Arthur Drury moved into sixth with his Cadillac-powered D&D special. At the completion of the third lap, less than two minutes separated the top six contenders. They were greeted by loud applause from the spectators as they rocketed down the half-mile stretch of Franklin Street.

End of lap 3:

1. P. Walters	Healey Cad.	16:16.2
2. E. Goldschmidt	Allard J2	0:12.5 behind
3. M. Collier	Riley - Mercury	0:59.6 behind
4. H. Ullrich	Bugatti T. 54 LM	1:10.2 behind
5. A. J. Hoe	Duesenberg J.	1.21.5 behind
6. A. Drury	D&D Special	1.54.1 behind

Now the leaders of the Seneca Cup had emerged. Barring a major upset, the eventual winner was among this group of six. In fact, during the fourth lap, these men started lapping the slowest drivers, such as Ken Hill (Merlin) and Ralph Knudson (Veritas). Meanwhile, Miles Collier was doing a superb job driving in third gear only and maintaining a solid third position. Then a seemingly minor mishap happened to Arthur J. Hoe. His Duesenberg's exhaust pipe began to break, threatening to fall off. As a result, he began to lose time, and positions. Arthur Drury was the first to pass him, then Charles Boynton surged from seventh to fifth, making the most out of his agile, Bristol-powered Frazer-Nash Le Mans to pass both Hoe and Drury. At the end of Lap 4, Walters had increased his lead by five seconds, but the race remained wide open.

End of lap 4:

1. P. Walters	Healey Cad.	21:34.1
2. E. Goldschmidt	Allard J2	0:17.9 behind
3. M. Collier	Riley - Mercury	1:15.6 behind
4. H. Ullrich	Bugatti T. 54 LM	1:32.5 behind
5. C. T. Boynton	Frazer-Nash LMR	2:34.1 behind
6. A. Drury	D&D Special	2:32.2 behind

The fifth lap saw the end of Arthur J. Hoe's hopes, when his "truant tailpipe," as a wag put it, finally forced him out. Arthur Drury dropped to the end of the field after a bad spin leaving sixth place to M. E. Abendroth and his Jaguar XK-120. Some of the able drivers who had started in the back of the grid were making strong progress through the field. Perry Boswell noted, "Cook, driving a blown MG, put up a real show, moving up 7 places in 7 laps to 9th position." As the race proceeded, with cars now spread out over the entire circuit, the skies darkened even more. Sudden wind gusts of cooler air made many spectators think that this time, umbrellas were going to become quite handy in the very near future. When Walters passed the start/finish line for the fifth time the entire circuit was still just moist in places and he had further widened his lead. Goldschmidt proved the only one able to keep the gap stable and below the half minute mark.

End of lap 5:

1. P. Walters	Healey Cad.	27:04.8
2. E. Goldschmidt	Allard J2	0:18.6 behind
3. M. Collier	Riley - Mercury	1:21.4 behind
4. H. Ullrich	Bugatti T. 54 LM	2:02.7 behind
5. C. T. Boynton	Frazer-Nash LMR	3:23.7 behind
6. M. Abendroth	Jaguar XK-120	3:33.9 behind

Now, after almost three hours of nerve-wracking tease, the long-threatening rain began to fall. It came gently at first, just enough to wet the track thoroughly in minutes. Yellow flags, as so many butterflies, flapped rapidly along

Watkins Glen, September 1950 - Charles T. Boyton II racing his Frazer-Nash LMR in the Seneca Cup. He finished 5th.

the entire course, advocating caution and forbidding passing. As Ken Purdy later explained to his *Sports Car* readers, some undoubtedly still puzzled, "Unlike track races, road races were run in anything, torrential downpours included, so there was no question of cancellation, but the prospect of wet roads on the curving downhill legs sobered most of the drivers."

Everybody indeed slowed down, but some less than others. Walters, whose fastest lap on the dry track had been completed in 5:13.5, took just an extra minute and a quarter (6:39.1) to complete lap 7, when rain fell the hardest. Goldschmidt, in comparison, slowed down from his best time by almost two minutes, completing lap 6 in 7:21.2. The rain began to abate just ahead of the hour mark, when the leaders were in their ninth lap. By the end of that lap, Walters had increased his lead over Goldschmidt by almost a full minute, gained another 24 seconds over Miles Collier and more than two additional minutes over Ullrich.

End of lap 9:

1. P. Walters	Healey Cad.	53:16.0
2. E. Goldschmidt	Allard J2	1:16.3 behind
3. M. Collier	Riley - Mercury	1:45.3 behind
4. H. Ullrich	Bugatti T. 54 LM	4:20.0 behind
5. C. T. Boynton	Frazer-Nash LMR	5:14.7 behind
6. M. Abendroth	Jaguar XK-120	N/A

About six minutes later, the rain had stopped completely. The track surface began to dry fairly fast, aided by the wind and the airstream of the remaining thirteen contenders. The green flag was waved at Walters just as he finished his tenth lap, in a cumulative 59:24.8. Racing soon resumed at full bore as each successive racing car passed by the Courthouse. Bob Grier was the last driver to take the green flag. Having found himself miserably drenched in his Le Mans-proven, but open, Allard J2 roadster, he had slowed down to a snail's pace. He would in fact not finish the race. Arthur Drury had dropped out during the seventh lap after his brief moment of glory.

By Lap 11, Walters was again turning times below the six-minute mark, reinforcing his chances for victory. The other top contenders were just happy to maintain their positions, particularly Erwin Goldschmidt, whose second place would ensure him of participation in the Grand Prix. The only change in the top six positions before the race ended was the disappearance of Abendroth, who dropped out for mechanical reasons while holding sixth place in the eleventh lap. This incident allowed Robert Wilder, driving "Old Grey Mare," to capture sixth place. After fifteen laps and almost one and a half hours of suspenseful racing, it was Walters, Goldschmidt and Miles Collier, followed by D. C. Peck's Bugatti Type 54 roadster, and Charles Boynton's Frazer-Nash. Walters had averaged a commendable, given the circumstances, 67.12 mph average. Nine participants were officially classified, driving the eclectic array of cars now typical of the races at Watkins Glen.

End of Seneca Cup – 15 Laps:

1. P. Walter	Healey Cad.	88:29.0	
2. E. Goldschmidt	Allard J2	1:41.0	behind
3. M. Collier	Riley - Mercury	4:24.0	behind
4. H. Ullrich	Bugatti T. 54 LM	7:03.0	behind
5. C. T. Boynton	Frazer-Nash LMR	7:03.5	behind
6. R. Wilder	Ladd	7.11.5	behind
7. B. Stevens	Jaguar XK-120	7:39.6	behind
8. H. A. H. Cook	MG TC superch.	10:33.5	behind
9. J. B. Sabal	MG TC superch.	N/A	

The rain had not proven much of a wild card in this race, as passing was barred during the downpour and the remaining drivers slowed down enough to avoid disaster. The final ranking was a relatively good indicator of what it took to win American road races in the unlimited category, regardless of weather conditions. As the top four finishers drove cars with engines ranging in displacement from 4.9 to 6.4 liters, and averaging roughly 240 hp in output, it was clear that horsepower was a key determinant. Even the MGs which finished the race, though almost two laps behind the leader, had supercharged engines giving them more horsepower.

Driving skill of course was also beginning to make a marked difference in the final classification. Bob Grier, though driving the Cadillac-powered Allard which had finished third against world-class competition at Le Mans in June, never managed to rank higher than twelfth in the Seneca Cup, dropped to last position shortly after the rain

Watkins Glen, September 1950 - Erwin Goldschmidt comes off Steuben Street at Milliken's Corner.

fell, then proved unable to finish the race. Phil Walters, in contrast, while he drove the most powerful car in the field, showed he could handle it well in all conditions. Walters had plenty of experience. Under the *nom de course* of Ted Tappett, he had proved one of the country's most talented midget and modified stock cars drivers. Now that he was driving in SCCA events, he had reverted to his true name, but lost none of his experience.

Of much political import to the nascent eastern racing community, Erwin Goldschmidt had qualified for the Grand Prix race by finishing second in the Seneca Cup. For some of the most exclusive SCCA members, the worst outcome for the Club had been realized. What if Goldschmidt now did well in the Grand Prix? Nothing, of course, could be done at this point, at least according to the rules. Non-SCCA members who qualified for the big race were forced to start from the back of the grid, regardless of their engine class. Goldschmidt and his Allard, therefore, would start with a big handicap. Would that last "firebreak" prove effective? Club members would first have to enjoy the pleasure of watching the Queen Catharine Cup before finding out the answer.

The First Queen Catharine Cup

It was 2 pm and 28 cars were lined up "Le Mans style" at a 45-degree angle against the curb on the east side of Franklin Street. This was the most plentiful grid at Watkins Glen yet. This was, of course, the "baby" event, the eight-lap race for small displacement cars. Given the relatively level performance of the cars involved, plus the high competitiveness of the field of drivers, everybody expected the first Queen Catharine Cup to be an exciting race. The weather remained threatening, the air was damp, the asphalt moist, as the trees in many places shed leftover rain and delayed evaporation.

The grid actually looked almost like that of an "MG Meet" as 21 of the 28 cars were of that make! Most had the standard 1250 cc engine, though two drivers — Rowland Keith and George Barrett — had created their own 1096 cc supercharged version. Ten of these MGs were the new TD model, the first significant improvement on that classic little racer since 1945. Adding to this overwhelming British contingent were two H.R.G.s and a Jowett Jupiter. The H.R.G. cars were Phil Stiles' Aerodynamic Special, and Fritz Koster's standard factory issue. Both had the 1496 cc four-cylinder Singer engine under the hood. Larry Whiting's Jowett had its standard 1500 cc four-cylinder "boxer" engine.

Against that British juggernaut, there were only four cars of a different national provenance: Kurt Hildebrand's VW Special, Paul Farago's gorgeous Fiat Special, the now familiar and still pretty Haynes/Keller Fiat 1100 Coupe,

Watkins Glen, September 1950 - A Cisitalia leads a pair of MGs through the railroad underpass in the early stages of the Queen Catharine Cup.

and Arthur Babin's supercharged Crosley — with the tiniest engine in the field at 721 cc. Many of the engine choices had to do with the driver's desire to capture a class win, something always important to competitive beginners; it also made them feel that the enormous amount of preparation required for a good race was truly worthwhile.

Rowland Keith, for example, lowered the displacement of his 1250 cc MG engine to 1096 cc by having cylinder liners fitted, which would have dropped the MG from class F to class G; but he then added an Arnott supercharger to the reconfigured engine, which kept his car in class F. The result of this 12 percent reduction in engine capacity, compensated by supercharging, was a proportionately bigger increase in horsepower, expected to be about 30 percent. The astute twenty-two-year-old man from Rhode Island knew that class F in the Queen Catharine Cup, though it allowed engines of up to 1500 cc, would be made up mostly of MGs equipped with the standard unsupercharged 1250 cc powerplant. He figured he would have a real advantage over Canadian, George Barrett, who had followed the same reasoning as Keith.

When the green flag dropped at 2 pm, the drivers dashed across Franklin Street, jumped into their racers, fired up their engines in a rush, engaged first gear, lifted the clutch with one foot as they pushed on the gas with the other, then roared off while dodging traffic, as their tires shrieked from acute friction. After the running start of the Seneca Cup, this was again a grand spectacle, a different delight. The crowd loved it. Rowland Keith was a tall man, and he used his legs well. He was one of the first to get into his cockpit, he had the first car roaring off. Right behind him was Fritz Koster in his H.R.G. They did not know it yet, but those two drivers would remain wheel-to-wheel for the entire race in a spectacular battle for overall victory.

As the leading pack weaved through the curvy downhill leading to Stone Bridge, it became obvious that no slack would be given by any of the drivers. Unlike the Seneca Cup, this was not a race where one possibly qualified for another event. This was not a race with a second chance. This was a race, assuredly, for lighter cars which ran out of breath as their speedometer needles tentatively flirted with the 100 mph mark. But it was a race of young lions with a deep desire to show their abilities.

Women, of course, were motivating part of that instinctual drive. Rowland Keith, for example, while driving to Watkins Glen, had gone out of his way, about forty miles, to pick up Margaret Cannon from Wells College at Aurora. She would man the pits for her friend's number 24 MG. He certainly planned to reward that attractive young lady for her efforts by winning a trophy.

Past Stone Bridge, behind Keith and Koster, Barrett was trying hard to run away from three unsupercharged MGs, when he got caught by the damp asphalt. He lost it, spun, and crashed straight into a large tree. Alden Johnson and Donald Stearns, who were right behind him, were caught by surprise. Their own MGs went astray and somehow piled up against Barrett's car, damaging its rear end, which was the only part that had remained intact. Blood was spilled once more at Watkins Glen, for the second time in as many hours. It was insignificant; just a split ear, some scratches and a few bad bruises. But it was enough to draw a number of ambulances, slow the race with yellow flags and cause some consternation. The first lap was only halfway through, and already there was damage.

The race resumed furiously, with Keith and Koster red hot, never being separated by more than a car length or two. Paul Farago, meanwhile, was doing a great job in his 1089 cc Fiat Special. Though his gorgeous dark blue roadster lacked in top speed, the Detroiter compensated by driving wisely, concentrating on winning class G. On the fourth lap, Koster managed to wring the lead from Keith. On the same lap, Larry Whiting briefly lost control of his last-placed Jowett Jupiter and damaged its front end. The damage was superficial, but Whiting called it a day. Several other drivers in the last tier gave haybales rude buffeting, but the damage was minor.

On lap 5, Keith regained the lead over Koster, though they were so close it was hard to tell who was going to be ahead at the next turn. About a minute behind them, it was Marsh Thomas (MG TC), David Ash (MG TD) and Carl Brocken (MG TD) vying for third place. On lap 7, "Milliken's Corner" witnessed another spectacular incident, as David Ash, Gus Ehrman (MG TD), Pete Crocker (MG TC) and Frank O'Hare (MG TC), all tangled in a smash

1950 Queen Catharine Cup. Paul Farago leading two MGs out of Stone Bridge in his Fiat 110 Special. He would win class G.

which sidelined all four contenders and drew yet more blood, though, again, just enough to bring ambulances and rattle nerves.

On the final lap, as Keith at last managed to create a lead of a few seconds over Koster, Thomas got out of Stone Bridge too fast and hit the haybales, losing third to Brocken, but recovering to finish the race in fourth. Behind him, the next two MG drivers were so close, they raced down Franklin Street side by side and finished in a dead heat, the timers unable to declare who was ahead. Of the 28 starters, only nine were classified, another sign of the intensity of the battle.

End of Queen Catharine Cup — 8 Laps:

1. R. O. H. Keith	MG TC Superch.	49:47.9	
2. Fritz Koster	H.R.G. Sport	0:13.3	behind
3. Carl Brocken	MG TD	1:50.0	behind
4. Marsh Thomas	MG TC	1:59.9	behind
5. E. R. Ogilvie	MG TC	5:02.7	behind
6. L. S. Beazell	MG TD	5:02.7	behind
7. R. Magenheimer	MG TC	6:02.5	behind
8. D. Whitcomb	MG TC	6:04.7	behind
9. P. Farago	Fiat Special	6:05.7	behind

The first Queen Catharine Cup ended thus. It was a genuine racing success, which had the public enthralled. The incredible dice between Keith and Koster had kept everybody on edge throughout the fifty-minute event. The other "races within the race" had the same effect, especially the great scrap between Ogilvie and Beazell for fifth place. However, there was a bitter aftertaste in most people's mouth. Crashes and the whining sirens of ambulances had marred the event. While in the end nobody had been seriously injured, when the medical vehicles were racing to the accident scenes passing momentarily subdued racing cars, spectators were not aware of the gravity level of the injuries.

But now the Grand Prix, the king of the races, was beckoning with the best cars and the best drivers. That would be a great show because the best actors would be on stage. Anticipation soon replaced anxiety.

Watkins Glen, September 1950 - The start of the Grand Prix. The oddly-matched front-row cars are off, as is the rest of the field. Tom Cole's silver Cad-Allard J2 (1950 vintage) and Bill Milliken's blue Bugatti T-54 (1932 vintage) seem to be on equal terms. Cole will beat Milliken to the first corner, though both would strangely retire from the race after similar mishaps, five laps apart, due to "overoptimism" at Townsend Road Corner.

The 1950 Grand Prix

The skies were still grey, the air still damp. The threat of more rain appeared to have decreased. It even seemed that a few sunrays might get through the cloud cover. The promise of a great race offered by the cars and drivers on the grid was very real. Lined up two abreast on Franklin Street along two village blocks were incredibly potent cars with rich racing pedigrees. Wrote Perry Boswell with an eagerness typical for those early days, "Here was a truly superb collection of sports cars, the class of entrants equal to those of any such race in the world! This is certainly true when you can list the following names in the plural, as a representative group of the 26 entrants: Ferraris, Alfa Romeos, Allards, Healeys, Jaguars." Now the clock was ticking towards 4 pm, and for a moment, Franklin Street almost turned silent.

In the front row as a result of the drawing were Tom Cole (Allard J2) and Bill Milliken (Bugatti T-54). Fred Wacker (Allard J2) was right behind Milliken, but next to him was an empty grid spot. The third powerful Allard J2, Erwin Goldschmidt's, was sitting in the back of the grid next to an MG. Though the engine displacement of his car should have put him in the lead group, the rules were that non-SCCA members who qualified for the Grand Prix had to start in the back. The gentlemanly bending of the rules that, for instance, Denver Cornett enjoyed after his spill at Stone Bridge in 1948, was not about to be applied to Erwin Goldschmidt. The outspoken and talented New Yorker knew he could still spring an unhappy surprise, especially in view of his brilliant performance in the Seneca Cup. If he could, he surely would do it with great pleasure.

The third row was made up of Bruce Stevenson (Meyer-Cadillac Special) and Briggs Cunningham who, in a rare exercise of owner's privilege, had decided to drive the most potent racer in his growing stable for the day's major race: the Healey-Cadillac. Phil Walters would be a Grand Prix spectator. Two XK-120 Jaguars formed the fourth row, with two red Ferraris behind them: the cycle-fendered Spyder Corsa driven by Sam Collier and the Touring-bodied 166 MM *barchetta* owned and driven by Jim Kimberly.

John Bentley, sitting aboard his Healey Silverstone, marked with racing number 59, described in a *Sports Car* article how it felt to be on that specific grid that day — if you were not Erwin Goldschmidt, "Yours is only one of 30 sports cars, tuned for racing to the hair-trigger of efficiency and equipped with an open, snarling exhaust. Yet, not one engine has started. The loud speaker is blaring out a string of incoherent sounds and the faces of thousands of people lining both sides of the street are working expressively as they chatter and stare ... Your throat feels a little dry and this strange mounting tension in the air is becoming almost a tangible thing. What's really going on in your mind? Are you scared? Are you already imagining hectic spins, crashes and heart-stopping instants where the right decision is perhaps the difference between an ambulance and a victor's checkered flag? ...

... Only one thing is certain: Those curves you took at 50 last evening — in a few moments now you'll be barreling through them at 80 and keeping your fingers mentally crossed. How will the car react? How much leeway have you got? Then, suddenly, the guy at your right in the black car starts his engine. Two, three, five, ten, twenty engines roar to life and there's a noise like feeding time in the lion's cage. Everybody is warming up. Won't be long now ... Then the flag drops, you snick in your gear and the car leaps forward, paced by a sound like a hundred B-29s taking off. This is it, and it's wonderful."

Cadillac Power

As the green flag was lowered by Nils Mickelson half an hour behind schedule at 4 pm, Tom Cole unleashed the full power of his large Cadillac engine, beating Milliken and his Grand Prix Bugatti to the first corner. The Dynaflow transmission was a clear handicap here. Fred Wacker and Bruce Stevenson, both also Cadillac-powered, started from row two with the expectation of roaring up Old Corning Hill in a hot challenge of the leading pair. Instead, Sam Collier and his Ferrari thrust forward from the fifth row and beat them to the first corner. Sam Collier was now driving a world-class racing car. He was in a top-level race in America and he was going to give it all to win. Behind him, as John Bentley wrote, "You're in a tight

bunch, already at the end of the straight, jockeying for position into the sharp right turn. You go highballing up the hill right on the tail of a blue car, picking up places over the slow stuff at your right." Thus, off went all 26 cars, from Cunningham's 6.4 liter Healey to Paul Farago's 1.1 liter Fiat.

Tom Cole and his Allard were first to cross the start/finish line, only 5:34.4 after the start. This was almost a full minute better than Miles Collier's first lap in the 1949 race! Bill Milliken's 1932 "Dynaflow" Bugatti followed a mere ten seconds later, with Sam Collier's Ferrari in hot pursuit only a village block behind. Less than two seconds after the Ferrari, Bruce Stevenson, Fred Wacker and Erwin Goldschmidt were involved in a hot battle, as the outsider from New York had skillfully used the power of his racer to pass 20 cars in his initial lap! Briggs Cunningham's Healey-Cadillac also appeared to be catching up from a slow start, passing by the Courthouse less than eight seconds behind Goldschmidt. In the back of the pack, Frank Griswold proved less lucky than in 1948, his new Alfa Romeo SS letting him down before he even passed the Stone Bridge. First lap was timed as follows for the leaders:

End of lap 1:

1. T. Cole	Allard J2	5:35.4
2. W. Milliken	Bugatti T. 54	0:10.0 behind
3. S. Collier	Ferrari 166 SC	0:14.5 behind
4. B. Stevenson	Meyer Cadillac	0:15.4 behind
5. F. Wacker	Allard J2	0:15.4 behind
6. E. Goldschmidt	Allard J2	0:15.8 behind
7. B. Cunningham	Healey Cad.	0:23.4 behind
8. R. Reider	Jaguar XK-120	0:24.1 behind

The Franklin Street stretch of the circuit measured a mere half mile, or a fraction of the Mulsanne straight, nonetheless it allowed drivers to reach near top speed before having to brake for the right turn at 14th Street. With the stupendous roar of those unmuffled 300 hp engines hitting both guts and eardrums simultaneously as they flashed by, for the crowd of thousands lining up the village's main street this was a grand spectacle.

Tom Cole's moment of glory at Watkins Glen proved

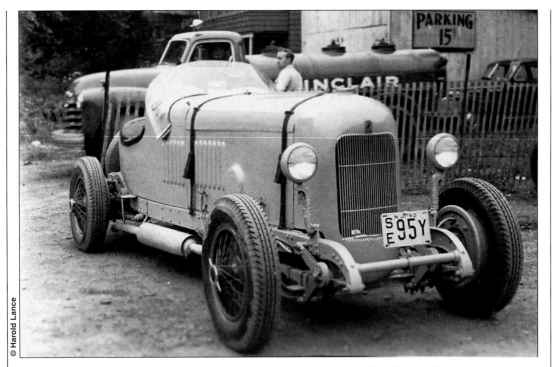

© Harold Lance

This was no longer a race for talented amateurs. The Watkins Glen events were now beginning to attain the much loftier, and riskier, level of European road racing.

Where The Buffaloes Roamed

Sam Collier, now focused on keeping his lead, shot past "the century mark" on his speedometer down the long straight past the railroad bridge. As he approached the fast bend at its end, he barely lifted his right foot, cutting tight at the apex. Suddenly, he felt his tires losing their grip as the Ferrari's wide, wood-rimmed steering wheel failed to make his little red racer respond the way he expected it to. Instead of taking the turn, the roadster glided almost straight across the gravel-strewn apex, spewing small stones from its rear. Straight ahead was the green wall of a gently sloping, wooded hillock. But Sam Collier only faced it for a mere instant. Before even reaching the left lane, the Ferrari spun ninety degrees to the right, and briefly went into a full sideways slide.

Sam Collier did the right thing, what every experienced driver would have done. He immediately went into full countersteer and applied power to regain traction. This is when fate struck. Instead of recovering into a safe trajectory, the Ferrari shot off straight to the right. In that direc-

short-lived. Perhaps a little over-confident, he entered Townsend's Road Corner, near Seneca Lodge, in a seemingly perfect four-wheel-drift, though with just a tad too much speed. On this narrow road with unforgiving shoulders, his Allard overshot the realtively easy turn, went off course and ended in a ditch. Cole was out for the day. Bill Milliken, driving "Doc" Scher's amazing Bugatti, was now in the lead, but not for long. Up Old Corning Hill, Sam Collier was charging hard in his red Ferrari and he overtook the blue Bugatti right at the beginning of the long straight. Seconds later, as their cars crested the hill to face the long, flat straight needling through the railroad underpass, the two drivers realized they were now vying for the lead. As Sam Collier rocketed under the railroad tracks, he checked his rearview mirror to see how hard Milliken was trying to regain the lead. What he saw in that tiny piece of reflecting glass was not only the horseshoe-shaped radiator of Milliken's Bugatti breathing down his neck, but, right behind it, the silver grin of Erwin Goldschmidt's Allard J2.

TOP: Watkins Glen, 1950 - This du Pont was the car driven by Charles Moran in the 1930 Indianapolis 500. In that race, Moran retired in the 22nd lap after hitting the wall. The wealthy Wall Street executive entered the restored car in the 1950 Concours d'Elégance.

BOTTOM: The site where Sam Collier's Ferrari went off as it looked, almost unchanged, nearly 50 years later.

© Philippe Defechereux

tion, there was no shoulder other than a soft, low berm of late-blooming wild flowers. There were no haybales, no hedge, no fence, nothing to counteract a moment of exhuberance. Luckily, there were no spectators either. Beyond, about a foot below the road surface, was a flat, vast, almost inviting expanse of cushy green meadow, with apple trees in the distance. Further yet, rolling hills of darker greens marked the border between earth and sky.

In hot pursuit about 80 feet behind the Ferrari, Milliken vividly remembers the next fifteen seconds, "This was only the second lap and I was trying to regain the lead. We all loved racing for the camaraderie, but, being a competitive bunch, we were also driving to win. Knowing there was gravel over the apex of that wide corner, I stayed more on the outside than Sam. The next thing I experienced was the sharp ding of a small boulder landing in my cockpit. Then I saw the Ferrari get into a slide and catapult end over end in the green meadow. Now focusing on the next turn and the approaching Stone Bridge section, I suddenly and joyfully realized I was in the lead. After my harmless roll-over on the hard asphalt of Fourth Street two years before, I was not overly worried about Sam. The open meadow seemed such a cushy landing spot."

Before the first Grand Prix in 1948, it was Milliken himself, strongly backed by Argetsinger, who had decreed that seat belts and helmets would be mandatory at Watkins Glen. It was a farsighted ruling, which the FIA would take many years to adopt internationally. Sam Collier should have been reasonably safe at Watkins Glen. Many drivers losing control in those days were hurt from impacting against a hard object as racing cars did not offer any protection from instant deceleration other than thin sheet metal and a light frame. Collier's Ferrari did not face any such objects on its hapless course. Though the vehicle had left the road at over 100 mph and cartwheeled at least twice, it had been allowed 200 yards of flat open space, carpeted by the rich grass that once fattened buffaloes, before exhausting its tremendous initial kinetic energy. There was no fire, no smoke, and no dramatic damage to the car.

These circumstances left a fairly favorable margin for much of the impact to be dissipated in relative safety. Sam Collier could have been fortunate at Watkins Glen. Fate,

The memorial plaque for Sam Collier at the precise point where the Ferrari left the road.

however, decided that the luck of this 38-year-old man born into great wealth had run out. His seatbelt anchor broke shortly after he left the road allowing the tremendous centrifugal forces to throw his body loose, most likely at the worst moment. As the driver was being jettisoned, he was sledge-hammered for an instant by the bouncing mass of red aluminum. Yellow flags went up, and the race continued at a slower pace. An ambulace arrived within minutes. The rescuers found the unlucky driver alive but motionless on the ground. Samuel Carnes Collier died shortly after his mangled body was wheeled on a gurney into Montour Falls Hospital.

The Race Goes On

The remaining drivers were not aware of the seriousness of the accident and neither was Miles Collier, who was officiating on Franklin Street. Many of the drivers saw the red wreck in the green meadow, but it did not seem a bad crash. In the split second allowed their minds by their 100 mph pace at that point, thoughts likely flashed through, such as, "Car almost intact, no fire or smoke, driver probably okay. Speed on! Concentrate on the next corner; watch the bastard behind you trying to overtake!" Or, as an MG driver in the earlier Queen Catharine Cup said, "Put your foot right into it, stay out of the haybales, and see what happens."

The leaders that reappeared on Franklin Street at the end of the second lap were quite different from the first six cars seen a little more than five minutes earlier. In fact, Bill Milliken and his formidable Bugatti were the only constant among the top six, though he was passed by the other "automatic" car in the race, Fred Wacker's Allard, just before the start/finish line. Indeed, outside of the venerable Bugatti straight-eight, "Cadillac Power" was imposing an early dominance in this Grand Prix, with Erwin Goldschmidt's own Allard J2 now leading the race, closely followed by Fred Wacker and Bill Milliken, then Briggs Cunningham's Healey only 22 seconds behind. Two Jaguar XK-120s sandwiched Bill Spear's Ferrari and John Fitch's Special in the next four positions, all less than a minute behind Wacker.

End of lap 2:

1. E. Goldschmidt	Allard J2	11:20.1
2. F. Wacker	Allard J2	0:03.7 behind
3. W. Milliken	Bugatti T. 54	0:03.8 behind
4. B. Cunningham	Healey Cad.	0:22.0 behind
5. R. Reider	Jaguar XK-120	0:29.4 behind
6. W. Spear	Ferrari 166 MM	0:37.3 behind
7. J. Fitch	Fitch Type B	0:42.3 behind
8. B. Stearns	Jaguar XK-120	1:03.1 behind

When lap 3 began, the three-way battle for the lead intensified throughout the third lap, with Goldschmidt, Wacker and Milliken never less than a few car lengths apart. They were averaging over 70 mph per lap! Bruce Stevenson stopped his Meyer Special on Franklin Street to report Sam Collier's accident. Miles Collier, worried about his brother's fate, left his post and began to walk up Big Bend to find out exactly what had happened. He would arrive at the tragic spot after the ambulance left.

Meanwhile, behind the three leaders, the next four cars remained in the same order, though these lost up to half a minute to the raging trio. Jim Kimberly, who had completed the first lap in twelfth position, was now moving his Ferrari up the field, finding himself in eighth position and looking at John Fitch's "Bitch" as his next victim just as he reappeared on Franklin Street.

End of lap 3:

1. E. Goldschmidt	Allard j2	16:55.4
2. F. Wacker	Allard J2	0:01.7 behind
3. W. Milliken	Bugatti T. 54	0:02.9 behind

4. B. Cunningham	Healey Cad.	0:30.9 behind
5. R. Reider	Jaguar XK-120	0:54.2 behind
6. W. Spear	Ferrari 166 MM	1:04.1 behind
7. J. Fitch	Fitch Type B	1:25.7 behind
8. J. Kimberly	Ferrari 166 MM	1:38.8 behind

During the next lap, the top six positions remained unchanged as less than one minute separated the four leading cars when they again passed by the Courthouse. The crowd, completely unaware of Sam Collier's fate, was going wild. Adding to the excitement, another ferocious battle was going on for seventh place between Fitch, Kimberly and George Huntoon. The latter, having recovered from a poor start, had brought his blue Alfa Romeo from sixteenth position to eighth at the end of Lap 4, between Kimberly and Fitch. But the three drivers were wheel-to-wheel and their positions were changing constantly.

As to John Bentley, he recalled that fourth lap thus, "... down the School House S, you're going too fast. You slide, correct — and lose time. There's No. 2 again [Argetsinger's Healey Silverstone], beginning to crowd you. At the T-road where the oily dirt is, he's stalking you close and you kick the gas too hard coming out of the right turn. Suddenly, the tail breaks loose and you go into a spin clockwise through 180 degrees. You cannon off the hay-bales and slide backward into a hollow the other side of the road. And that's it, brother. In one careless instant, all your hopes are wiped out; all your preparations have become so much waste of time. Eight cars go by and you cannot even start the engine. The pinion's jammed and you've buckled both rear fenders. It takes five minutes and as many people to dig you out of the soft earth and rock the car while you free the starter. Five minutes is nearly a lap and from then on, you haven't a chance of catching anyone."

During the fifth lap, Milliken passed Wacker, taking the Bugatti to second place and only five seconds behind Goldschmidt, who established a new lap record at 73.49 mph. Wacker, though, was right behind the Bugatti at the end of the lap. The battle for the lead remained furious. The rest of the six leading contenders managed to keep their positions, while, behind their group, Kimberly put fifteen seconds between himself and Fitch who himself had re-passed Huntoon to regain eighth.

More Drama

The sixth lap saw several dramatic developments. Milliken, who had just completed a 72.96 mph lap, was going for the lead. That immense amount of work performed on that beautiful Bugatti during the summer was not going for naught. To boot, the Dynaflow transmission, just as he and his engineers had predicted, was working perfectly. Finally, Bill Milliken truly loved Bugattis. "I am a firm believer that it is more thrilling to awake at the sound of a Bugatti than to die to the note of a Bentley," he had said. Goldschmidt's red Allard was just a few car lengths ahead of him as the two drivers began to tackle Old Corning Hill for the sixth time. The first serious turn, Townsend Road Corner, was ahead. That was where Tom Cole had lost it a short thirty minutes before.

The danger for leading drivers at that moment is that their minds are still filled with the thrill of roaring down the flat, straight stretch of Franklin Street at full throttle between two files of cheering spectators. The hill ahead is an exciting climb through the woods, with more spectators cheering you on. Tom Cole may have overdone it just for that reason. Now it was Milliken's turn. As he began to turn right, the tail of "Big Bug," the nickname he had given his beloved mount, began to move toward the outside, where there is a drop off. Milliken applied power to regain such grip which he thought was necessary, but the heavy Bugatti continued to drift out of control, "in a case of centrifugal force catching up with the coefficient of friction between rubber and damp macadam," as a journalist later put it. Then, the Bugatti's front wheels hit the right shoulder sending the French car into a rolling spin. The ill-fated Grand Prix racer flipped, then landed in a ditch wheels up in the air, facing downhill.

Milliken recalls the next moments, "It all happened very fast. For the second time, I found myself upside down in a Bugatti, but this time it was really scary. The moment I realized what position I was in, fuel dripped on the hot engine and flames began to spread ahead of me. This time, I had trouble figuring out which way to release the safety aircraft belt buckle. At first, I tried it the wrong way, and I could not get myself free. The spreading fire helped to concentrate my mind very fast, and I finally wriggled out from under the car before it was too late." The fire continued for a while before firefighters could come to the rescue and extinguish it. While Milliken was unharmed, the Bugatti was not. With barely 35 miles of racing accomplished since its last "hospitalization," the hapless Grand Prix car found itself with seriously bruised skin, bent axles, a broken wheel and serious fire damage under the hood. Back to the hospital it would have to go: good thing it was owned by a wealthy doctor!

So now it was Goldschmidt, Wacker, Cunningham, three Cadillac-powered cars as the three leaders. Goldschmidt, however, instead of having a pursuer on his tail, now commanded a measurable advantage over his two closest challengers. On that same sixth lap, Bill Spear also lost it, though in his case he was able to recover without physical damage. Given the intensity of the battle in which he was involved he lost three positions in the incident. George Huntoon had now passed Fitch and gained an advantage of five seconds over Kimberly's Ferrari.

End of lap 6:

1. E. Goldschmidt	Allard J2	33:21.6	
2. F. Wacker	Allard J2	0:19.5	behind
3. B. Cunningham	Healey Cad.	1:18.7	behind
4. R. Reider	Jaguar XK-120	2.03.6	behind
5. J. Kimberly	Ferrari 166 MM	2:20.6	behind
6. G. Huntoon	Alfa Romeo 8C	2:43.3	behind
7. J. Fitch	Fitch Type B	2:49.0	behind

Things calmed down a bit in the ensuing three laps. The top positions remained unchanged. Goldschmidt put together very hot laps laps and established another new record on lap 8 at 73.95 mph, gradually increasing his lead over his pursuers. This part of the race, leading to the hour mark, also saw two other noteworthy contenders dropping out. First was Bruce Stevenson, whose Meyer-Cadillac gave up on his seventh lap. His gallant gesture on lap two, when he stopped on Franklin Street to tell about the Sam Collier accident, and which had cost him at least five min-

TOP: Watkins Glen, September 1950 - Bob Reider's Jaguar XK-120 misses a turn and hits a tree in the early stages of the Grand Prix race.

BOTTOM: Watkins Glen, September 1950 - Seconds later, spectators and officials rush to help Bob Reider. In this case, no big harm was done, other than to the ego and the wallet of the driver. Even the tree survived.

utes, was not rewarded. Cameron Argetsinger's turn came a lap later when his Healey Silverstone lost a cylinder. The second tier battle provided the biggest excitement. Kimberly, Huntoon and Fitch kept battling it out in a spectacular manner with Kimberly and Huntoon keeping the advantage over Fitch after nearly fifty minutes of racing.

End of lap 9:

1. E. Goldschmidt	Allard J2	49:37.6
2. F. Wacker	Allard J2	0:52.2 behind
3. B. Cunningham	Healey Cad.	1:42.1 behind
4. R. Reider	Jaguar XK-120	2.53.3 behind
5. J. Kimberly	Ferrari 166 MM	2.53.6 behind
6. G. Huntoon	Alfa Romeo 8C	3:59.5 behind
7. J. Fitch	Fitch Type B	4:16.1 behind

Lap 10 provided the next series of dramatic developments. First, Briggs Cunningham decided to make his move. Just as Goldschmidt was slowing down to the 72 mph per lap range to avoid a mistake, Briggs began to move up from his position, completing lap 10 at a 73.67 mph average, lap 11 at 74.20 mph, and lap 12 at a superb 74.67 mph. This allowed him to pass Wacker's Allard down Big Bend and regain twenty seconds on Goldschmidt. Lap 10 also proved to be Bob Reider's last lap, as his XK-120 crashed against a tree soon after his

tenth pass by the Courthouse.

As all this was going on, Fitch was devastated to see his oil pressure drop to zero in the turns. He chose to pit so as not to risk seeing his engine blow and not even finish the race. This stop cost him four positions and allowed Bill Spear and his Ferrari to recapture the sixth spot he had lost four laps earlier, a position he kept through lap 12.

End of lap 12:

1. E. Goldschmidt	Allard J2	65:55.7
2. B. Cunningham	Healey Cad.	1:24.9 behind
3. F. Wacker	Allard J2	1:27.3 behind
4. J. Kimberly	Ferrari 166 MM	3:19.0 behind
5. G. Huntoon	Alfa Romeo 8C	5:02.8 behind
6. W. Spear	Ferrari 166 MM	5:54.0 behind

The final three laps were suspenseful as Cunningham continued to reduce the gap separating him from Goldschmidt corner after corner. The great sportsman from Connecticut completed lap 13 in 5:18.2, averaging 74.69 mph; then lap 14 in 5:17.2, establishing a new record for the race at 74.90 mph. Though Goldschmidt was now lapping nearly 15 seconds slower than Cunningham, he still held an advantage

of 56.3 seconds over his pursuer when they roared down Franklin Street for the last time before the winner would see the checkered flag.

Cunningham put on a superb last effort in that final lap, establishing yet a new record of 5:16.9, or an average of 74.97 mph. He regained another sixteen seconds over Goldschmidt, which obviously was not enough to snatch victory from the unlikely but deserving leader. Cunningham put in his bid too late in the race and Erwin Goldschmidt, a man disliked by many in the SCCA leadership and a non-member of the club, won the 1950 Grand Prix! Behind the leading pair, Wacker finished third, making it a full Cadillac-powered podium. Four Italian cars followed the Anglo-Saxon trio, Jim Pauley having been able to insert his Alfa Romeo-powered Nardi-Danese into seventh position. John Fitch was the last classified driver in eighth. His pit stop had also cost him the class D win, and the joy of finishing ahead of the group he had been battling the whole race.

End of Grand Prix - 15 Laps:

1. E. Goldschmidt	Allard J2	82.24.8
2. B. Cunningham	Healey Cad.	0:48.0 behind
3. F. Wacker	Allard J2	1:55.5 behind
4. J. Kimberly	Ferrari 166 MM	3:45.7 behind
5. G. Huntoon	Alfa Romeo 8C	5:15.7 behind
6. W. Spear	Ferrari 166 MM	7:27.8 behind
7. J. Pauley	Nardi-Danese	N/A
8. J. Fitch	Fitch Type B	N/A

So ended the third Grand Prix of Watkins Glen. All three events had seen exciting racing, great feats of talent and many dramatic moments. Had a professional European motorsport journalist been there to write the story, he would undoubtedly have called the day a tremendous success. But the mood on Franklin Street, then later at Seneca Lodge, where the awards ceremonies took place, was as somber as the weather.

Most people learned quickly about the injuries caused in the first lap of the Seneca Cup in the early afternoon. It was unnerving but not overly serious, and soon ascribed to simple bad luck. Then there was the unfavorable weather and even rain, which damped some of the enthusiasm. That

was just a natural phenomenon, though; organizers could not be lucky with the weather every year. Next came the the smashes and crashes of the Queen Catharine Cup. While nobody was seriously hurt, a lot of people were seriously scared. After that came the awkward placement of Goldschmidt at the back of the Grand Prix grid. Few spectators knew what actually caused the Allard number 98 to be placed there, rather than among its peers at the front of the grid. They did know that the car had finished a strong second in the Seneca Cup. Of course, all key SCCA members knew what was going on and a lot of nerves were rattled by that incident. Now, as the aftermath was setting in, the news of Sam Collier's death was spreading rapidly.

Death! Road racing was not a great aristocratic party just for fun after all ... At once, those passionate amateurs, those disciplined, though lofty men had to confront two serious facts: not only could they die while enjoying their favorite pastime, but they could also be responsible for injuring, maiming, or perhaps even killing innocent people who were not at all part of the club. The spectators had a reality check of their own. They could get killed watching those wealthy people driving their expensive machines! The ticket price to attend the race may have been low, but the actual price to be paid for being there could be astronomically high.

By the European standards of the day a driver's death and a few minor spectator injuries over a whole day of racing was in fact a good safety record. By American standards, especially political, it was an awful outcome. It was not that a beloved leader and racing driver had died "in his true colors," as Sir Henry Birkin, an early British enthusiast, would say; it was the sudden realization by organizers that despite the safety and communications effort they had made at great cost, and these were remarkable for the day, death was still at the door of their club.

The Aftermath

Sam Collier's death and the other accidents caused a lot of commotion within the SCCA community. The reactions were generally similar, but the solutions proposed covered a very wide spectrum, showing that in these early days, no one yet knew for sure how to insure perfect safety in a road race.

In the November-December issue of *Sports Car*, Perry Boswell wrote, "It seems quite evident to this writer that the so called 'amateur' sports car racing is rapidly becoming a thing of the past. This is indicated by (1) the wholesale use of salaried professional mechanics and (2) the come-what-may all-out driving of the cars in the Grand Prix. ... It seems to me that one of two courses needs to be taken, namely road racing should turn professional, or lap speeds should be slowed."

Jim Hoe stated his views, "I attribute a great deal of the trouble experienced through the day to lack of practice. For my part, had I taken the railroad crossing at speed just once before the race, my tailpipe weakness would have shown up and would have been corrected, thus saving me disqualification. ... A practice period should be mandatory. If the local police refuse this practice period, the race should be called off. ... Drivers who have not been around the course in practice should not be allowed to race."

Peter Crocker, whose MG was involved in the four-car pile-up during the Queen Catharine Cup, was more intense), "The things I would like to see improved are: (A) crowd control (I thought it *!*!!). People were allowed entirely too close to the road, especially in the corners and outside the town. ... Next year, I'd like to see Police deputies or Guardsmen with Billy Clubs every 100 yards around the course, with instructions to use them if necessary."

Paul J. Timmins proposed an even more radical solution, "The prime reason for these races is NOT for spectator entertainment! The main idea is to give our members a chance to do some competition driving on the public roads without the normal law and traffic restrictions. ... Remember, all of our driving members would be just as keen about the racing business if there were NO SPECTATORS!"

In answer to this sort of critique, Argetsinger wrote, "There are a great many problems, but I firmly believe that all problems have solutions, and these are no exception." [He went on to describe in details a series of improvements already planned for the next year, such as 13.2 miles of fence, both sides of the road, all the way around the circuit, more police; and a complete medical plan, including a field

hospital]. Then Argetsinger went on, "The problem of: are they too fast and how to slow them down, is a serious one. The answer must be carefully studied and not arrived in haste. My own present thought is that lengthening the races and thereby taking them out of the sprint category would place the premium on mechanical reliability and driver steadiness. I hope to see the Grand Prix next year a minimum of 25 laps (165 miles) and preferably 30 laps (198 miles)." In writing these words, Argetsinger was clearly confirming his original intention of bringing "European-type professional road racing" to Watkins Glen. This was quite a different direction from that represented by Paul J. Timmins, who had quite a few followers among SCCA members.

What Did It All Mean?

The third Grand Prix of Watkins Glen punctuated a year which turned out to be a major turning point for American road racing.

• In a mere three years, road racing had spread through much of the country, poised to become a major national sport. At Watkins Glen, American road racing even reached close to the best European level. The number of participants, the Le Mans-tested breeding of many cars fielded, and the quality of the organization all proved that. Surely, the quality of participants and cars applied only to a minority of the field, but it was clear that this was only a beginning.

• In spite of safety measures way ahead of those in place in Europe — helmets would only be required by the FIA in 1952 and seat belts much later — a driver's death had happened, as well as injuries to several spectators. While in Europe death was an accepted part of the sport — in 1950, six deaths occurred on various European circuits, including that of famous French champion Raymond Sommer at Cadours — Americans clearly had a different attitude toward that aspect of any sport. So did the pro-amateur status members of the SCCA, who never quite imagined the sport of road racing being anything else than "harmless fun on open roads." Paul J. Timmins was a typical spokesman for that group.

- The beginning of a schism was therefore appearing within the ranks of the SCCA. As indicated by the reactions of some of the participants in their *Sports Car* comments, one camp was coalescing around the strong wish to keep the sport strictly amateur and gentlemanly. The other camp, spearheaded by Argetsinger, wanted to make American road racing an integral part of the great international championships — especially endurance and Formula 1 — and that led them away from the amateur status. The year 1951 would witness the full fracture between the two camps.

- On the technical side, new solutions were being tested. Aerodynamics was beginning to gain in importance as top speeds approached the 130 mph mark. Cunningham's "Le Monstre" might have been ugly, but it was a serious attempt to deal with the problem of drag. In fact, one of the Cunningham timers at Le Mans calculated that if "Le Monstre" had not lost one half hour in a sandbank, it would have finished fifth or six, way ahead of the standard Cadillac coupe. The Fitch Type B was much more aerodynamic than an MG. The Healey Silverstone, though cycle-fendered, was a nicely streamlined car. It would take fifteen years, however, for this "black art" to begin to turn into a science.

Automatic transmissions were used for the first time in a race. They were of two types: Milliken's Dynaflow and Wacker's Hydramatic. The Dynaflow was a torque converter, using a fast flow of oil through a turbine-like device to transmit power from the engine to the wheels. The Hydramatic system was a more traditional geared transmission activated automatically by hydraulics. While the techniques were different, the purpose was the same: to free the driver to concentrate on racing and passing, without having to worry about and labor at using a clutch (and in the case of the Hydramatic, shifting gears). It worked more or less at the Glen, but this revolution was not pursued. Automatic transmissions consume power, and therefore lower top speed. When in 1951 airport runways became the main venue for American road races, top speed became paramount and everybody reverted to the standard gearbox. It

Sebring, December 31, 1950 - The Aston Martin DB2 entered by Bill Spear leads Kimberly's Ferrari 166 MM into a corner during the night hours. The DB2, co-driven by Rand/Marshall, would end up 16th in the race.

would take almost fifteen years for the technology to reappear on an American race car: the Chaparral.

An Extraordinary Year

All things considered, it had been an extraordinary year and its peak was definitely Watkins Glen. Yet, the American season was not finished as the country affords year-round good weather in several of its regions. The first Pebble Beach race, near Monterey, California, was held on the private Del Monte estate on November 4. It was an SCCA sponsored event and it was well attended, though none of the participants had ever been seen in the east. There were four races and the big one, the Pebble Beach Cup, was won by Phil Hill in his Jaguar XK-120.

On December 31, Alec Ulmann and his team staged the first ever race at Sebring. While Ulmann hoped to turn his race at Sebring into a serious endurance event ("the Little Le Mans"), this first race was limited to six hours. Still, it would be the first endurance race of modern times in America.

New Year's eve on December 31, 1950, saw a particularly grand celebration at Sebring among a happy bunch of racing enthusiasts. Many wondered if 1951 could ever be better.

Watkins Glen, 1951 - The "Le Mans Start" grid for the Queen Catharine Cup. Identifable from right to left: Al Coppel's MG TD Special (#23); Peter Iselin's H.R.G. (#37); David Viall's Lester MG (#19); Kurt Hildebrand's VW Special (#92); Bob Magenheimer's MG TD (#10); Hector Sheffer's red Siata GS (#24); then the MG TCs of Ed Kinsley (#63) and Reg Ogilivie (#29). The green MG TD (#65) at the far left is Gus Ehrman's; he would finish 5th. GM's Le Sabre show car is highly visible behind the grid.

chapter four
The Great Controversy

Red Assaults And Stormy Times

One week before the third Watkins Glen Grand Prix, on September 15, 1950, the Korean war theater witnessed the beginning of a spectacular reversal of fortunes. That day, United Nations troops, led by General MacArthur, effected a surprise landing at Inchon, near Seoul, way in the rear of the bulk of North Korean forces. Within nine days, the capital city of South Korea, held captive by communist troops since June 28, was free. Six weeks later, the allied troops had not only liberated all of South Korea, but they had pushed all the way through North Korea, reaching the Yalu river on October 27. That river marked the southern border of the People's Republic of China. The war seemed won.

It was not. In early November, the Red Chinese launched a massive assault across the Yalu, quickly pushing back the allied forces. As the allied retreat continued, President Truman declared a state of emergency on December 16, proclaiming that "the full and rich life guaranteed by the Bill of Rights was put in jeopardy by the menace of Communist imperialism." But the mighty red tide was still rising to full force. The communist juggernaut crossed the 38th parallel on New Year's day, 1951 and recaptured Seoul three days later. A strong allied counterattack soon stabilized the front near the South Korean border

"You're driving in a race because speed gives you a bigger thrill than all else on earth - and because, in time, these races will help gain public acceptance of a better, safer, more beautiful automobile."

John Bentley

and Seoul was freed again on March 14th.

These heated battles witnessed the first major deployment of helicopters in military actions as well as the first dogfights-for-kill between jet fighters: Sabres versus MIGs. The swept-wing North American Sabre quickly gained superiority over its Soviet rival and in so doing became a new popular symbol of continued technological leadership for Americans. The jet fighter, its shape and name would soon be adopted by Detroit manufacturers hoping to capture some of the halo of its success.

Meanwhile, MacArthur was not taking his recent setback with equanimity. In the early Spring, without White House approval, he began to talk openly about attacking China and using atomic bombs if necessary. On April 11, 1951, president Truman took the bold step of removing the Pacific War hero and Inchon victor from all his commands. This was not a popular decision. It got the American president a terrible drubbing in much of the press while MacArthur, upon his return to America, received a triumphant welcome. The popular general was even given an exuberant ticker tape parade in New York. These tense events were taking place as the red scare reached hysterical levels across the American nation. The tumultuous trial of Ethel and Julius Rosenberg, the couple accused of passing on to Russia the secret of the atomic bomb, ended in New

York on March 30, 1951 with a guilty verdict. Five days later, Judge Kaufman handed them the death sentence.

Adding to the scare and controversy, communist insurgents were expanding yet another conflict in a region of Asia situated about 2,000 miles southeast of the Korean conflagration. General Giap and his Viet Minh guerrillas tried to capture Hanoi in mid-January, but the French, energized by the arrival of general de Lattre de Tassigny, repulsed the assault and forced Giap into retreat. *La Guerre d'Indochine*, as the French called it, was reaching full scale level. The 18th parallel, dividing the northern and southern part of what would within a few years be called Vietnam, soon joined the 38th parallel in the Korean peninsula and Check-Point Charlie in Berlin as the hair-trigger dividing lines between two opposite visions of human society. Further east, in Central Asia, China officially absorbed Tibet on May 19, 1951 when formal surrender documents were signed in Peking. Truman had some solid foundations to back up his statements about global communist imperialism.

In comparison, Europe was relatively calm politically. The Iron Curtain had stabilized from the Baltic sea to the Aegean sea. NATO, with its new headquarters in Paris formally opened on July 23 by general Eisenhower, provided assurance that the containment was sustainable. In fact, the

The strictly standard Peugeot 203 (wagon) which successfully completed a seventeen-day treck from Paris to Cape Town and back to Paris via Algiers, in January, 1951. Total distance was about 15,000 km, or 9,300 mi. Messrs. de Cortanze and Mercier, of France, were at the wheel.

unplanned and cynical political border would remain unchanged for almost forty years. In addition, the Marshall plan, now in full swing, was beginning to lift Western European economies, calming social unrests. Accordingly, in 1951, international car racing began to approach the popular intensity it had known during the 1930's.

Season Opener

As had become traditional, Argentina opened the new racing season. First, two Formule Libre races were staged in late February, the Buenos Aires Grand Prix on the 18th and the Evita Perón Grand Prix on the 24th. For the first time since 1939, Mercedes-Benz was present in force with three of their formidable pre-war, three-liter supercharged twelve-cylinder W154 Grand Prix racers. These had been thoroughly updated, including the fitting of new pistons and a more aerodynamic nose. The house of the three-pointed star was testing its nerve for an eventual victorious return to the Formula 1 championship. Local driver Froilan Gonzales, though, driving a much lighter supercharged two-liter Ferrari 166 C, won both races. The Mercedes racing team and their leader Alfred Neubauer had a lot of thinking to do.

On March 18, it was time for a sports car race, called the Juan Perón Grand Prix. The event would consist of 40 laps on a circuit carved out of outer city avenues and surrounded by parks. The main straight was a wide thoroughfare split by a bushy divider and called *Avenida Costanera Norte*, which in fact gave its name to the circuit. Several East Coast American enthusiasts, forlorn at the long lack of racing in their wintry region, flew to Argentina for the occasion. Among them were six by now familiar names: Kimberly, Spear, Rand, Wacker, Fitch, and Cole. The first three would race Ferraris, the other three Cadillac-powered Allards. The Argentinian General himself was the host and he made sure all American drivers and accompanying people stayed in the best hotel: the Alviar Palace. Louis Firpo, a boxing champion who once fought Jack Dempsey, was assigned to them as official entertainer. Juan Perón made sure the Americans did not have to pay for anything, which of course was not in abeyance with the strict SCCA rules. The "extra-territoriality" of Argentina provided a convenient cover.

Interestingly, the Allard J2 that John Fitch brought down was the silver car that Cole had badly damaged at Watkins Glen at Townsend Road Corner almost six months earlier. Cole, who had since obtained a brand new Allard, had accepted Fitch's offer to cobble the wounded racer back together and borrow it for the Argentinean race. Cole had actually not bought his new Allard. It was given to him by John Perona, owner of the famous "El Morocco" night club in New York. A racing enthusiast and fun-lover, Perona had also been invited to attend the race in Buenos Aires. John Fitch has a vivid memory of a particular skit Perona loved to perform for friends, taking advantage of the close likeness of his last name to that of General Perón, "Perona would click his heels while making the fascist salute by raising his right arm. All present would immediately respond with the shout 'Heil Perona.' Everybody would always get a good laugh, Argentinean friends included."

Local drivers entered an eclectic group of cars, such as an Alfa Romeo 8C-2300 by Adolpho Cruz, a Healey Silverstone by Jose Collazo, two Jaguar XK-120s by Roberto Mieres and Jorge Camano, and a Delahaye by Miguel Schroeder. In addition, Eric Forrest Greene, a Briton living in Argentina, entered a 4250 cc Bentley, while Roberto Bonomi fielded a Cisitalia. This made the

Buenos Aires, March 18, 1951 - John Fitch, driving Tom Cole's old Allard J2, about to win the Juan Perón Grand Prix. This would be his first international victory. Several SCCA members participated in the race and were lavishly lodged and entertained by General Perón and his wife Evita. This was a "no-no" for the SCCA and would accelerate the onset of the "Great Controversy."

Juan Perón Grand Prix a "North America versus South America" challenge, which is exactly what the organizers had intended.

The start of the race was spectacular as several of the most powerful cars jockeyed for the lead through most of the first lap. John Fitch emerged as a solid leader at the beginning of lap 2, pursued closely by Cruz's Alfa Romeo and Wacker's own black "Eight Ball" Allard. Soon, attrition took its toll, with Cole being sidelined by transmission problems, and Mieres by engine failure. By mid-race, Fred Wacker was pushing hard and gaining on Fitch, but in so doing he spun in a turn. The Chicagoan recovered, but he had lost too much time to threaten Fitch again. Meanwhile, the former P-51 pilot set fastest lap and broke all kinds of records. The only thing he did not break was his sputtering Allard. He won the race brilliantly, marking his first international win. Fred Wacker finished second and Schroeder third. The two Ferraris finished, respectively, seventh (Bill Spear) and eighth (Kimberly); their smaller engines simply could not overcome the top speed of the Allards in the long straights that made up part of the course.

The Argentinean spectators cheered the finishers wildly for they had enjoyed a very exciting race. Fitch was as elated by this reception as by his first major victory. At the award ceremonies, he was kissed on both cheeks by Evita Perón who, as he likes to point out with a grin, "died shortly thereafter" — in fact she died on July 26, 1953, or sixteen months later. This remark, of course, is typical of Fitch's wonderful dry sense of humor. He likes to tell of another ironic moment which happened just as he took the checkered flag, "My patched-up Allard expired on the way back from the circuit. A radiator mount broke and this drained the coolant entirely. The gearbox got stuck in second gear. As race car designers like to point out, the silver Allard had behaved as the 'perfect' racer: it won the race then promptly fell apart. Had it not, it would have been over-engineered and therefore likely too heavy to win."

Much more important to Fitch, Briggs Cunningham, who was then looking for another talented driver to complete his team for his second assault on Le Mans, took note. Upon Fitch's return to Connecticut, Cunningham called him: would he agree to co-drive with Phil Walters one of the three brand new cars now being prepared for Le Mans in June? The answer, of course, was yes, even though Elizabeth Fitch was now only three months away from giving birth to their first child. John Fitch would end up leaving for France three days after the birth of his first son, named John, who was born on June 7, 1951.

As to Fred Wacker, he sold his black Allard to an Argentinean, intending to use the money to buy himself a brand new one when back in the States. That is exactly what he did, only to learn soon after taking delivery of his new race car in Chicago that Evita Perón herself had cancelled the sale of his first Allard — no one remembers why — and the British racer was shipped back to Wacker's home in Chicago. Says he, "I now had two Allards, which from a financial viewpoint, I needed like a hole in the head."

The First Cunningham Racer

By March, Briggs Cunningham was indeed well on his way to completing the next step in achieving his dream: win at Le Mans with an American-made sports car driven by Americans. He had actually taken a major step on October 1, 1950, when he purchased outright the Frick-Tappett Motors Company. That was the Long Island shop which had prepared the two Le Mans Cadillacs. "Tappett" was of course Phil Walters while Bill Frick was renowned as the best mechanical mind on the east coast. One month later, Cunningham opened his new "factory" at 1402 Elizabeth Avenue in West Palm Beach, Florida, a stone's throw from one of his many residences. Year-round temperate weather would make it easier to test prototypes or components whenever they became ready. The official company name was B. S. Cunningham Co. Competition Cars.

On March 5, 1951, or two weeks prior to John Fitch's victory at the Juan Perón Grand Prix, Cunningham closed the Frick-Tappett Motors shop in Long Island and Phil Walters moved full time to West Palm Beach in order to supervise the entire operation. George Desler had been managing the company before Walters' arrival. He had already assembled a staff of around twenty people who had set out to meet an impossible deadline: design, build, test

and ship three new competitive racing cars so they could be on the starting grid at Le Mans on June 23.

A first prototype, the C-1 had been completed in November, 1950. The intention was for this first Cunningham to be both a test bed for the Le Mans racer and a prototype for a private customer car, as the Le Mans regulations then required that any participating make have a production of at least ten cars per year. The C-1 was a two-seater coupe designed to carry the large Cadillac V-8, the Cadillac three-speed transmission, a Ford-based front independent suspension, a specially designed de Dion rear axle and four coil springs. It was a heavy load and as a result, the chassis was a massive affair made of 3″ diameter steel tubes reinforced by a heavy cross-shaped brace in the middle, plus front and rear cross-members. With a wheelbase of 105″ and a track of 58″, the final car would have a dry weight of over 3,400 lbs., not a promising figure.

Then another blow had to be absorbed. In November, the Cadillac division of General Motors advised the Cunningham Company that it would stop supplying it with its V-8 engines — even though Cunningham had already ordered close to eighty of the Cadillac powerplants! This decision was made by the top executives of General Motors, over Ed Cole's objections of course, and in spite of the fact that Frank Burrell, one of Cadillac's top engineers, had been essentially assigned to the Cunningham Le Mans project from the beginning. He had even been part of the first expedition to France! This renunciation was a clear reflection of G.M.'s ambiguous feelings about racing, though the principal reason given Briggs Cunningham was that "The company was too busy fulfilling military orders from the Government for the war in Korea." General Motors could afford to be flippant about racing. All senior company executives knew their giant corporation would soon announce profits of over $800 million, the third yearly record in a row. What shareholder could complain?

Chrysler Power

Panic briefly struck the fledgling team until Cunningham heard from Paul Farago of Detroit that Chrysler might have the answer. Farago was a race car tuner, designer and driver who had the ear of influential

TOP LEFT: Sebring, December 31, 1950 - Robert T. Keller (right) and Paul Farago, with companions, next to the Fiat 1100 with which they finished third (Index). Robert T. Keller was a Chrysler executive and his father K.T. Keller the Chairman of the company. Both men would prove precious connections for Briggs Cunningham. Farago facilitated the deal.

BOTTOM RIGHT: A Cunningham C-3 Vignale at the 1952 Watkins Glen Concours d'Elégance. Though beautiful, the car was priced too high for the market at the time. Only about 30 were built.

people at the Chrysler Corporation — he would eventually build the Dual Ghia with them. He reminded Cunningham of Bob Keller and his participation in the two previous Watkins Glen Grand Prix in a Fiat 1100. A Yale buddy of Cunningham's, Bob Keller was then a mid-level executive at Chrysler. His father, the legendary K.T. Keller, was president of the Chrysler corporation, having succeeded its founder, Walter P. Chrysler! Better yet, Chrysler was just beginning production of its own new V-8, better to compete with the new and popular G.M. unit. The Chrysler V-8 was of similar dimension and layout as the Cadillac engine — "oversquare" and 5626 cc or 331 ci — but it had hemispherical combustion chambers with valves inclined on either side, giving it better breathing and therefore an extra 20 hp in its standard issue — 180 hp total. Due to its then unusual chamber shape, that engine would soon be known as the "Chrysler Hemi."

Both Kellers proved eager to help Cunningham, being only too happy to steal great publicity from General Motors for a new engine they had not even officially introduced to the public. A supply agreement was soon signed, and the Chrysler-Cunningham team quickly went about to modify the engine in order to give it extra racing power. Extensive tuning was performed on the basic unit, then four Zenith carburetors were fitted. The end-result was a V-8 that could produce 230 hp at 5300 rpm. It was more complex and expensive than its Cadillac competitor — its hemispherical chambers requiring four rocker shafts, eight intake and exhaust pushrods as well as eight intake and exhaust rocker arms — but it seemed like a winner. In fact, the "Hemi" would make great racing history.

The biggest challenge left to the Cunningham team was design, build and test three competitive C-2 roadsters, the cars that would race at Le Mans, in less than four months! At the same time, several additional C-2 chassis would also have to be built and eventually fitted with a coupe body and luxurious interior. They would be called C-3s and were to be offered for sale to private customers so that the Cunningham Company could qualify as a "car manufacturer" according Le Mans criteria. Bill Frick had now joined Phil Walters in West Palm Beach along with Bob Blake, an outstanding metalsmith who once had his own shop, and Briggs Weaver, a former designer and head engineer of du Pont Motors. The B. S. Cunningham Company now had a staff of thirty-two people.

Enormous time pressure and American practicality led the team to borrow the best possible assemblage of existing parts from various American manufacturers. The Chrysler engine was mated to a Cadillac three-speed transmission

which itself was connected to a Ford differential! Cadillac Alfin drum brakes were used, along with Chrysler Oriflow shock absorbers and Oldsmobile coil springs. The worm-and-roller steering also came from the Chrysler parts bin while a Cunningham Company-designed de Dion rear axle was used for improved handling. A fairly conventional aluminum body was designed by Phil Walters and Jack Donaldson, then built in the shop by Bob Blake.

Ironically, this multi-corporate "of-the-shelf" approach, though chosen out of sheer practicality by a few good brains within a very small private company, convinced the left-leaning French press, and soon its readers, that the Cunningham team was the spearhead of a national American effort to conquer and wipe out all opposition in international road racing. Little did the French public understand the much more modest Cunningham reality, let alone were they at all aware of the petty rivalries that were about to split the American ruling organization for road racing severely apart.

Le Mans-Bound

Three Cunningham racing roadsters were completed between March and May. The C-2 turned out big and relatively heavy, weighing 3150 lbs. with full load of fuel and driver on board. It sported a clear modern American look, with a large, smoothly rounded front end, oval grill and

John Fitch driving a team Cunningham C-2 just past Stone Bridge during the parade laps at Watkins Glen in September, 1951. Except for the higher "normal" windshield, the removal of extra headlights attached to the bumper bars, and some extra horses, the car was exactly as it raced at Le Mans three months earlier.

long vertical side panels followed by curvy rear fenders. It made an Allard look like a miniature museum piece, but the British racer weighted 1,700 lbs. less! The aerodynamic advantage of the Cunningham could not compensate for such a drastic difference in mass. After minimal testing in Florida, the trio of cars was shipped by rail to New York, then by boat to Le Havre, then driven to Le Mans where they arrived just in time to participate in the trials preceding the June 23-24 race.

During this same period of time, the Cunningham team also built the coupe version for "normal customers," the C-3. The West Palm Beach group, however, quickly found out their C-3's production costs were overwhelmingly high. Later, Cunningham contracted the *Carrozzeria Vignale* of Turin to design a coupe body for the official C-3 during the years 1952-53. Completed chassis and drivetrains would be shipped to Turin, fitted with the new bodies and a luxurious interior, then re-shipped to West Palm Beach for final detail work. They were eventually put up for sale at $10,000 — an extremely high price for the time. The C-3 was actually a nicely styled car and about thirty were built through 1953. The powerful and comfortable American roadster drew a great deal of attention, but very few customers because of its price.

In order to win at Le Mans, a racing team must not only have the right cars and talented drivers, but also be extremely well prepared based on solid experience with the race. Cunningham's second attempt at Le Mans was too hurried and proved a disappointment. The three pairs of all-American drivers, Walters-Fitch, Rand-Wacker and Cunningham-Huntoon, had more than enough talent. Thanks to the Chrysler Hemi, the C-2 could reach 152 mph on the Mulsanne straight (as against "only" 144 mph for the new Jaguar C-Type) and its handling was decent. A rainy night, however, sealed the fate of two of the white behemoths. Both Huntoon and Rand went off the road and were forced to retire. That left only one Cunningham in the race, still carrying great hopes. From the 14th hour, Walters-Fitch were running in second position behind the last remaining of the three factory Jaguar C-Types entered: the Walker - Whitehead machine. The two sidelined works Jaguars had suffered from the same ailment: total loss of

oil pressure resulting in a seized engine — later discovered to be caused by the breaking of a copper oil line vibrating too roughly at high engine revs.

Says Fitch about those anxious moments, "We assumed the third Jaguar C-Type would suffer from the same ailment and that it was just a matter of time until it too would retire. It was not to be, and instead it was the Cunningham that caught the bug at the 20th hour while holding second place. At that point, a rod bearing problem developed in the Chrysler engine which made the oil pressure drop dangerously. After a brief pit stop, it was decided that no repair was possible. The car would have to be nursed carefully in order to even finish." For a team to have at least one car finish was critically important: it guaranteed them the automatic right to race again the following year as long as their new cars met the ACO's rules and regulations.

Walters-Fitch nursed their ailing car and managed to finish, but only in 18th position behind Ferraris, Aston Martins, Talbots and several Jaguars, including the last remaining C-Type of Walker-Whitehead which won the race. Fitch comments, "What a coup if an American car had won Le Mans on the first time out with a dedicated racing sports car!" Indeed, the repercussions across the Atlantic would have been huge, and one can conjecture that the "internationalist point of view" would have received a massive boost. Alas, it was not to be.

The three C-2s were re-shipped to America to compete in the less demanding venues of Elkhart Lake and

TOP LEFT: LeMans, 1951 - The winning Jaguar C-Type of Walker-Whitehead. This was the new Jaguar's first outing and it managed to beat the Ferrari right out of the gate.

BOTTOM RIGHT: Sebring, December 31, 1950 - Luigi Chinetti driving Briggs Cunningham's Ferrari 195 S, a fine example of the Touring body. Chinetti co-drove the car to 7th overall (Index).

Watkins Glen. In the interim, the Cunningham team, with Bill Frick in the lead, tried to extract even more horsepower from the Chrysler engine, while beginning design work on the next racer.

The European Season

Jaguar had finally beaten Ferrari at Le Mans. The C-Type, the first car specially built by Jaguar to win the French classic and other major endurance events, triumphed there on its first outing having been readied and road tested only three weeks before the race. In contrast to the fledgling Equipe Cunningham, however, the Jaguar team, including chief executive Sir Williams Lyons, had accumulated several years worth of experience and detailed technical data at Le Mans.

The C-Type's predecessor, the XK-120, also continued to demonstrate Jaguar's winning power. It helped the remarkably talented Stirling Moss win the Silverstone International Trophy in May. Belgian jazzman and driver Johnny Claes won the Spa sports car race ten days later in a similar car, then Belgian journalist Jacques Ickx, father of a six-year-old named Jacky, won the grueling Liège-Rome Liège Rally with another XK-120 in mid-August. On September 15, Stirling Moss gave the C-Type its second major victory at the famous Tourist Trophy at Dundrod. Jaguar was having a very good year.

Though it lost at Le Mans, Ferrari still posted an enviable record in 1951. The Maranello company had further

increased the displacement of its famous V-12, racing it principally in two versions: a 4.1 liter version powered the new, bigger Ferrari 340 America, while a 2.6 liter version was fitted in the existing chassis and called 212 Export. Both models were still most often dressed in *Carrozzeria Touring* spider and coupe designs, though Vignale was beginning to create new body shapes for Ferrari as well. Between April 1 and the end of the year, Ferrari would accumulate over twenty victories, including the *Giro di Sicilia* (212 - G. Marzotto-Crossara), Monza's *Coppa Intereuropa* (212 - Villoresi), the *Mille Miglia* (340 - Villoresi-Cassani), the *Tour de France* (340 - Pagnibon-Barraquet) and, last but not least, the second Carrera Panamericana (212 - Taruffi-Chinetti). In the Formula 1 championship series, Alberto Ascari finished second to Juan Manuel Fangio's Alfa.

Promising Fledglings

Two upstart sports car makers were also beginning to gain awareness in the ever-expanding community of racing aficionados. The first was OSCA, founded by the three surviving of five Maserati brothers in 1947. Count Orsi, the financeer who had come to their financial rescue ten years earlier had forced them to sell their business name and company. The Maserati brothers took the bold step of leav-

BOTTOM LEFT: Rees Mackins driving an early OSCA MT4 at Elkhart Lake in 1952.

BOTTOM RIGHT: Porsche 356 "Gmünd" coupe of 1949. This car from the Collier Collection is fitted with aerodynamic wheel "spats" used for speed record runs.

ing Modena in December, 1947, and returning to their native Bologna, where they set up the *Officine Specializzate per la Construzione di Automobile*, acronymed as OSCA. Their early cars were pretty little racers, with a standard engine capacity of 1100 cc. OSCA won its first two major overall victories in 1951: the *Coppa Dolomiti* in July and the Monza Grand Prix in September. The new Italian firm also accumulated countless class victories throughout the year, thus beginning to make a name for itself. The Maserati brothers were working hard on getting their revenge.

The second new marque to be noticed around race tracks was Porsche. Founded in 1946, Porsche Konstructionen GmbH was now producing the Type 356 in small numbers in Gmünd, Austria. Early in 1950, Dr. Ferdinand Porsche was urged by Charles Faroux, the leading organizer of the Le Mans 24 Hours, to consider a participation in the French classic. At the time, Porsche was considering moving back to its original building, promised to be vacated by occupying Allied troops, in Zuffenhausen, a suburb of Stuttgart, which they eventually began to do in September. There was no time for a factory representation at the 1950 French classic. Then Dr. Porsche died at the age of 75 on January 18 of 1951. By then, his son Ferry and the new Porsche team were well in place and poised to

continue developing the company. Official Porsche participation was considered for the 1951 Le Mans race. The factory decided it was not yet ready for such an effort, but vowed to support serious enthusiasts.

French importer Auguste Veuillet, founder and owner of the Sonauto foreign car dealership in Paris, proved the most dedicated. He entered two specially prepared 356 SL coupes which would race in Germany's official racing color, bright silver. They were aluminum-bodied Gmünd coupes, race-tuned with the help of Porsche GmbH. One of the cars crashed during practice and could not take part in the race, but nonetheless the first participation of a Porsche in the famous 24 hour race was a success. The lone 1086 cc Gmünd-built car, co-driven by Auguste Veuillet and friend Edmond Mouche, finished 20th and won its class. Following that feat, two 356s finished the Liège-Rome-Liège Marathon third and tenth overall in mid-August, and a similar car finished third overall in the tough Tour de France behind two Ferraris two weeks later. A great rivalry, and a long tradition, had just begun.

Within this fascinating kaleidoscope, French makers were practically absent. Only one company sporting the French racing blue hue had any degree of success in 1951: Talbot. At Le Mans, it fielded no less than five barely disguised 4.5 liter Grand Prix racers and managed to place second and fourth. The other Talbots did not finish. In fact, only Talbot among French makers won a race of any repute

Credit: Collection Jean-Paul Delsaux

TOP RIGHT: The Gordini T15 S of factory team driver Robert Manzon at the Nürburgring sports car race in 1950. They won their class (up to 1100cc). Amédée Gordini was a passionate mechanical genius but, unlike Enzo Ferrari, not a savvy businessman.

BOTTOM LEFT: The Talbot-Lago T26 GS of Louis Rosier racing at Rouen in 1950. The car is essentially a Grand Prix racer with minimal adaptations to meet CSI sports car criteria (headlights, fenders, two seats, etc.). Louis Rosier and his son Jean-Louis won the 1950 Le Mans in that machine.

Credit: Klemantaski Collection

in 1951: the *Coupe du Salon* at Montlhéry in October, where the opposition was weak. In the Formula 1 World Championship, Talbots were simply invisible among the top finishers. Gordini had an appalling season, scoring only minor class wins and meeting with disaster at Le Mans. Though the team fielded four racers in the French classic, all equipped with Gordini's best 1.5 liter engine, and used the talent of drivers such as Maurice Trintignant and Jean Behra, none of the Simca-based cars finished the race! At the end of the year, Simca decided to drop out of racing entirely, leaving Amédée Gordini in dire financial straits.

So in 1951, the European public witnessed the return to full-blown racing, or the beginning of the "modern era," as some put it. The traditional nationalistic rivalries were fully reignited, but this time without the propaganda tactics of the pre-war years. It was again British racing green versus Italian red, French blue and German silver. American white with the blue stripe had just been added to the mix, to everyone's delight. Everyone in Europe, that is. There was a strong movement within America's SCCA lead group to remain contentedly isolationist, write their own provincial racing rules, and stay away from those "loony foreigners."

The Great Controversy

The Goldschmidt affair had been the first major row to rock the previously tightly knit group of enthusiasts who ran the SCCA. As Fred Wacker rightly asserted later, that affair had more to do with Goldschmidt's rough manners than with his ethnicity, "The SCCA had several Jewish members, Max Hoffman being one of the most prominent." Nonetheless, the "Goldschmidt affair" had split the upper layers of the club into two camps. Egos were both bruised and on the line. At the end of 1950, Alec Ulmann, a certified internationalist by background and spirit, did something that some of the most conservative members simply thought outrageous: he organized and ran America's first endurance race at Sebring, with the intention of eventually inviting foreigners to participate. He even sought and received the support of the AAA. Cameron Argetsinger, rich with his experience of running Watkins Glen, helped him with organizing the event. Bill Milliken, though he held serious doubts about the AAA, based on his earlier experience with them at Pikes Peak — finding their rules "rigid and petty," helped with key technical aspects.

It was Ulmann's trip to Le Mans with the Cunningham team in 1950 which had rekindled his great interest for international endurance racing. The Russian émigré had attended several Le Mans 24 hour races in the thirties and had then been infected with the passion for the sport. He was convinced that road racing had a great future in America. In fact, he had started looking for a venue where an American version of Le Mans could be organized even before his first trip to France with the Cunningham team. In Ulmann's mind, such a race would have to be staged in the early winter to complement the European calendar, so sunny climes were a must.

At the time, Ulmann's main business was to buy surplus military aircrafts and then recondition them for civilian use or prep them for sale to small nations. Florida was a state familiar to him. In the Spring of 1950, he had visited Hendricks Field near Sebring. A friend of his, Col. C. D. Richardson, was already maintaining an aircraft part store at the decommissioned World War II Boeing B-17 bomber training base. Ulmann was looking for a place where to store and fix the surplus airplanes he was buying, fixing and selling. He needed hangar space and lots of tarmac. Sam Collier flew in from West Palm Beach with his private Beechcraft Bonanza. Then the two friends and Bob Gegen, the SCCA Florida regional executive, surveyed the field from the air. It seemed like the perfect site for Ulmann's business as well as for his passion. Hendricks

Field had long runways, vast possibilities for road course layouts, plus a village of service buildings, mess halls, barracks, and even a church!

To quote Alec Ulmann from his book, *The Sebring Story*, "It was then and there that the idea germinated in my mind of duplicating, on a smaller scale, the Le Mans 24 Hours endurance race, emulating the Le Mans principle of condensing within a circuit all the sporting potential of a point-to-point race with its inherent problems." He soon signed a long term lease for the former military base. Ulmann was following Argetsinger's steps.

After the 1950 Le Mans race, Ulmann visited the Paris-based headquarters of the FIA and had lunch with Auguste Pérouse, then president of the organization's *Commission Sportive Internationale* (CSI). He was seeking the FIA's support for his project. Though he remembered the food to be fabulous, Ulmann was shocked to hear that as far as the FIA was concerned, their only valid partner in America was the AAA, not the SCCA. This was so even though the AAA only ran one *Grande Epreuve*, the Indy 500, which, except for engine capacity limitations, did not conform at all with FIA rules!

In contrast and thanks to Argetsinger and Ulmann, Watkins Glen did, and Sebring would, conform to all FIA rules But tradition is tradition, especially for the French. As far as Auguste Pérouse and the CSI were concerned, colonel Arthur Herrington, a Washington D.C. resident and Chairman of the AAA Contest Board, was the official contact in America and he would have to be formally approached about this very official matter. Then, there was also the proverbial dismissive French attitude. To quote Ulmann again, "And, after all, this was America, far off, where things were done differently and where racing cars ran only one way, round and round an oval, at terrifying speeds that seemed to them in Europe, phony."

Upon returning to America, Ulmann decided to go ahead with his project anyway, and even to base the Sebring rules on the International Code prescribed by the FIA. He would, however, keep the first event low key and only invite American road racing drivers. His true hope was to be officially free, one day, to invite some of the most famous international works teams and talented

© Harold Lance

were falling further and further behind or disappearing entirely. The small Renaults, the D. B. Panhards and the Simca Gordinis would thus have a shot at a prize. Needless to say, it was not a good idea for V-8 crazy Americans whose domestic manufacturers, with the exception of Crosley, did not produce a single small car! Fortunately for Ulmann, most participants would come to Sebring for the fun anyway; plus for the thrill of participating in an American road race which would start in the early afternoon and end in darkness. With, in addition, an expected distance of over 350 miles after six hours of racing, Sebring could only enthuse the passionate pioneers who had sent in their applications. Complex rules or not, the joy of racing was the most important criteria of all.

December 31, 1950 turned out to be a cold but sunny day in South Florida. A little less than 3,000 spectators showed up for the event. It was just as well, for there were no grandstands, no pits except for folding tables tied together by 2 x 4 planks or anything but the most basic facilities. Twenty-eight cars were eventually qualified to

A gorgeous Delahaye at the 1950 Watkins Glen Concours d'Elégance. This was a Type 145, one of two such cars built in 1949-'50. The body is by Henri Chapron. The car had a 12-cylinder 4.5 liter engine originally designed for world championship racing. This is a fine example of how the French car industry could have kept its leadership, but for wrong-headed government taxation policies.

take the Le Mans-type start. The big-engined cars took the lead early but, according to the index formula, it was not the real lead. At any rate, the race went on with some spectacular moments, including a noisy outburst from Erwin Goldschmidt when his Allard, then with Cole at the wheel, was disqualified after he sent a mechanic to fix the car stalled in a turn far from the pits, a strictly forbidden move. As darkness fell around 6 pm, the bizarre reality that the Kimberly-Lewis Ferrari 166 (1995 cc), though several laps ahead on distance, was trying to catch up with the Koster-Deshon Crosley Hot Shot (724 cc), leading on the index, set in. Even more strange, the overall leading car on distance at that point was the Wacker-Burrell Cad-Allard which, due to its large engine size, was running in eighth on the index.

Laughter, then Political Trials

In the end, though Wacker's Allard won on distance with a total of 111 laps, or 388.5 miles, the little Crosley was declared the winner with only 89 laps completed (311.5 miles) as its index gave it the most favorable position. The Kimberly-Lewis Ferrari 166 was declared second (though fourth on distance with 108 laps) and the Keller-Farago Fiat 1100 was declared third, though it completed only 85 laps. Everyone nonetheless had a grand time and the New Year's celebrations that night were particularly festive in Sebring, Florida, then a town of barely 7,000 people. Few of the participating SCCA members realized that New Year's Eve that a mighty political storm was abrewing in their club, fed precisely by the event in which they all had just reveled.

As far as some powerful members of the SCCA were concerned, Alec Ulmann had committed a triple sin in staging the first modern endurance race in America. First, he had worked hand in hand with the AAA, "that roughneck, bloodthirsty professional drivers' association" through Herrington and Clemenger; he had also accepted the help of an experienced Royal Automobile Club member, Fred Royston, a foreigner! Second, he had invited participants not only from the SCCA ranks, but also "outsiders" such as Erwin Goldschmidt. Third and probably most damaging, he had, in his own words, "precipitated a head-on collision

American V-8 engines. Commented Ulmann, "John Bentley, ex-Englishman, echoed their thoughts in the matter: 'This is not Europe and it is 1951, and the surest way to promote fair club competition is to use classifications to fit the cars now available in the United States. Hence, the SCCA-revised classes make a good deal more sense than the International FIA-imposed ones'."

Ulmann, morally supported by Cameron Argetsinger, Miles Collier and George Rand among others, decided then and there to go his own way, such was his conviction that intercontinental sports car racing abiding by the FIA rules was the only way to go. The "Great Controversy," a portentous schism that would last eight years and set back intercontinental sports car racing substantially, had just begun.

A Paper Battle Rages

The fact that Ulmann had, on his own, met with FIA officials in Paris, then established a rapport with both Colonel Arthur A. Herrington and Jim Clemenger of the AAA, had sealed his eventual death sentence as a SCCA member. Through these contacts, the AAA, which had ruled all forms of racing in America for over fifty years, and the newly powerful but independent SCCA, became entangled in a mighty power struggle. Though the spoken words have not been recorded, a heated exchange of letters between Colonel Herrington and D. Cameron Peck was on the docket and was in fact fully printed in the March - April, 1951 issue of *Sports Car*, next to strong comments from Peck and further backed by a long, last-minute memorandum by him inserted in the issue. These written exchanges between the heads of the AAA and the SCCA are undoubtedly toned down by the more polite form required for official correspondence, but they leave no doubt as to the animosity and intensity of the actual personal conflict and the verbal exchanges that surely took place.

After summarily removing Ulmann as Activities Chairman, reducing him to a mere member, Peck and Felton still felt that the strongly dissenting minority within the "rebels" needed a more blatant warning. They deemed that the SCCA had to send a formal message to Colonel Herrington in order to clear matters entirely. In a letter

with the office of President Cameron Peck and his stormy petrel, Colonel George Felton, the retiring Vice-President."

In a fashion which would have been expected in the Kremlin, the SCCA dropped Ulmann from his duties as Activities Chairman early in January, then erased his name from all descriptions of the first Sebring race in the report featured in the first 1951 issue of the club's publication, *Sports Car*. Shortly thereafter the newly elected SCCA Contest Board, with Bill Milliken as Chairman plus George Huntoon, George Weaver and Russ Sceli as members, issued a decree confirming the abandonment of International FIA car classifications, replacing them with displacement classes more amenable to the then available

Sebring, December 31, 1950 - At 3 pm, seconds after the "Le Mans start" of the Six-Hour race. MGs, Jaguars, Aston Martins and Allards rush towards the first corner.

European champions. Ulmann proceeded with great diplomatic caution, while keeping that idea in mind. He disclosed his plan to the AAA representative in New York, Jim Clemenger and enlisted him in the venture. He welcomed formal counsel from Fred Royston, a member of England's Royal Automobile Club. He contacted and worked with Colonel Herrington, and actually found him "enormously helpful."

Next he went to Chicago to pay a visit to D. Cameron Peck, the then president of the SCCA, in the hope of influencing him. Peck, however, was the man who had told Argetsinger earlier, "We cannot have Goldschmidt race at Watkins Glen." Peck's response to Ulmann was brutal. Wrote the Russian émigré afterwards, "I was told that SCCA was not going to debase its image by joining that roughneck, bloodthirsty professional driver's organization [the AAA]. That foreign drivers and foreign teams coming to America was a pipe dream."

The First Sebring Race

Ulmann went ahead anyway. In the late Summer, he mobilized a group of SCCA enthusiasts which eventually included Argetsinger, the Collier brothers, George Huntoon, Bob Gegen and Smith Hempstone Oliver. America's first endurance race, which was to be called The Six Hours of Sebring, was scheduled for December 31, 1950. It would be run on a 3.5 mile circuit marked by haybales and a few signs on the airport's vast area, start at 3 pm and end at 9 pm. Just as at Watkins Glen, the starter would be Nils Mickelson. Soon, the effort to recruit participants was in full swing, and entries began to come in. When Sam Collier died at Watkins Glen on September 23, it caused consternation among the entire racing community. In honor of the great and dedicated racing enthusiast, Ulmann decided to rename the first Sebring race The Sam Collier Memorial Grand Prix of Endurance.

By the announced deadline, thirty entrants were officially accepted, coming from states as diverse as Texas, Wisconsin, Ohio, New York, and even Ontario, Canada. Many figures familiar to the Watkins Glen spectators were among them: Chinetti, Spear and Kimberly would drive Ferraris; Fred Wacker and Erwin Goldschmidt Cadillac-

© Frank Campanale Collection

Sebring, December 31, 1950 - View of pit row shortly before the start of the first Sebring race.

powered Allards, with Tom Cole assigned as the main driver for the Goldschmidt car. Phil Walters would drive Cunningham's Healey Cadillac, while Cunningham himself and George Rand would drive Aston Martin DB2s, a car that had done particularly well at Le Mans in June — one had finished third overall and five out of five finished the race. Bob Keller was paired up with Paul Farago in the former's Fiat 1100 coupe; Milliken would drive an MG TC and Kurt Hildebrand would race his Volkswagen Special.

Ulmann had only one strange idea in his otherwise great scheme, but it was very strange. Having been impressed by the "index of performance" race within the race that Charles Faroux had established at Le Mans, he decided to make the Sebring Six Hours a race entirely based on a formula designed to equalize all participants regardless of their car's engine size. The final ranking would thus be determined by a complex equation adjusting actual distance covered by a coefficient based on the exact cubic centimeter capacity of the car's engine. The winner would be the driver who exceeded his handicap by the most amount of miles as a percentage of his minimum expected mileage determined in advance by the formula. This was a surefire way to make it very hard for the public to figure out who was in the lead, who was trailing and what the actual ranking at any time really was!

Charles Faroux had originally devised a similarly arcane index of performance to give some French manufacturers a chance to win some prize at Le Mans as the national big-engine makers (Bugatti, Delahaye, Delage, Talbot)

"Our methods are not those of a dictator, who would attempt to propound these rules and foist them upon you." ...

"The whole tone of your communication would seem to imply the meaning that you are an organization controlling all sports car activities in the United States." ...

"We deeply regret that you do not see your way clear to accord your colleagues in the sports car, or amateur racing activity, the courtesy of sitting down with them and with us to consider this whole proposed course of action in a temperate and businesslike manner." ... *"Had you had the opportunity of attending one of our meetings, as your colleagues have done, I am quite sure that you would have occasion to considerably revise the opinions and assertions set forth to the members of your Sports Car Club of America."*

"We propose to continue our conversations with your colleagues. If as a result of these talks it should be determined that it is advisable for us to assume control of amateur automobile racing in the United States, it will be our intention to do so."

With this letter, D. Cameron Pecks' ship had taken a few torpedoes in its hull and was put on the defensive. Peck, though, had the comforting thought that a voting majority of SCCA officers stood behind him. His response to Herrington, dated April 9, was written accordingly while it also unleashed some heavy fire on the "Ten Petitioners," now standing alone in the open (excerpts):

"I appreciate your frankness and the complete expression of your opinion." ...

"I realize that a 'controversy' if such it must be called, does not exist between SCCA and AAA as such, but rather between the majority of SCCA's members and a small minority within our club who are using AAA's name and prestige." ...

Jim Kimberly in 1951.

"We appreciate your assurance that AAA does not seek to take control of amateur automobile racing." ... *"No representative of SCCA was ever instructed to by-pass AAA and to obtain direct recognition from FIA. That one SCCA official did so on his own initiative is correct."* ...

"We have found the International Rule Book a reasonably satisfactory framework within which to operate, but have never hesitated to make whatever changes would bring about the fairest and most sporting competition among our members."

"We are glad to have you state that your 'methods are not those of a dictator.' Neither are ours." ...

"However, we view with some amusement your assertion that 'if as a result of these talks it should be determined that it is advisable for us to assume control of amateur automobile racing in the United States, it will be our intention to do so.' Talks with groups representing a small minority of the organized enthusiasts in this country hardly justify taking control of anything."

Herrington, of course could not resist firing back at Peck. In a letter written the very next day (April 10), he first stated that there obviously seemed to be an element of misunderstanding, then he wrote with calculated ambiguity:

> *"The AAA has not sought and does not now seek to take control of amateur automobile racing in the United States."*

> *"When a group of gentlemen, who are active in amateur racing in the United States, come before us of their own free will and accord and request a hearing from us to determine whether we would consider taking over control of amateur automobile racing in the United States, it is only common courtesy that they should be given a hearing."*

> *"If as a result of these conversations, a majority of the sports car clubs of the United States indicate a desire for the AAA to assume control of amateur automobile racing in the United States, it will be our intention to comply with their request and to proceed with the organization of such activities as are necessary to accomplish their desires."*

That last paragraph summarized the *Casus Belli* for the Peck faction of the SCCA. By pluralizing the word club in the phrase "sports car clubs," Herrington implied that other clubs such as Cal Club or, worst of all, the MSCA to which Erwin Goldschmidt belonged, could join together and form a rival national road racing club which would have both AAA and FIA approval and could drive the Peck-run SCCA into oblivion. The declaration of war was printed in the March-April issue of *Sports Car* in which Peck had a memorandum of his own inserted, dated April 16, and which rebutted the "Dissident Declaration" paragraph by paragraph.

The Next Defeat of the Internationalists

Now was Argetsinger's turn. In the late Spring, the planning for the fourth Watkins Glen Grand Prix began to accelerate. Argetsinger's point of view was well-known: he was an internationalist and had envisioned an event such as "The 24 Hours of Watkins Glen" from day one. Under his flawless guidance, the 1950 Watkins Glen Grand Prix had successfully passed the FIA test. The 1951 event should

Cameron Argetsinger (left) and D. Cameron Peck in an intense discussion at Watkins Glen in 1950. Ironically, Argetsinger wears a SCCA patch, while Peck wears the AAA logo!

therefore be an international race sanctioned by the FIA and open to all qualified drivers with a valid licence. The next deciding body in the national decision tree was the Watkins Glen Board consisting of the early founders, and including Bill Milliken as the only out-of-towner on account of his critical contributions from the early days. The final decision on which way to go had to be made by June. Meetings would take place in the Village Board Room. The SCCA faced a gigantic crossroad. In April and May, long and numerous telephone and written discussions took place between the key protagonists. The isolationists lobbied very hard.

The first Board meeting took place in early June. Cameron Argetsinger would present his strongly-held point of view. Two very important friends came into town to support his cause: Miles Collier who flew in in his Beechcraft Bonanza for this single purpose, and Ken Purdy, the foremost automotive writer in the nation at the time. To the arguments already stated, Argetsinger added that with the FIA's sanction, Watkins Glen would have safer and better races and would get more assistance than from just the SCCA. To the Village officials of Watkins Glen, that small community in Upstate New York, it probably seemed far-fetched compared to a formula that had worked so well for them three years in a row. The Board split its vote 3 to 3, underlining the seemingly impossible dilemma the club was facing.

A second meeting was called. Bill Milliken, Chairman

© Bruce Craig

TOP LEFT: Phil Walters in his OSCA at the start of the Bridgehampton race in 1951.

TOP RIGHT: John Fitch in the Fitch-Whitmore Jaguar, a much lightened racer based on XK-120 drivetrain and mechanicals.

was held on April 22, 1951 and served as the effective season opener for the east. There were 46 participants, almost half driving MGs. The main race was won by Preston Grey in a Cadillac Allard; Roger Wing came second in a Jaguar XK-120 and Jim Hoe placed third in his Duesenberg J Special.

The second eastern race was held in Bridgehampton on May 26. Tom Cole once again won with his Allard; Phil Walters finished second in a Cunningham-owned Ferrari 195 Inter; and Erwin Goldschmidt finished third in his own Allard. John Fitch was fourth in his new creation, the Fitch-Whitmore Jaguar Special. Coby Whitmore was a famous magazine illustrator and a good friend of Fitch. They had raced as a team in a Jaguar XK-120 at the first Sebring race, and thought they could radically improve the performance of the vaunted British roadster.

The pair of friends would do so by reversing the by-now traditional method of improving a European sports car's performance: remove the small original engine, replace it with a big American V-8, then adjust the suspension for higher cornering speeds. Instead, Fitch and his friend decided to keep the Jaguar chassis, suspension and engine intact — with the exception of minor tuning — and to replace the production body by a much lighter and narrower aluminum shape contained inside the wheels. Cycle fenders provided the regulatory cover to meet sports car regulations. Fitch and Whitmore drew the body shape by working together. The end-result, built by metal specialist Andy Salada, was an attractive two-seat roadster which weighed 800 lbs. less than the stock XK-120. The fourth-

place finish at Bridgehampton, the car's first race, made the pair of friends feel optimistic.

Midwest Mixer

On August 30, it was back to Elkhart Lake, this time on a new circuit following the Watkins Glen format: the start/finish line in the middle of the village's main thoroughfare, then a challenging 6.7 mile circuit traced in roller-coaster fashion in the hills surrounding the village and leading back onto the main straight. This would be the first genuine "endurance" race after Sebring: the main event, called "The Elkhart Lake 200," would require the drivers to go around the long circuit 30 times for a total of 200 miles.

There were two sensations among the entries. First was the presence of the three Cunningham C-2s, veterans of Le Mans and to be driven by Fitch, Walters and Cunningham himself. Bill Spear would drive his new Ferrari 340 America, which he had also driven at Le Mans. He lent friend Steve Lansing his other Ferrari, the 166 MM. Second was the challenge of a strong California contingent. It was led by two special light-weight Jaguar XK-120s owned by west coast importer Charles Hornburg. The cars had unique aluminum alloy bodies and were to be driven by Phil Hill and Jorge Malbrand. Mike Graham, a British-born California resident, brought his Allard J2 from Harry Chapman of Los Angeles who would later become an OSCA distributor.

Credit: Road America

A view at the villarge street corner at Elkhart Lake in 1952. The general landscape does not look very different from Watkins Glen, which was the original intention. A pack of Jaguar XK-120's and a Nash-Healey are about to be challenged by Phil Walters' Ferrari two-tone Vignale Coupe seen in the back. Walters would finish second to Phil Hill's C-Type Jaguar, the first time Hill beat Walters.

The first "Elkhart Lake 200" was a hard-fought race. The John Fitch-Cunningham C-2 combination, though, proved unbeatable. Michael Graham finished second in the Allard, followed by Phil Hill and Jorge Malbrand in their Jaguars. Bill Spear and his Ferrari were 5th, ahead of Cunningham in his own C-2. The third Cunningham, driven by Walters did not finish due to engine failure. The crowd of spectators was huge, some objective estimates putting it as high as 30,000. Most important, the first direct rivalry between easterners and westerners turned into an additional thrill. Despite its political problems, the SCCA was able to plan and implement a calendar which by now was beginning to take the shape of a truly national road racing championship. The next race on that calendar was Watkins Glen on September 15. It was by all accounts the SCCA's prime event of the year. For better or worse, it would prove a decisive weekend in the history of international road racing.

Fate Comes Into The Picture

Cameron Argetsinger, despite the defeat of his strongly-held internationalist point of view, remained a key player within the SCCA during the first half of 1951, the bitterest phase of the "Great Controversy." He fully intended to remain active and influential, to continue racing and, hopefully, to win a big one. In the early summer, he bought an Allard J2 in order to catch up with the competition. He bought the car from Cal Connel, a Detroit Cadillac dealer and tinkerer, who had earlier prepared Erwin Goldschmidt's winning Cad-Allard. Argetsinger's new Allard had already won the Giant Despair hillclimb earlier in the year and the young lawyer could not wait to drive it in a race. One of the first things he did was to show it to his friend Sam Cobean. Cobean was a cartoonist for *The New Yorker*, a colleague of Charles Addams, and he and his wife, Anne, owned a summer cottage near Watkins Glen. They had become good friends with the Argetsingers and this is how Sam Cobean came to draw the original Watkins Glen circuit map featured in the early race programs. Sam Cobean himself owned a bright red Jaguar XK-120. He and Cameron were always keen to compare notes on their respective racers.

On July 2, Cameron Argetsinger dropped his new Allard at Smalley's garage to have some work done on it. Sam dropped by in his Jaguar and offered Cameron a ride back to his lakeside home. In no time, the two friends were riding side by side in the open-topped roadster, with Sam at the wheel. As they were going up Lake Road, Cobean proceeded to pass a slow car. Right after he began his maneuver, the other driver, seemingly unaware of being passed, proceeded to turn left. Cobean swerved to avoid a collision but he could not keep the Jaguar on the road. As is often the case around Watkins Glen, a tree stopped the out-of-control vehicle. The force of the impact was strong but not catastrophic. Cameron Argetsinger was ejected from his seat, suffering bruises and a concussion.

Fate, however, was not so favorable to Sam Cobean. The shock had projected him forward toward a steering wheel which, at that relatively moderate deceleration level, was more likely to provide some protection than to hurt him badly. Alas, there was the cone-shape horn button pointing toward the driver's chest at just the wrong angle. Sam Cobean died on the spot from one of the unlikeliest stab wounds anyone might ever think of. He was 38, the same age as Sam Collier, at the time of his death at Montour Falls Hospital.

Cameron Argetsinger was transported to the same hospital and recovered quickly. However, his doctor was worried about the concussion which had knocked his young patient unconscious for a few minutes. The doctor's final verdict, "You must forgo any racing until next year." So now not only was the founder of the Watkins Glen Grand Prix on the losing side in the political war which was tearing through the SCCA, but by way of a dumb and tragic accident, he would not be able to race in the fourth annual Grand Prix. The sudden loss of a dear friend obviously dampened his spirit even further. This unfortunate event gave the "amateur-only" majority in the SCCA even more freedom to organize the forthcoming Grand Prix exactly as they wanted.

Early September 1951, New York Finger Lakes Region

In the week preceding the fourth Grand Prix, and despite the strong pull to keep SCCA racing "amateur only," the list of participants and registered cars showed that the Watkins Glen race was attracting machines and drivers with more than respectable international exposure.

First among those, of course were the three Cunningham C-2s, veterans of Le Mans and Elkhart Lake. They would be driven by Briggs Cunningham himself, along with his two best drivers, John Fitch and Phil Walters. Showing the thorough internationalization of the Watkins Glen event in a different way was the fact that there were only five "American-made" racers in the entire 1951 field of almost one hundred machines: three specials and two Crosley Hot Shots, the latter of course entered in

BOTTOM LEFT: Briggs Cunningham driving his own C-2 during the parade laps at Watkins Glen on September 15, 1951. The three C-2s would end up first, second and fourth in the Grand Prix.

BOTTOM RIGHT: Jim Kimberly driving Briggs Cunningham's Ferrari 166 SC during the parade laps for the Grand Prix at Watkins Glen on September 15, 1951. Kimberly, whose own two Ferraris were then under repair, borrowed this one from his friend. It was the car in which Sam Collier crashed a year before.

the Queen Catharine Cup. The three "big-bore" specials were entered in the Seneca Cup, not the Grand Prix. John Bentley would drive the now familiar Meyer Offenhauser, Denver Cornett the same Ford Special he had fielded in 1950 and Saxon Marsh an Altemus Special with innovative technology designed to improve handling.

The gaggle of Ferraris on the entrants' list was the next indicator of the "Europeanization" of Watkins Glen. No fewer than seven made-in-Maranello racers were entered, with engines ranging from 2.6 liter for Charles Moran's 212 Inter to 4.1 liter for Bill Spear's 340 America. Both Moran and Spear had driven similar Ferraris at Le Mans in June. Jim Kimberly, who now owned two Ferraris, ironically had to borrow one of Cunningham's for the Watkins Glen weekend: both of his Italian thoroughbreds were in the shop for varying reasons. The Ferrari Kimberly was lent by Cunningham was the one which remained uncommitted from "Mr. C.'s" growing stable: the 166 SC in which Sam Collier had died a year earlier. The fateful car had been repaired, though it still showed minor unsightly creases on its sheet metal.

There would be seven more Italian-made cars in the 1951 field: three small Siatas, a Bandini-Fiat and the well-known Keller-Haynes Fiat 1100, all entered in the Queen Catharine Cup. In the "big-bore" category, two Grand Prix Maseratis were entered. First was the inimitable "Poison

"Lil," George Weaver's Maserati V8RI. He would race it in the Seneca Cup possibly under the mantra "Hope Springs Eternal." Second American V8RI owner, Phillip Cade, would field his own pre-war Italian ogre in the same race. In order to hedge his bets for a second victory at the Glen, Weaver would also compete in the Queen Catharine Cup aboard a Max Hoffman-entered, highly tuned Jowett Jupiter. That car, in its unusual white livery, was just one member of a vast British contingent at the Glen.

Besides the usual herd of MGs, the British automobile industry would be represented by six Allard J2s, six Jaguar XK-120s, two Jowetts — including Weaver's, two H.R.G.s, one Healey Silverstone, one Lea-Francis, one Connaught and even a Morris Minor. In addition, as Formula 3 cars (500 cc) for the first time were be allowed to race in the Seneca Cup, three were entered, all British: two Coopers and an Effyh. The German automobile industry was absent of any "official" representative car. Only two entries could claim some teutonic genes: Kurt Hildebrand's VW special and a BMW roadster entered by E. J. Tobin. Finally, there were no French cars entered, confirming the decline in international reach of that nation's once great automobile industry.

That was the field for 1951. It was remarkable in many other ways. There were no pre-war cars, with the minor exceptions of the two Grand Prix Maseratis and a trio of American specials. In fact, many of the major entries were brand new designs or newly produced cars, including the three Cunninghams, many of the Allards and Jaguars, and Bill Spear's Ferrari 340. Here was another clear sign of the rising competitive level of road racing at Watkins Glen. D. Cameron Peck's biases notwithstanding, the gap between American and European road racing was closing fast.

The 1951 Watkins Glen Program

With the growing popularity and sophistication of their Grand Prix event, the Watkins Glen Race Committee decided to expand their program in many ways. Most modifications reflected the experience acquired in the previous years and were intended to increase safety and organizational professionalism. The biggest change was the addition of an extra day to the formerly one-day affair. The official series of events would begin Friday at 11 am with a dri-

The pretty though oddly colored Siata Daina Coupe of Fred Proctor Jr. The owner entered and drove the 1400cc car in the Queen Catharine Cup, finishing 12th.

ver's meeting. There the competitors would receive final instructions for race day. In addition, starting grid positions would be drawn and quickly publicized.

Then, from 2 to 5 pm, there would be what the official program described as a "probable practice period," where each driver would complete a minimum of five laps in order to become familiar with the circuit and its various topological challenges. Finally, the Concours d'Elégance would be held on that same evening, starting at 7 pm and ending with a parade of the participating cars. Thus, the Concours would not crowd race day and risk creating unwanted delays for the three races scheduled for Saturday.

Race day, Saturday the 15th, would start at 10:45 am with the "unrestricted" Seneca Cup, to go eight laps or a distance of 52.8 miles. The inaugural race was expected to last about one hour. At 12:15, small-bore cars (under 1500 cc) and their drivers would have the field to their own with the start of the Queen Catharine Cup. This event, intended to become a serious "small displacement" or "beginners" race, was scheduled for fifteen laps or 99 miles, as long a distance as the first Grand Prix of 1948. Finally, at 2:30

pm, the start of the fourth Grand Prix of Watkins Glen would be officially given. This time, the main race would come close to meeting the basic criteria for a European endurance race: it would require the winner to complete thirty laps of the demanding circuit, or 198 miles (319 Km). This was expected to take just short of three hours, a far cry from the 1948 main event which counted only 8 laps and saw Frank Griswold win the race in less than fifty minutes.

Sabre Rattling

There would also be one unique automobile, a concept car, present at the Glen that weekend, though it was not part of the Concours nor would it participate in any of the races. It was the Le Sabre, "the car of the future" as seen by General Motors. It was a stunning automobile designed by the team of Harley J. Earl, the colorful head of design for the world's biggest car company. The styling of the large two-seat convertible roadster was unmistakably inspired by the F-86 Sabre jet fighter of Korean war fame. The hood resembled the jet fighter's nose section, beginning with a central air scoop jutting out ahead of the front bumper. The latter sported two conical "bumpers" on each side of the central scoop, an apparent design cue taken from the two long torpedo-like extra fuel tanks the F-86 often carried under its wings to extend its range. The Le Sabre sat low on a 115 inch wheelbase and its rear fenders ended in a triangular shape inspired by the jet fighter's swept rudder. Even the car's color, light silver grey, was meant to evoke the polished aluminum skin of its winged namesake (see photo page 94).

Just as fascinating as the car's sweeping styling were the numerous innovations carried inside the dazzling shape. No less than fourteen electric motors were fitted to power a vast number of "gadgets." Among the most startling such innovations were a rain sensitive plate under the seat fabric which automatically raised the convertible's top at the first rain drops; thermostatically-controlled electric seat warmers; doors that opened at the touch of a button, built-in hydraulic jacks besides each wheel and even fenders that lifted up on hinges to aid in tire-changing. No less than sixty controls and gauges helped operate and monitor this

vast array of amenities. In order to afford all this luxury without a tremendous weight penalty, light aluminum and magnesium alloys were used extensively. The convertible still weighed 4,000 lbs. The car's V-8 engine was supercharged and had a 10-to-1 compression ratio producing 300 hp. The Le Sabre could theoretically reach up to 150 mph — though any wise motorsport journalist would have wanted to test that promise first on the vast and obstacle-free Bonneville Salt Flats.

This latest G.M. concept car represented the epitome of the fast-emerging American design philosophy: large size wrapped in striking styling, and loaded with as many gadgets as possible to pamper and comfort driver and passengers. The big engine size was intended as much to provide enough power for smoothly accelerating the enormous mass of the car. Handling, cornering and performance braking were furthest from the designer's mind. The Le Sabre, for all its futuristic gadgets, had an "off-the-shelf" front and leaf-spring rear suspension system; standard drum brakes and a rail-frame chassis. Fuel economy was not even a concern.

Peugeot's new 203, quite representative of the most advanced post-war European family production car design, stood in sharp contrast. Though sitting on a respectable 102 inch wheelbase and capable of holding a family of five without crowding, the new Peugeot was powered by a fuel-efficient 42 hp 1290 cc four-cylinder engine with overhead valves. It had unibody construction, rack and pinion steering, a four-speed gearbox, hydraulic brakes and coil-spring-only suspension. It weighed only 2,028 lbs. With talented drivers and a boosted engine (1425cc supercharged delivering 90 hp), it could race from Liège in Belgium to Rome and back, peaking at speeds of up to 100 mph, twice crossing the thousand-hairpin-turns Alpine range, and safely finish the 3,000 mile marathon. It would take Detroit four decades and two "oil shocks" to incorporate in the core design of its mass production cars some of those standard European design technologies, such as unibody frame, which both save weight and add to safety. Meanwhile, the Atlantic ocean would remain a wide chasm between two vastly different automobile cultures.

Political Oblivion and New Safety Measures

To those who had either attended or participated in previous Watkins Glen Grand Prix events, it must have been a bit strange to peruse the 1951 program booklet. The name Argetsinger appeared only once in those sixty-odd pages, buried in a standard article recalling the history of the lower Finger Lake region, the geology of the gorge, and the birth of road racing in 1948. While the previous program listed Argetsinger in the official Grand Prix roster page as both General Race Chairman and as one of five members of the Activities Committee — both senior SCCA positions — his name was nowhere to be seen in the 1951 roster. The ingratitude was palpable, but Argetsinger would stay above the fray. He would attend all parts of the 1951 event and remain on friendly terms with all but the most obdurate members of the isolationist faction. Erwin Goldschmidt was not so lucky. The title holder of the previous Grand Prix was simply not invited, as he was "not a

The strictly stock Peugeot 203 with which Mmes. de Cortanze and Sigrand won the *Coupe des Dames* (Ladies Cup) in the grueling 1951 Monte Carlo Rally.

member of the SCCA."

The stamp of Argetsinger and Bill Milliken, however, was everywhere to be seen in the enhanced safety measures adopted for the 1951 races. Two areas had received particular attention: crowd control and circuit-wide telecommunications. To insure that the expected crowd of nearly 40,000 spectators would not go even more out of control than the smaller crowd of the previous year, Captain Herschel Gay of the State Police had been put in charge with two hundred police and firemen from Watkins Glen and the neighboring villages under his supervision. In addition, one hundred soldiers from nearby Sampson Air Force Base were brought in to help contain spectators all around the 6.6 mile course.

An even bigger investment was made in a circuit-wide telecommunications system. Designed by Pennsylvanian Dewey Alter, both a telephone engineer and racing enthusiast, and supervised by communications expert Fred German, the outcome turned out to be the first modern safety-oriented telecommunications system in road racing history. When finished in early September, it consisted of thirty-one "safety stations," each manned by four people, all connected instantaneously by twenty-eight miles of telephone wire! This network was also connected to the public address system so spectators as well as participants could be speedily made aware of any emergency, then take immediate appropriate action. A total of 112 carefully selected volunteers and professional technicians were needed and recruited to operate the system. In addition, the race course was divided into four "safety districts," each having at least one ambulance, a fire truck and a tow truck at the ready. The lessons of 1950, it seemed, had been well learned.

Saturday September 15, 1951

The crowds were unbelievable. It seemed that the entire course was lined on both sides with throngs of excited spectators. Franklin Street looked more like a busy outdoor market on sale day than a racing circuit's main straight. Some observers estimated the total count at over 100,000 spectators! This undreamed-of popular success actually made officials nervous. Could their well-planned

Credit: C.H.A. Davison; credit E. Davison Collection

and elaborate safety measures be overwhelmed? The previous day had already witnessed some incidents. These had forced the cancellation of the five practice laps that all participants were supposed to have taken in the early afternoon. Mere parade laps at slow speed were allowed instead. In view of this, the Race Committee decided to allow Grand Prix drivers to go for two hot laps just before the official start of the big race.

The Concours d'Elégance, though, had gone quite well the previous evening. The number and quality of cars impressed everyone. The Vintage Class was won by a 1929 Mercedes-Benz owned by D. C. Paterson Jr. A 1932 Packard, property of Merl Brindle, took the top award in the Classic Class. Dr. Samuel Scher won the Modern Class with his new and gorgeous 1951 Rolls Royce roadster. Finally, Max Hoffman, ever the great public relations wizard, won the Trade Class with a 1951 Porsche 356 coupe. Hoffman had been first to realize the potential of the American market for that unusual sports car. He had imported the first three in the early fall of 1950 and they sold quickly. In fact Briggs Cunningham bought two as gifts for his favorite ladies: his wife and the wife of best friend Sam Collier. In the current year, Hoffman had imported 31 Porsches and advertised them as "The German

Automotive Jewel." The Concours of Watkins Glen was a perfect setting to promote the car. Within three years, Hoffman Motors would account for 30 percent of Porsche's total sales worldwide!

Now the sun was rising clear above the hills bordering the eastern bank of Seneca Lake. The crisp autumn air began to warm up a bit. New groups of spectators were still arriving to witness the great event, including by train. As clocks and watches neared the 10 am mark, Bill Fleming and his Chief Stewart Colonel Field decided to tour the course to check out the situation. To quote Bill Fleming's post race report, "[we found] the spectator situation on Old Corning Hill completely out of hand. Two policemen were patrolling a stretch of road approximately one half-mile

long and people were in the road and in very dangerous places. The loudspeaker system did not reach them, and some of us went up and yelled through megaphones to try to get some semblance of order. Colonel Field, after a particularly eloquent plea got a rock thrown at him for his trouble."

Just at that point, the normally cooperative New York Central Railroad unwittingly added to the confusion. Bill Fleming again, "The excursion train from Rochester was also late and blocked the road [at the famous railroad crossing] for considerable time while it unloaded its passengers. How long it took I do not know for it seemed an eternity to me." Remembering the unfortunate incidents of the previous year, the Race Committee decided to delay the start of the Seneca Cup and to use the time to get the "spectator situation" under better control. The Watkins Glen Grand Prix was clearly at risk to become the victim of its own amazing success, but for a good reason: spectator safety was one of the primary concerns.

Officials finally felt ready to allow the start of the Seneca Cup at 11:45 am, a full hour behind schedule. A bright sun was now shining near its autumnal apogee and the excitement among spectators and participants alike was palpable. On Franklin Street, the noisy formation on the grid, deafening as it was, caused a great relief among the thousands clumped along its sidewalks: the races were about to begin!

The Seneca Cup

The first event was of course the "unrestricted" category race, where all kinds of machines — and all sorts of drivers, as long as they were SCCA members — were allowed to participate. Accordingly, the grid was a rather eclectic assemblage of machinery. On top of the horsepower range were two Maseratis V8RIs: George Weaver's "Poison 'Lil" and sister car owned and to be driven by Philip Cade of Winchester, Massashussets. At the other end of that range were three "crickets" or Formula 3 cars powered by 500 cc engines: two Coopers and one Effyh. These were tiny open-wheeled machines with surprising agility and gumption. Next to the big cars, though, they looked like toys. Their drivers had to have extra courage to get on

TOP RIGHT: Bruce Stevenson, founder of the Bridgehampton race, driving the Meyer Cadillac Special (formerly Meyer Offenhauser). Meyer entered the same car in the Seneca Cup for John Bentley to drive.

BOTTOM RIGHT: Watkins Glen, 1951 Seneca Cup front row of the grid: the Altemus Stabilizer Special conceived by John D. Altemus and with Saxon Marsh at the wheel (left), next to the former Miller Indy two-man racer, now Ford Special, owned and driven by Denver Cornett (right).

the race course among their much larger competitors.

Then there were the "specials." First were John Meyer's Meyer Cadillac (5.4 liter V-8) to be driven by John Bentley, and Denver Cornett's Ford Special (4.6 liter V-8). This was the same car he had driven the previous year, but now it sported a shiny silver paint job, as opposed to the maroon of 1950. The third special, designed by John Altemus of New York City, was the most intriguing. Called the Altemus Stabilizer it had unusual pendulum-like device inside its open-wheeled, cycle-fendered body. Acting on the rear suspension, the mobile mass was designed to transfer weight from one side of the car to the other each time the vehicle was taking a turn. Following the same movements as a sidecar crew in a motocycle race, the weight would be transferred to the left side in a right turn and vice

versa, theoretically keeping the inside wheels more firmly on the ground — reducing camber — and offsetting some of the centrifugal forces acting on the car in the turn. This certainly was an intriguing concept and the twisty Watkins Glen course was the perfect place to test its practicality. Saxon Marsh was the appointed driver.

There was a risk of the weight getting out of control, though, making the car unpredictably fly off the road in a turn. The Technical Committee, headed by Bill Milliken, had to make the decision on whether to approve the car or not. Milliken and George Weaver decided to take the Altemus for a tour of the circuit before making their decision. Off they went, immediately feeling that the device was less than perfect. The twisty uphill stretch past Stone Bridge was particularly hairy, though the two friends were also having a jolly good time. They finally made the decision to allow the car to race, but it would have to start from the back of the grid so at least an incident in the first turn would be avoided.

Three Ferraris would also vie for victory, two belonging to Briggs Cunningham. "Mr. C." would drive the 166 SC in which his friend Sam Collier had been fatally wounded a year earlier. John Fitch would drive Cunningham's blue Ferrari 195 Inter Coupe. That car was powered by the 2.3 liter version of the famous V-12 released in late 1950 and had raced at Sebring with Luigi Chinetti at the wheel. Bill Spear would drive the third Maranello-made car, a 166 MM Touring Barchetta. He was, however, only allowed as a non-official entry for reasons that remain unknown. Two Allard J2s would provide strong opposition, one Cadillac-powered to be driven by George Harris, and one Chrysler-powered to be driven by Fred Zeder. Finally, among the possible victors were also Ken Hill and Robert O'Brien, both driving Jaguar XK-120s.

The complete grid, including three MGs, a Healey Silverstone and a Jowett Jupiter, was supposed to be made up of 30 cars. Alas for Phil Cade, his Maserati V8RI suffered from a terminal — for the day — mechanical ailment on its way to the grid. Both car and driver had to sit out the race. This left George Weaver wondering one more time about the reliability of his own Maserati V8RI as Nils

Watkins Glen, 1951 Seneca Cup - Denver Cornett's Ford Special in turn one pursued by the ever fuming Maserati V8RI of George Weaver. Weaver, in his fourth year of trying with his famous Maserati, would glean his second victory at the Glen in that race. He would go on to win the Queen Catharine Cup in a Jowett Jupiter less than two hours later.

Mickelson waved the "start your engine" flag from across the Courthouse. Powerful engines at last began to roar to life, ready for a serious race. Shortly thereafter and for the fourth year in a row, at about 11:45 am, Mickelson stepped from the sidewalk onto the asphalt of Franklin Street and unfurled the green flag. Then, as every other signal up and down the grid turned positive, he raised then lowered the green standard in a flourish, unleashing a sonorous, fuming and mighty cavalry.

George Weaver and his potent Maserati shot forward into the lead even before the first turn, followed by John Fitch in Cunningham's blue Ferrari and John Bentley in the Meyer Cadillac. By the time the little Coopers and the Effyh passed the starting line emitting their high-pitched howls, the crowds were in a high state of excitement. Less than six minutes later, Weaver's black and red Maserati, just as in the 1948 Junior Prix, reappeared first at the corner of Fourth and Franklin Street. Weaver's first lap average turned out to be over 77 mph, or 13 mph faster than his first Junior Prix lap! Experience, and better track surface were having a striking effect on performance.

Weaver remained in control of the eight-lap race throughout, while behind him, John Fitch, John Bentley, Phil Weaver, Briggs Cunningham and George Harris vied furiously for position. On the fourth lap, Ken Hill, hotly pursued by John Fitch, lost control of his Jaguar XK-120

and bounced into the fields near the fateful apple orchard. Fortunately, there were no spectators or safety officials in the immediate vicinity. Unfortunately, there was no one to provide quick emergency help. Despite the competitive pressure on him, Fitch stopped his Ferrari and ran towards the wreck to assist Hill. After the tall former fighter pilot found his fellow competitor to be all right, he ran back to his blue berlinetta and went on racing full bore.

There were many other incidents during the cup, each raising yellow caution flags around the entire course. This lowered the overall averages but insured a perfect safety record. On the sixth lap, despite a spin due to a deflated tire and an ensuing pit stop, John Bentley was holding fourth position in the Meyer Special. Then the car's fan belt broke bringing the big Cadillac engine's cooling water to the boiling point in no time and therefore sidelining both car and driver for good. John Bentley thus joined the ranks of fourteen cars — half the field! — which would not finish the 52.8 mile race.

Within the lead group, "Poison 'Lil" kept charging on. Weaver never gave up the lead. He crossed the finish line a winner, with a superb average speed of 75.79 mph, exactly 41 minutes and 44 seconds after the start. Despite his sportsman-like stop, Fitch finished second. Bill Spear was third across the line, though he was not classified as his entry was unofficial. A Ferrari nonetheless took third place: Briggs Cunningham's 166 SC with its owner at the wheel. In a certain way, "Mr. C." was honoring the memory of his late friend Sam Collier in the best possible way. First behind this triple-headed Italian steamroller was the George Harris Allard J2 which finished almost eight minutes behind the winner. First class 6 finisher was David Ash, of Stony Point, New York, a remarkable tenth overall with a mere stock MG pitted against cars with engines three to four times bigger.

In this Seneca Cup, the 500 cc cars were placed in a category of their own, Class 9. The winner of that class was Roland Keith who drove Alexis Du Pont's Cooper. His win was doubly deserved as in the last lap problems with his gear shift lever forced him to keep only one hand on the steering wheel, his left, while his right hand reached backwards in the engine compartment to insure proper shifting!

Watkins Glen, 1951 Seneca Cup - A stalled Cooper F3 being attended by spectators somewhere along Old Corning Hill.

Phil Walters finished second in class in the Cunningham-entered Cooper. Gordon Lipe was third in his own Effyh. At the award ceremony, a special prize was given to John Fitch, the Sportsmanship Award, for his stop to provide help to Ken Hill after the latter left the road.

New Delays and More Sabre Rattling

The Seneca Cup had taken place without major incident. But the organizers were not done yet dealing with time-consuming problems, almost all of a Keystone Cop nature. Once again, Bill Fleming's letter is the most accurate source of information:

"Between the Seneca Cup Race and the Queen Catharine Cup Race, other difficulties arose. They started when, although the course itself was clear, it became necessary to remove the wreck of an XK-120 (Ken Hill's) from its resting place on the side of a road into a field. While this was being done, a spectator either fainted or had an epileptic fit and an ambulance had to be dispatched to remove her to the hospital. Dr. James Norton had to make a tour of the course to distribute blood plasma to the aid stations and just as he came in and the race was ready to start, a trap door on Franklin Street caved in under the weight of spectators and dumped two or three of them in a coal bin, requiring the dispatching of another ambulance to see that they were properly attended. Fortunately, none was injured and after first aid, the ambulance was able to return to its station. These happenings occurred consecutively, not simultaneously, so that, trivial as most of them were, they ... consumed a considerable amount of time."

Officials became quite anxious about keeping the crowd both interested and under control. As a result, they made two key decisions. First, they decided that the distance of both the Queen Catharine Cup and the Grand Prix would be reduced, so the Grand Prix would not run into darkness. They lopped off four laps and twenty-six miles from the Cup, making it an eleven-lap event of 72.6 miles. Then they cut down the Grand Prix length by half, reducing it back to its previous year's length of 15 laps and 99 miles. These were courageous decisions, given the original determination to move gradually toward true endurance distances.

The second decision was to use G.M's Le Sabre as a diversionary tactic to entertain spectators while all the time-delays were being taken care of one by one. So the General Motors showcase was called in for a tour around the circuit. Even though it ended stalled on Franklin Street and had to be towed back to the corporate transport truck, the futuristic-looking car fulfilled its new purpose, as cheerleaders often do during intermission. The Le Sabre's attractive curves kept the crowds excited, distracting their impatience as they waited for the start of the race.

The Queen Catharine Cup

As in its first run the year before, the Cup for small displacement machines would begin with a Le Mans-type start. Many thought the race would be a replay of the intense battle between H.R.G.s and MGs as witnessed in 1950. This time, however, there were other serious contestants to challenge Fritz Koster's H.R.G. (1486 cc Singer engine) and the fifteen "normal" MG TCs or TDs in the field (1250 cc MG engine). First among them was the white Jowett Jupiter "Le Mans" (1486 cc Jowett engine) entered by Max Hoffman and to be driven by George Weaver. The clever New York importer had added "Le Mans" to the car's model designation to enhance its appeal based on the fact that one Jowett Jupiter, out of three entered, had completed the Le Mans race in June, finishing in 23rd position. Hoffman had bought those bragging rights, as his car was that very specimen which completed

Watkins Glen, 1951 Queen Catharine Cup - The happy third finisher David Viall (left) in his Lester MG Special.

the 24-hour French ordeal. This new vintage of Jupiters also sported a new streamlined body.

Second, there were two MG Specials, one being a Lester MG. Harry Lester was a British motorsport enthusiast based in Thatcham, England. His modified MGs were built on TD mechanicals highly modified and clad in an open-wheel body with cycle fenders. David Viall of Alexandria, Virginia, would drive that car, while Alfred Coppel of Los Altos, California, would drive another similarly modified 1951 MG TC. Coppel was an automotive writer. He had designed the car himself, including the body shape, and turned it into a highly competitive machine. Completing the lead British contingent would be a Connaught L3 (1500 cc Lea-Francis engine) to be driven by British émigré Harry Grey. Connaught was another small British firm established after World War II to produce small series of racing cars. All early Connaughts, including Harry Grey's, were based on Lea-Francis mechanicals.

Italy was also well represented in the lead-contender group. A pretty 1400 cc Siata Daina coupe, oddly painted in an unflattering dark brown color, was entered by Fred Proctor of Westport, Connecticut. Another 1400cc Siata Gran Sport, this one a red roadster looking like the twin of a Ferrari 166 Barchetta, was entered by Hector Scheffer of Park Ridge, Illinois. There was a third Siata in the field, a pretty blue roadster. Its owner, Tony Pompeo, had fitted it

TOP LEFT: Watkins Glen, 1951 Queen Catharine Cup - The Crosley-engined Siata roadster entered by Tony Pompeo and driven by Otto Linton during the parade lap.

BOTTOM RIGHT: Watkins Glen, 1951 Queen Catharine Cup - The Fiat 1100 S shared by Bob Keller and Paul Farago at the first Sebring race and otherwise co-owned with Dick Haynes. The latter ran a restaurant called "Little Harry's" on East Jefferson Avenue in Detroit where many sports car enthusiasts used to congregate. Charles H.A. Davison and Harold Lance were among those.

with a 750cc Crosley engine so that its appointed driver, Otto Linton of Exton, Pennsylvania, could vie for a Class 7 win only, not the overall victory. The fourth and last Italian contestant was the silver-green Fiat 1100 Coupe of Bob Keller and Dick Haynes, veteran of two previous Glen events as well as the first Sebring endurance race. The sole "German" entry was the VW Special which Kurt Hildebrand had raced in 1950 and since improved.

A total of 33 cars were lined up diagonally along the eastern side of Franklin Street when the organizers finally decided the Queen Catharine Cup could start. Crowd control, especially at Old Corning Hill, had continued to be a problem, and now the day's schedule was about one and a half hours behind, meaning the second race was going to get started at just about the time it had been intended to end — 2 pm. Spectators nonetheless remained obviously joyful, the pressure bearing mostly on the Race Committee.

When Nils Mickelson lowered the green flag, the 33 Catharine Cup drivers ran across Franklin Street and hurriedly jumped into their waiting cars. First off were two regular MGs, Magenheimer's and Hawley's, but at the first turn, George Weaver managed to wriggle his white Jowett into the lead position. Weaver, undoubtedly charged up by his earlier victory, quickly built a comfortable distance between himself and the pursuing pack. The main suspense turned to the fierce battle waged by the two drivers who trailed Weaver at the end of the first lap: Coppel in his own

MG Special and Viall in the Lester MG. For the first time, Watkins Glen was the scene of a duel between a west coast member and an east coast member, both driving comparable cars. The vast crowd was soon entranced by this battle, until Coppel's car, for which this was the inaugural race, suffered from a terminal connecting rod failure in the fifth lap.

Fortunately for the spectacle, by the time Coppel was sidelined, Fritz Koster's H.R.G. and Hector Scheffer's red Siata *barchetta* had made up most of the distance they had given up to Viall in the early laps. Even though Weaver and his white mount kept roaring into a more and more comfortable lead, the battle for second was vivid and exciting enough to keep the spectators fully entertained. Also, attrition was taking its toll. Two cars, including the highly vaunted Connaught, completed only one lap. By the time Coppel retired, he was the eighth driver to be forced out. Though less spectacular than a heated duel between drivers, seeing cars expire in the midst of battle was part and parcel of the drama that makes racing so exciting.

As the race went on, the pattern by now established remained essentially unchanged. Just a little over one hour after the start, exactly in 63:10.8 minutes, George Weaver was first to get the checkered flag, scoring his second victory in the same day. His race average was 68.95 mph, a new record for the category. What a deserved turnaround for the Bostonian who had suffered from such bad luck (some also say lackadaisical preparation) in the three previ-

ous years! Behind him, David Viall succeeded in keeping second place, finishing just short of two minutes behind Weaver and 0:41.0 ahead of Koster and his H.R.G. Scheffer and his pretty Siata finished fourth one and a half minute behind Koster, but a mere ten seconds ahead of fifth finisher Gus Ehrman in an MG TD.

The other two Siatas also distinguished themselves. Otto Linton won his class in the Crosley-powered blue roadster. Despite its small engine, his car was also declared the noisiest in the field! Fred Proctor's Siata Daina finished 12th though he was much better positioned at the beginning of the next to last lap. Mid-point through it, Proctor was about to pass an MG when the driver of the British car inadvertently cut into the Siata's intended trajectory. In order to avoid an accident, Proctor voluntarily took to the ditch. That gentlemanly act cost him several positions but justifiably won him the second Sportsmanship award of the day. Though not as exciting as the first Queen Catharine Cup, this had been an excellent race with plenty of thrilling moments and, most important, no serious incidents.

"People, People Everywhere!"

The above phrase was used as a subheading by a writer in *Road and Track* who gave an account of the fourth Watkins Glen race weekend in the November, 1951 issue of the magazine. Indeed, while an intermission of only half an hour had been planned between the second race and the Grand Prix, persisting problems with crowd control caused further delays. Bill Fleming explained further, "All this time, the spectator situation at Old Corning Hill was still very bad and we were trying to clear it up. We later learned that 15 auxiliary police from Corning (a village twenty miles south from Watkins Glen) who had been assigned to the patrol of this area phoned at 9:30 Saturday morning to say that they wouldn't be there, which was the reason for the poor policing in this area." This provides another glimpse at how complex the organization of those early races really was.

So the fourth Watkins Glen Grand Prix race would start two hours behind schedule, at 4:30 pm. The necessity to cut the planned number of laps in half was compelling. No one could protest, and practically no one complained.

Watkins Glen, 1951 Grand Prix - Fred Wacker's second "Eight Ball" Cad-Allard J2 in the parade lap. His first Allard was painted black, then he switched to red in 1951. The car's Hydramatic transmission would prove too much of a handicap in this Grand Prix. Wacker finished 12th after a great start.

What helped, of course, was the strong anticipation of seeing the "big boys" and the fastest road racing machines in America in action. Leading that group would be the three Cunningham C-2s, veterans of Le Mans. Since the June race in France, the West Palm Beach engineers had succeeded in extracting even more horsepower from the new Chrysler powerplant. By fine-tuning cam timing as well as intake and exhaust porting, they had made the "Hemi" produce 270 hp at 5500 rpm, a seventeen percent increase! The odds were that the Grand Prix winner would be the driver of one of these three cars, though at least another ten drivers thought they themselves had at least a shot at it also.

First among those was Bill Spear and his potent Ferrari 340 America. The newest and biggest of the Ferrari sports cars, the 340 was powered by a 4101cc V-12 engine producing 220 hp at 6000 rpm. With an overall weight of just under 2000 pounds, the car was capable of fantastic accelerations and had a top speed of 137 mph. It had also proved reliable as a similar car in the hands of Villoresi and Cassani had won the Mille Miglia in April against formidable opposition. The three other Ferraris lined up for the Grand Prix — Kimberly's, Charles Moran's and Logan Hill's — were of the older 2.0 or 2.6 liter types and therefore were not expected to vie for overall victory.

The five Allard J2s, either Chrysler or Cadillac-powered, were also serious contenders. After all, such a car was the Grand Prix title holder. Fred Wacker's new J2 was the

odds-on favorite. His first Allard's Hydramatic transmission had been transferred to the new one which still would sport racing number 8 — as in Eight Ball. Wacker, however, had switched paint scheme from black to bright red, better to be noticed by spectators. Also, G.M.'s Frank Burrell had again made sure that the Hydramatic transmission would shift up instantly, as well as shift down, unheard of features in those days. George Harris and Joseph B. Sabal were the other two Allard J2 drivers considered to have a chance, however slim, of winning. Another competitive Chrysler-powered J2 was a forfeit, as driver Hal Ullrich had crashed it badly the day before just south of Montour Falls. He had suffered only minor cuts and injuries, but his British racer was totaled. Fred Zeder, with his own Chrysler-powered J2, was the lucky fellow who was granted the empty spot.

Finally, two young and promising drivers, Sherwood Johnston and Walter Hansgen, both driving Jaguar XK-120s, were seen as possible dark horses. The Grand Prix field of twenty-five cars also included a Lea-Francis, Harry Grey's repaired Connaught, three MGs — including one powered by a 2.2 liter Ford V-8 "60" engine — and a BMW roadster. The only ingredient missing for a truly fabulous race was the presence of at least a few European aces and famed factory cars. D. Cameron Peck and his allies had annihilated that wonderful possibility five months earlier.

The Grand Prix Set Up

The grid formed two abreast in a tremendous explosion of howls, booms and rolling thunder. The combined unmuffled outburst of over 4,000 horsepower unleashed within a strip of Franklin Street no longer than four hundred feet in length echoed loudly up the surrounding hills. This instantly caused anticipation to rise among tens of thousands of spectators. The now traditional drawing from the hat had placed a Cunningham and an Allard J2 in the front

Watkins Glen, 1951 Grand Prix Grid - On the front row are Briggs Cunningham's own C-2 and George Harris' Cad-Allard J2. Bill Spear's Ferrari 340 America is on the second row while the other Cunninghams are further back. No matter, driver talent and car performance would dictate the final ranking.

row with, respectively, Briggs Cunningham and George Harris at the wheel. Behind them were Bret Hannaway's Allard and Bill Spear's Ferrari 340. Two Allard J2s occupied third row: Fred Wacker's and Joe Sabal's. The Cunninghams of Walters and Fitch had had an unlucky draw and found themselves in fourth and fifth row, alongside Preston Grey's Allard K2 — row 4 — and a Walt Hansgen's Jaguar XK-120 — row 5.

The Race Committee, having learned from the experience of the previous years and the failure of the previous day, were now ready to let the drivers go for two "hot" practice laps before the official start. As agreed by all, the Grand Prix participants would be flagged to leave the grid and go for those two laps, with a hiatus of a few seconds being enforced between each pair of cars. So after Mickelson lowered the flag, off they went, two by two, but quickly mixing and passing as they went up the hill, as no special restric-

tions had been given to the drivers. As the pack of potent racers passed through each section of the course in succession, spectators applauded wildly, waved hands and gave a heart-warming reception to all participants.

About fifteen minutes after the first pair of cars was released, the grid reformed perfectly on Franklin Street, each car occupying its assigned rectangular box painted in white on the smooth, dark asphalt. This part of the show seemed eerily quiet in comparison to what had just been witnessed. Adding to the tension, the perfect geometry of the white lines and the disciplined alignment of cars by pairs stood in sharp contrast to the thunderous mayhem which everybody knew was about to be unleashed.

Now was the time for Nils Mickelson to take to the street once again with his famous green flag. Other than the obviously American architecture of the houses lining Franklin Street, the scene could easily have been mistaken for the start of a major European road race. The cars not only looked the part, most were directly issued from the top rungs of European sports car factories. And the crowds! Franklin Street almost looked like downtown Brescia during the start of the famous Mille Miglia. "People, People Everywhere!" indeed.

Thus in an ironic twist of history, the vision Cameron Argetsinger had promulgated in 1947 was now plainly realized, a mere four years after he first started it, but the young lawyer was no longer officiating, and an unfortunate accident had even deprived him of the pleasure of taking part in the racing. The missing ingredient for a true European-type race, professional participation of at least a few of the best overseas works teams and drivers, sure was not his fault. It could easily have been added to the stew by Argetsinger, Ulmann and a few others. Though none of the happy spectators had any notion of this, the SCCA had taken a fateful turn at a vital crossroads. It would affect the sport unfavorably for years to come.

Go!

When Mickelson dropped the green flag, the sounds of hell broke loose in and around Watkins Glen. Bill Spear's potent white and blue Ferrari darted through the front row pair and quickly took the lead. Cunningham mangled his

Watkins Glen, 1951 Grand Prix - The Chrysler-powered Allard J2 of Joseph B. Sabal during the parade lap. They would finish a creditable 5th.

start and lost the advantage of his front row position in mere seconds. By the time the lead drivers roared away from the Stone Bridge, about half way through the first lap, it was Spear, Walters, Wacker, then Fitch. Hannaway and his Allard were fifth, and that was the order when those lead cars completed the first lap at high revs between super-heated crowds of spectators. This early Ferrari-Cunningham-Allard-Cunningham-Allard locomotive formation, with talented drivers at the wheel of each machine, promised an exciting race.

Despite great individual driver efforts, the order was the same at the end of lap two. At that point, Cunningham had surprisingly dropped from 7th to 9th. Between the four leaders and "Mr. C.," a battle for position was emerging between four Allard J2 drivers: Hannaway, Zeder, Harris and Sabal. Then behind those top nine, a thrilling dogfight was shaping up between two Jaguar XK-120 drivers: the silver roadster of Walt Hansgen and the black sibling of Sherwood Johnston. There was plenty of spectacle to please everyone.

The lead changed in the third lap. Phil Walters, probably the most able driver in the field — John Fitch being a close second — managed to pass Spear's Ferrari in Big Bend. Walters rushed past the Courthouse to start his fourth lap three seconds ahead of the 340 America. Behind them, the remaining eight of the top ten kept their positions. In contrast to the earlier years, all participants were still very

much in the race at this point. Here was another clear sign that preparation and seriousness had increased dramatically in a very short time.

The fourth lap witnessed a further gradual Darwinian culling of positions. Fitch and his Cunningham passed Wacker's "Eight Ball" Allard to gain third place behind Spear's Ferrari. Now that the competition had become a lot more serious, Wacker, it seems, found himself more handicapped than helped on this twisted course by his Hydramatic transmission. Lower down the ranks, both Briggs Cunningham and Walt Hansgen passed Joe Sabal's Allard, which now occupied 10th position. All twenty-five starters were still in the race. The fifth lap saw two important changes. Fitch was on a roll and passed Spear to claim second spot behind teammate Walters, making it seem like the beginning of a Cunningham steamroller. Then the first two dropouts met their fate. Both were MGs, the first a "blown" TC driven by Roland Keith, then the other the Ford V-8 powered roadster of Willard Christy. However boosted their powerplants might be, the lovely little

Watkins Glen, 1951 Grand Prix - Walt Hansgen's silver XK-120 Jaguar gives a hot chase to Fred Wacker's "Eight Ball" Allard just getting into Stone Bridge.

British-born racers were now clearly out of their league in the Grand Prix.

Lap 6 witnessed one single dramatic development: the fall-out of Bret Hannaway's Allard in that gallant internicine J2 battle. Engine trouble was the cause. This boosted the four top ten contestants who were behind him one position ahead in the ranking. The Allards of Harris and Zeder were now fifth and sixth, respectively, followed by Briggs Cunningham, Walt Hansgen, then Joe Sabal. The driver who took the freed-up spot in the top ten was Sherwood Johnston. He was gunning to catch up with Hansgen's silver XK-120 two positions ahead of him.

During the next four laps — 7th to 10th, the process of pure Darwinian selection became paramount as none of the lead cars encountered significant mechanical problems. Only the combination of driver talent and car performance played a role. In those conditions, while the top three spots remained unchanged, Briggs Cunningham poured it on and moved up one position per lap so that when he crossed the start/finish line for the tenth time, he was in 4th position! Bill Spear's big Ferrari was now the only car splitting the trio of American-made sports cars, the first of their breed. In the middle of the top-ten group, four Allards were having their own fight. Three changed places as George Harris managed to pass Fred Wacker to reclaim fifth position, then Fred Zeder fell to seventh. All the while, Sabal clung to eighth place. Just behind those four Allards, three Jaguar XK-120s were now engaged in a fierce battle for at least the Class 3 (3 to 4 liter) victory: Hansgen's, Johnston's and Robert O'Brien's driven by motorsport writer John Bentley.

The next two laps, 11th and 12th, saw two more spectacular developments. Fred Wacker, who was experiencing more and more trouble with his Hydramatic transmission, found himself in a double spin at Corning Road Turn on the 12th lap, which he eventually completed in tenth position, down from fourth on lap 9. Though Frank Burell of G.M. had tuned this unique Hydramatic to shift up instantly and even to shift down, the standard gearboxes proved superior on the tough Glen circuit.

Soon after Wacker dropped back, Phil Walters gave a further demonstration of his talent by clocking an all-time

Credit: Richard Irish Collection

record lap in 04:55.0, averaging an astonishing 80.5 mph. Meanwhile, Johnston seemed to be keeping the upper hand over Hansgen in the incredibly fierce Jaguar battle, from which O'Brien had dropped as he fell to 11th behind Wacker. The Johnston-Hansgen duel got so heated that the latter was black-flagged on lap 11th for bumping Johnston's car in a corner. Hansgen was forced to pit. Remarkably, by the completion of lap 12th, twenty out of twenty-five participants were still very much in the race with only three more laps to go.

The Finish

Wacker dropped further behind on lap 13, which allowed Kimberly and his red mount, Briggs Cunningham's old Ferrari 166 SC, to fill in the last spot in the top ten group. This meant that four Equipe Cunningham cars were now at least temporarily in the Grand Prix elite. Within that group of ten, all other positions remained unchanged. The same was true in the penultimate lap, except for the fact that Joe Sabal managed to pass George Harris to gain fifth place overall and, of no minor import, first rank in the Allard battle.

As the final lap began, it seemed the final order had

Watkins Glen, 1951 Grand Prix - Charles Moran and son driving his own Ferrari 212 *barchetta* during the parade lap before the Grand Prix.

already been decided, barring an unforeseen incident. The top four positions had remained unchanged for the previous five laps, and roughly one minute separated each one of those four leading cars as they passed by the Courthouse and the white flag ("one lap to go") was waved at their drivers. A little more than five minutes later, Phil Walters took the checkered flag at a record average speed of 77.65 mph, having completed the fifteen laps in 76:29.6 minutes, or a stunning 05:29 (5.57 mph) improvement over Goldschmidt's winning time achieved over the same distance a year before. Whether the "Chrome-Plated Chariot Club" members, as one wag called them, liked it or not, reality was fast overtaking the position of the amateur-only faction.

John Fitch brought his Cunningham C-2 to second place, one and a half minute behind Walters. Bill Spear and his Ferrari finished third, more than half a minute behind Fitch. The third Cunningham, driven by team owner "Mr. C." finished fourth and the rest of the top ten each carefully kept their position:

End of Grand Prix - 15 Laps:

1. Phil Walters	Cunningham C-2	76:29.6
2. John Fitch	Cunningham C-2.	1:28.4 behind
3. Bill Spear	Ferrari 340 America	2:07.0 behind
4. B. S. Cunningham	Cunningham C-2	4:20.3 behind
5. Joe Sabal	Allard J2 (Chrysler)	N/A
6. George Harris	Allard J2 (Cadillac)	N/A
7. Fred Zeder	Allard J2 (Chrysler)	N/A
8. Sherwood Johnston	Jaguar XK-120	8:38.2 behind
9. Walt Hansgen	Jaguar XK-120	N/A
10. Jim Kimberly	Ferrari 166 SC	N/A

Amazingly, twenty cars finished the race. Fred Wacker ended up in 12th position, behind John Bentley in O'Brien's Jaguar XK-120. Wacker was followed by the two remaining Ferraris, the two liter models driven by Logan Hill (car owned by Bill Spear) and Charles Moran. Sherwood Johnston won Class 3 while his direct competitor, Walt Hansgen, shortly thereafter had his Competition License (No. 300) suspended by the SCCA Contest Board "because of hazardous and incompetent driving during the 1951 Watkins Glen Grand Prix." Harry Grey and his

Connaught managed a minor achievement by winning Class 5 ahead of Paul Ramos' supercharged MG TC, even though Grey only finished in 19th place.

Taking Stock

The fourth Grand Prix weekend proved an astounding success. Some automotive writers claimed there were up to 350,000 spectators crammed around the course! The overly modest Chamber of Commerce said 30,000. The exact truth will never be known, but based on a rough averaging of the various "honest" estimates (*Sports Car* magazine's number was 150,000 to 175,000; *Road & Track's* was 150,000 and the Sheriff's 200,000), it appears safe to say that at least 100,000 people were in and around Watkins Glen that weekend, and quite possibly as many as 150,000. That is an extraordinary number given that in May of the same year, the famous Indianapolis 500 had drawn a crowd of just 160,000. Even Cameron Argetsinger had not predicted that a popular phenomenon of that magnitude would develop so quickly.

The second part of the success was the safety record: nobody was hurt. Given the circumstances, the seriousness of the crowd control problem and the 130-plus mph top speed of many participants, it can reasonably be said that either divine intervention or incredible luck played a role in this outcome. Of course, the intelligent security measures that had been planned and were effectively in place had a lot to do with a perfect record. However, the planning had been done based on a projected attendance figure of less than half of what turned out to be the actual number. Therefore, at least some luck was involved. Many of the drivers with international experience, such as John Fitch and Phil Walters, indeed agree that a collision between spectacle (faster and faster racing cars), and spectators (unaware of danger and in numbers not envisioned so soon), portended a possible disaster. The SCCA was holding a tiger by the tail.

Backing the argument about faster cars, several speed records were indeed broken on September 15, 1951 at Watkins Glen. The most memorable of course was Phil Walters' new all-time fastest lap average of 80.5 mph, but there were several others. The next one was that the first

four of the Grand Prix finishers bettered the previous year's Grand Prix record of 72.1 mph. Then the Queen Catharine Cup's winner, George Weaver in the 1.5 liter Jowett Jupiter, finished the eleven-lap race at an average of 68.95 mph, an improvement of over 5 mph over the winner of the previous year's equivalent event, which had only eight laps! The same was true for the Seneca Cup. Phil Walters had won the 1950 fifteen-lap event in Cunningham's formidable Healey-Cadillac clocking a 67.13 mph average. While the 1951 the Seneca Cup was admittedly cut down to eleven laps, two drivers bested Walters' previous record. George Weaver won the race in his famous pre-war Maserati at an average of 77.65 mph — a fifteen percent improvement — while John Fitch brought Cunningham's Ferrari 195 Inter into second at an average of 70.30 mph. Fitch accomplished this in spite of his stop to check on Ken Hill, and with a 2.3 liter engine, less than half the displacement of the Healey's engine!

The first tangible consequence of this popular success was to reinforce the argument of the "amateur-only" camp. If the status quo in terms of regulation could bring about such a popular response, who could now say with credibility that changing the rules likely would lead to the withering of the sport? Truth be told, the extraordinary popular success of the 1951 Grand Prix had nothing to do with changing or not changing the rules. The fourth Watkins Glen event was simply riding the powerful wave that Argetsinger, Cunningham, Ulmann and the Village elders had initiated in 1948. Practically no one among spectators or the fledgling motorsport press had any inkling that a mighty power struggle about the core principles of the SCCA had taken place in the preceding months. All they knew is that road racing, especially with exotic European machines peppering the field, was the latest, most exciting sport Americans could join or watch. The majority in place within the SCCA, however, was not going to let that opportunity pass them by.

In the September-October issue of the club's *Sports Car* magazine, which reported on the 1951 Grand Prix, D. Cameron Peck wrote a one page editorial which at once affirmed his side's point-of-view and framed any SCCA-AAA dialogue in the narrowest possible terms:

Finally, Peck addressed the issue of member dismissal, as the Ulmann affair had caused a lot of ruffled feathers:

"The procedure for dismissal of members for cause must be streamlined and responsibility placed on the regions themselves, subject to review by the national officers."

At the end of that editorial, Peck also announced his resignation "as President and Director of SCCA." Peck cited "the tremendous pressure of my business affairs, and an essential reduction in the number of my activities for reasons of health" as the main two causes for his decision. Though only in his thirties, he would retire satisfied. He had, with his final editorial, officially sealed the fate of the dissenters. Peck's version of the "Monroe Doctrine" had triumphed for now. Then, following the Club's By-Laws, he handed over his duties to Fred Wacker, then the Club's Vice President. An election would be held early in the new year to nominate a new president.

What Did It All Mean?

The year 1951 was the first in nearly half a century to offer circumstances that were ideal for the future development of international motorsport. For the first time since the infancy of both the automobile and car racing, there was now a real chance to align European and American standards and regulations. By 1951, road racing as a sport had sufficiently developed in North America, both in organization and popularity, to join the international league and help create a true intercontinental championship spanning at leat three continents. This undoubdetly would have made motorsport a prime sport in America, as it was and still is in Europe, fifty years earlier than what actually happened. In 1951, one can say that the proverbial "critical mass" had been reached in the United States, and plenty of visionary people were pushing for it. Alas, it was not to be for quite a while.

There is no use in assigning blame, though it is important to understand the reasons for this missed opportunity. From the historical facts laid bare in details for the first time here, one can safely conclude that opposite attitudes rooted in decades of separate history on both sides of the

"Every aspect of professionalism must be avoided, including such borderline matters as payment of expenses for appearance. Either we keep this game an amateur one, or we will see it fall into decay and disrepute. Our standards of amateurism should be reduced to writing and published for distribution to all future members."

"the affairs of AAA and SCCA impinge, of necessity, at only one point, namely where international competition enters the picture, or where SCCA members wish to secure FIA permits to race abroad. ... To this end a meeting will be held in the near future between three members of the AAA Contest Board and three members of the SCCA."

Watkins Glen, 1951 Grand Prix - Roger Merrill's Jaguar XK-120 in the parade lap. By 1951, the XK-120 had definitely replaced the MG T series for racing amateurs or beginners wishing to compete in the big-bore categories. The first post-war racing Jaguar, though, was already outclassed by more modern machines. Merrill finished 15th in the Grand Prix.

Atlantic ocean were fundamental to the missed connection. On the American side, despite the enormous popular success of the fourth Watkins Glen Grand Prix and other road races across the country, motorsport was still an afterthought for the general public and press, especially compared to baseball and football.

The Indianapolis 500 was a great national event again, but it was more an annual party weekend than anything else. Oval racing certainly was not a deep passion gushing daily in the American people's bloodstream, as road racing had been to Europeans for four decades. The newfangled SCCA road races on the east and west coasts were beginning to create a groundswell movement, but they were still the primary domain of the wealthy few in terms of participants. How could, for example, someone earning a living on a G.M. assembly line ever root for, say George R. Harris III (1951 Seneca Cup), even though said George Harris drove a Cadillac-powered car? Hank Aaron would win the working stiff's heart over a wealthy "sportsman" any day.

Then, on the other side of the Atlantic, there was a different kind of arrogance, but one that led to the same outcome. The seat of power for international racing matters was in Paris, and had been since the early days of the automobile as the French were the early leaders both in car technology and racing organization. For the French-dominated FIA in 1951, the only American race worthy of any attention was the Indy 500 — on account of its popularity, not the technology of the racers fielded — and that meant the only partner in America was the AAA and its president, Colonel Herrington. Lifting a finger to help expand road racing as a popular sport in America was considered a waste of time. Road racing in Europe and Latin America were booming, surpassing in intensity, popularity and passion any other sport but soccer. What would be the benefit of investing a lot of political capital in supporting a Yankee participation? The hapless American efforts at Le Mans showed that these people had little to contribute anyway, other than the great noise of their big engines.

Thus, the group of visionary internationalists within the SCCA were twisting alone in the wind. They held to their vision too passionately to rejoin the "mainstream" other than as race participants. They were going to have to wait out a major turn in the direction of political winds, or, if they could afford it, carve their own way alone. Few in either camp realized what major crossroad intercontinental motorsport had just been rushed through, but the consequences would reverberate until the end of the millenium.

The Other Outcomes

One thing that the fourth Watkins Glen Grand Prix at least made certain was that the fledgling sport was fast gaining in grassroots popularity in America. That gave a lot of heart to those who were betting with their time, money or both to plunge ahead with whatever activities they had involving them in the sport. Alec Ulmann decided to go on his own and develop his "Little Le Mans" vision, with the AAA and FIA as partners. With his long term lease, he now practically owned Hendricks Field. He would stage the first "Twelve Hours of Sebring" early in the 1952 season, before the European weather got warm and the racing calendar busy, hoping to attract as many top teams from across the ocean as possible. In the late Fifties, Ulmann's event would turn out to be the main connecting dot between Europe and North America in terms of road racing.

By 1959, Ulmann made the first attempt in history to stage an International Formula 1 United States Grand Prix. It was run on December 12 at Sebring. It was a popular and financial failure. The following year, Ulmann arranged for the Grand Prix to be staged at Riverside in California, where a few international sports car races had attracted a large public in previous years. He succeeded no better. In 1961, the baton would pass back to Cameron Argetsinger and the village of Watkins Glen. They both had kept the flame aburning and staged two successful Formule Libre events in 1958, 1959 and 1960. The FIA handed them the prize of the United States Formula 1 Grand Prix in 1961. They would do a magnificent job of it for two decades, until 1980.

Another important consequence of the 1950-51 road racing seasons was the firm implantation of European makes in the American automobile market place, especially on the two coasts. Anything on four wheels that was sophisticated, fast and winning steadily came from Europe,

pure American guts, spirit and know-how. He would be followed by Lance Reventlow and his Scarabs, then Jim Hall and his Chapparrals. Both were succesful on American soil but failed to conquer Europe. It would take the enormous resources of the Ford Motor Company, fueled by the bruised ego of its Chairman, Henry Ford II, finally to turn the tables and beat the Europeans at their own game. And that would take fifteen years and millions of dollars, until the epochal 1966 Le Mans race.

Still, Cunningham was the man who singlehandedly blazed that trail. He fielded the first successful "Equipe" in America, the equivalent of a European winning works team, as early as 1949. In the second Watkins Glen weekend, "Mr. C." had no less than three cars entered: his just-acquired Ferrari 166 SC which he himself would drive, bringing it to second in the Grand Prix; his pre-war Bu-Merc, lent to George Roberts who finished third in the same race; and finally his supercharged MG which Sam Collier brought to fourth in the Seneca Cup. Two years later, in 1951, Briggs Cunningham had five cars entered, including three bearing his own name, plus two Ferraris. His three "Cunninghams" were veterans of Le Mans and Elkhart Lake by the time they arrived at the Glen. "Mr. C." did invent the first truly American road racing team.

Of all of this, of course, most of the protagonists and even less so the general public were aware. The main conclusion right after the 1951 Watkins Glen Grand Prix among racing enthusiasts and their growing audience was "More of the same, please, this is terrific and highly exciting." They would not be let down, but things would not go exactly as planned either.

with very few exceptions including, of course, the Cunninghams — though they never won in a European venue and never became a commercial success. By 1951, not only were MG, Jaguar, Ferrari, Aston Martin and Porsche familiar names to the automotive cogniscenti, but the Volkswagen Beetle was slowly beginning to make an impression on the American public. An important segment that Detroit would take four decades to appreciate had been carved out in the American psyche.

Last but not least, the "American Special" based on old componentry was beginning to prove a clear dead end. The Meyer, Altemus and other "Ford Specials" failed to accomplish much. There were a few exceptions on the West Coast, but these drivers were taking advantage of less intense competition from European racers. Cunningham was the first American to try to outdo the Europeans with

Max Hoffman in a Lea Francis with a company representative at Watkins Glen. Hoffman rarely saw a new European make he did not like and became an importer of marques such as Jaguar, Porsche and BMW.

America Begins to Dominate Part of The Road Racing Calendar!

Well, "more of the same" surely happened in the months that followed September 15, 1951, to an extent that few enthusiasts in America would have ventured to predict even one year before. In fact, in the seven months that followed the fourth Watkins Glen Grand Prix (Mid-September, 1951 to Mid-April, 1952), twelve notable sports car races were staged in Europe and North America, of which only three took place in Europe! Here is the calendar with the race winners:

September 16, 1951	Monza Grand Prix Feature Race 1st: Giulio Cabianca in OSCA MT4	Italy
October 7, 1951	Coupe du Salon - Montlhéry 1st: Guy Mairesse in Talbot Lago T26 GS	France
October 21, 1951	Reno Race 1st: Bill Pollack in Allard J2	USA
October 28, 1951	Palm Springs Cup 1st: Don Parkinson in Jaguar XK-120 Special	USA
November 20, 1951	Carrera Panamericana II 1st: Taruffi - Chinetti in Ferrari 212 Inter	Mexico
December 9, 1951	Palm Beach Shore Race 1st: John Fitch in Ferrari 340 America	USA
December 9, 1951	Torrey Pines Race 1st: Michael Graham in Allard J2	USA
March 8, 1952	Vero Beach 12 hours 1st: Kimberly - Lewis in Ferrari 340 MM	USA
March 9, 1952	Tour of Sicily 1st: P. Marzotto - Marini in Ferrari 166 MM	Italy
March 15, 1952	Sebring 12 hours 1st: Kulok - Grey in Frazer-Nash LMR Mk. II	USA
March 23, 1952	Palm Springs Race 1st: Chuck Manning in own Mercury Special	USA
April 20, 1952	Pebble Beach Race 1st: Bill Pollack in Allard J2	USA

Even though the deciding majority of the SCCA had opted against international participation, North America, with sunny climes in its southern and western regions in the middle of northern hemisphere's winter, was beginning to replace Argentina as the place of choice to race once the European season shut down in October. European professional drivers were still not allowed, and would not be for some time to come, but a long-lasting pattern was being set, with few realizing it.

Watkins Glen, September 1952 - Phil Walters in C-4RK number 1 during the Grand Prix "hot laps" approaching School House Corner.

chapter five

The End of the Road

Trouble in Africa, Stalemate in Korea

Between the end of the fourth Watkins Glen Grand Prix and the start of the first truly international road race of 1952, the Mille Miglia on May 3, important changes in both consumer-goods technology and international politics affected the daily life of people in the west in increasingly visible ways.

Television became an international medium for the first time on October 30, 1951, when the visit of Great Britain's Princess Elizabeth and her husband the Duke of Edinburgh to Windsor, Ontario, was telecast across the Detroit River to the NBC's nearest local station, then to the chain's national network. While the Detroit River is not much of a distance for electronic waves to bridge, this was a first that would become the norm across continents in a short time. Eventually, it would greatly enhance the popularity of all forms of sports, including motorsport.

This was a time for England to be in the news in many parts of the world. Four days prior to the Windsor visit, Winston Churchill, at 77, defeated the Labor Government in a national election. He would replace Labor Prime Minister Clement Attlee. The ousted PM was blamed by the electorate for a trade deficit growing so fast that the British Pound was losing the confidence of England's major trading partners. Clearly, those MGs and Jaguars and

"Too often in this demanding sport, unique in terms of ability, dedication, concentration and courage, someone pays a penalty for trying to do just that little bit better or go that little bit faster. And too often someone pays the penalty just for being in the wrong place at the wrong time when a situation or a set of circumstances is such that no human being can control them. However, that's the way it is. We accept it ..."

Bruce McLaren

(Eulogy for Jim Clark, April 1968 - McLaren himself was killed two years later in a freak accident during testing runs at Goodwood. Both champions raced at Watkins Glen's Formula 1 events in the mid-1960's)

Healeys and Austins coming to the United States by the boatload in exchange for U. S. dollars were not enough to stem the bleeding incurred in other parts of the British economy.

The beginning of the unraveling of the African portion of the former British Empire can also be traced back to that period. On December 24, 1951, Libya formally gained independence under King Idris, who was named head of a parliamentary political system. The former Italian colony had become a protectorate under British and French rule after 1943. Lybia then became the first nation to be organized under the auspices of the new United Nations in 1949. Egypt was the next link in the chain to weaken. Following severe anti-British riots, Egyptian strongman Mohammed Naguib staged a bloodless coup in Cairo in July, 1952, ousting King Farouk and proclaiming himself Commander-in-Chief of the army. A certain Colonel Nasser was one of the leaders within the group of rebellious officers. The grip Great Britain had long held on the strategically vital Suez Canal was beginning to loosen.

On February 8, 1952, King George VI of England died. This turned his eldest child and star of the first international telecast in history into Queen Elizabeth II. A month prior to that, British Overseas Airways Corporation, better known as BOAC, inaugurated the commercial jet age with its "Empire Routes" and the new Comet 1. At about the same time, American technology also made a leap forward having to do with air-flow, but this one was earth-bound: in mid-July, General Motors announced the successful development of air conditioning for cars and said the extra convenience would be available as an option on select 1953 models. Those big V-8s would be needed more than ever! Also very much part of the American landscape were record dollar amounts in the form of record corporate earnings or gross sales. On February 18, 1952, Goodyear became the first tire company in the world to top the one billion dollar mark in sales. Few motorsport enthusiasts probably even heard about this astonishing figure at the time, but it was very good news for their ever-growing international community.

The most important news in politics between the 1951 and 1952 racing seasons was the truce agreement signed by the two opposing sides in the Korean war on November 28, 1951. While it would take two and one half more years of episodic combat and painstaking negotiations to reach a full armistice, the path had been cleared to squelch the fire of the last hot spot of the early cold war years. When on March 10, 1952, General Fulgencio Batista regained power in Havana after a surprise coup, no one imagined that Cuba would, within nine years, become the next and most dangerous flashpoint of a war that would last nearly forty years.

The Early 1952 International Racing Season

The first genuine major international road race of 1952 was undoubtedly the 19th Mille Miglia, staged on May 3rd across the northern half of Italy. A startling total of 501 cars — with two men per car for most entries — took the start; 275 finished the grueling marathon. The extraordinarily large number of entrants allowed to race was considered a great risk and had the Italian press dubbed this edition of the classic event "The Race of the 1,000 Drivers" or "The 30,000 Horsepower Race." Among the participants were, of course, hordes of Italian cars beginning with no less than twenty-six Ferraris (!), seven OSCAs, a large number of Lancias including four of the beautiful and fast 2.0 liter Aurelia B20 coupes (one with Villoresi as lead driver had

Charles Hornburg's Jaguar C-Type, to be driven by Phil Hill, at Elkhart Lake in 1952.

finished second the previous year) several Alfa Romeos, Siatas and Cisitalias, plus legions of Fiats of all kinds and sizes. Alfa Romeo, Ferrari, Lancia and OSCA all had works cars and talented drivers officially representing their marque.

Most important, however, was the fact that England, France, and for the first time since the end of World War II, Germany, were represented by high-caliber factory and private teams. Aston Martin entered three DB2s with Tom Wisdom, Reg Parnell and George Abecassis as lead drivers. Jaguar, which had unsuccessfully fielded a pair of XK-120s assigned to Stirling Moss and Leslie Johnson in 1951, now entered one C-Type, again entrusting Stirling Moss with their hopes. Donald Healey entered his own pair of Nash-Healeys with Leslie Johnson and him as principal drivers. Frazer-Nash was represented by the private entry of former Ferrari driver Franco Cortese. He would drive his own Le Mans Replica racer with which he had won the 1951 Targa Florio, making it the first British car ever to win one of the great Italian classic endurance races. It would also be the last.

© Julian Silverberg

On the French side, the lone official team was Panhard, successor to the famed Panhard-Levassor manufacturing firm. The post-war Panhards were fast little front-wheel-drive machines powered by an air-cooled flat-twin engine. Called the Dyna Panhard, the new series of cars had experienced some success at Le Mans in their class. A pair of 745cc-engined Dynas were entered in the Mille Miglia, aiming for a class win. Several other French makes, such as Peugeot and Renault, were represented, but only by a small number of private entrants. Two were considered to have a remote chance at overall victory because of their powerful engines: Jean Blanc's Talbot and René Cotton's Delahaye.

Teutonic Come-Back

Most striking of all in this expanding international participation was the presence of two official German teams: Porsche and Mercedes-Benz.

Porsche would field three 356 coupes, a model which had now been raced privately in several countries for three years and was growing fast in reputation. A number of private entrants would improve the odds of the Zuffenhausen company to win its class. The reappearance of a new Mercedes works team was the most stunning news. The

By 1952 356 Porsches were common participants in "small bore" competition. Even the first 356s were successfully campaigned by privateers. In 1950, Prince Joachim von Fürstenberg, Ferry Porsche, Count Berckheim, Prince Fritzi zu Fürstenberg and Count Günther von Hardenberg (from left) in a two-car team at the Midnight Sun Rallye in Sweden.

three sports cars were brand new, had never raced before, and were only presented to the press on March 12, 1952. Based on the first new post-war Mercedes sedan, the 300, which had been introduced in April, 1951, the new sports car from Stuttgart was a gorgeous, slippery coupe called 300 SL.

The decision by Mercedes to follow the "start from an existing car" rather than "start from scratch" route was due in great part to the Jaguar C-Type victory at Le Mans which took place two months after the 300 sedan introduction. Mercedes-Benz management was greatly impressed. The C-Type was a relatively simple racing evolution of an existing car, the XK-120, whose core mechanical elements were clothed in a lightweight, streamlined body shape attached to a lightweight frame. Conversely, the unsuccessful Mercedes experience at the 1951 Buenos Aires races had shown that, in order for a car to compete successfully in the new Formula 1 championship, the Stuttgart firm would need to develop a totally new racer from the ground up. Updated pre-war Grand Prix machines simply would not do. Mercedes-Benz, however, could not afford such an investment so soon after the war.

Less than one month after the much celebrated Jaguar victory in France, the Mercedes-Benz management committee officially chose the arena of international sports car competition to rejuvenate its victorious racing image. The company would develop a new sports car based on the 300 sedan mechanicals, including its six-cylinder in-line 3.0 liter engine. The new model's main goal would be to win major endurance races across Europe. Famous Mercedes R&D chief Rudy Uhlenhaut had a revolutionary vision about how to transform a sedate luxury sedan into a winning sports car. The three-pointed star was on its way back to the greatest race courses in the world.

The 300 SL was a two-seat coupe with an extremely aerodynamic body. In fact, its drag coefficient was a mere 0.25, a number that engineers still found hard to achieve on cars of that size forty years later. The wind tunnel at Stuttgart University, used extensively, had served well. This was part of the bargain that Alfred Neubauer had reached with his management and Uhlenhaut at the onset of the car's design. Neubauer had not been enthusiastic

about using the 300 sedan's engine and mechanical components. The six-cylinder powerplant was originally never conceived as a potential racing engine, on top of which the sedan's suspension and drivetrain were rather heavy, coming from a large luxury car. Neubauer wanted to win, not just race. He agreed on the "300 solution" provided Uhlenhaut and his team could deliver a chassis that would be both extremely rigid and lightweight, plus a body with superior aerodynamics.

By the time the first three works cars appeared in Brescia for the 19th Mille Miglia, it was clear that the German team had succeeded. One unique feature symbolized the innovativeness of every major decision Uhlenhaut and his team made to achieve that goal. The famous "Appendix C" of the FIA, which had to be met in order for any car to be authorized in major endurance races, required doors of a certain size. As the Mercedes engineers were developing an advanced tubular frame chassis, it became clear to them that the lateral parts of the frame had to remain deep throughout the length of the chassis. That meant no conventional doors were possible. Therefore, the 300 SL's doors did not open sideways, but, rather, they opened upwards from the bottom rim of the side windows, being articulated on a longitudinal beam in the center of the roof! The Stuttgart engineers called them *Flügeltüren*, or "wing doors." The British press soon coined the transla-

TOP LEFT: The Mercedes-Benz racing team aces at Bern, Switzerland in 1938. From the left: Rudy Uhlenhaut (head engineer), Karl Kling, Manfred von Brauchitsch, Rudy Caracciola, Dick Seaman (drivers), Max Sailer (director), and Alfred Neubauer (racing chief). Seaman would be killed at Spa at the Grand Prix of Belgium in 1939. The others would live through the war and help reform a winning racing team.

BOTTOM RIGHT: May 27, 1952 - Bremgarten, Switzerland. The Bern Grand Prix for sports cars preceding the Formula 1 race. Karl Kling takes the 300 SL number 18, painted green, around a curve. He will win the race in front of Hermann Lang (car painted light blue) and Fritz Riess (car in silver). The fourth 300 SL, Rudy Caracciola's, was painted deep red. This is the only race where Mercedes-Benz fielded 300 SLs or SLRs in colors other than silver.

tion "gullwing doors" to describe the remarkable feature, and that phrase would stick.

Thus, the "vertical door" solution was arrived at so that the "roof portion" counted as part of the door's size. Quipped Neubauer, "Nowhere is it written [in Appendix C] that a door must open only sideways." The Italian organizers could not find anything in the rule book that would prohibit this design, and the new cars were allowed to race in the Mille Miglia. Mercedes-Benz, though, was well aware that this "fighter cockpit access" would be much tougher to sell to the Le Mans scrutineers. The company engineers already had a possible solution in mind.

The 1952 Mille Miglia

The 978 mile race turned out to be one of the most thrilling Mille Miglias ever. Works Ferrari driver Giovanni Bracco, driving a new 250 S Berlinetta powered by a prototype 3.0 liter version of the famous V-12, took the early lead out of Brescia. At the fifty-mile mark, one Mercedes was out (Hermann Lang had crashed), but Karl Kling's silver machine was a close second to Bracco. Behind Kling, the next of the three works Ferraris, a 225 S driven by Paolo Marzotto, was putting the pressure on the German. After that, it was two Lancias, three Ferraris, then Stirling

Moss in the lone works Jaguar. The long and fast descent down the Adriatic coast allowed Kling to grab the lead, while Bracco suffered from tire problems, dropping down to fourth. At Pescara, when the course veers west and inland across the Apennines towards Rome, Kling had an eight-minute lead over the first Ferrari, now a 225 S driven by Castellotti. Behind the Italian were four more Ferraris — including Bracco's — then the second 300 SL driven by Rudi Caracciola, then the Stirling Moss Jaguar. Millions of Italians were glued to their radios, where the race was reported live for the twelve hours it would take to be completed.

At Rome, which lies 580 miles into the demonic race, Kling still had the lead and behind him were Taruffi (works Ferrari 340 S), Bracco, Fagioli (Lancia B20), P. Marzotto and Moss. At Florence, with about three quarters of the race completed, Kling was still in the lead, while three of the four pursuing Ferraris were out: Taruffi's, P. Marzotto's and Biondetti's. Only Bracco still gave chase to the silver rocket, about four minutes behind it. He was Enzo Ferrari's last card. The Italian public was in a trance. The next car after Bracco's was Fagioli's Lancia, too far behind to still have a chance at overall victory. The terrain ahead, though, offered splendid opportunities for great drivers and cars to upset the odds: the Apennine range had to be crossed once

Credit: Mercedes-Benz

May 27, 1952 - Bremgarten, Switzerland. Rudy Caracciola in the 300 SL number 16, locked a wheel in a turn, left the road and crashed straight into a tree. The 51-year-old driver suffered a badly broken leg and this ended his career. Note the "short" gullwing doors. They would be more enveloping for Le Mans in order to permit faster egress.

more, including the famous steep and sinuous Futa and Raticosa passes leading to Bologna.

This was Bracco's moment. The chain-smoking Italian, fortified with occasional sips from a flask of brandy, launched a terrific assault against the Mercedes and its driver. When Bracco reached Bologna, about fifty miles north of Florence, he had not only seized the lead, but also put two minutes between himself and his German rival! Luck was also on the Italian's side after Florence as Kling was slowed by a pesky wheel hub for a while. The final segment between Bologna and Brescia was relatively easy. Though their respective engines both displaced the same three liters, Bracco's V-12 delivered 230 hp at 7500 rpm against the 171 hp at 5200 rpm of Kling's in-line six. The Italian and his Ferrari crossed the finish line after racing almost without interruption for twelve hours, nine minutes and forty-five seconds! Kling and his Mercedes followed nearly five minutes later, then it was Fagioli's Lancia followed by Caracciola's Mercedes, both more than a half hour behind Bracco. Stirling Moss did not finish, as he crashed his car (without injury to himself) in the Raticosa pass.

Ferrari also won the 2.0 liter class in the "International Sports" category with a 166 MM Berlinetta entered privately by Brivio-Cassani. The works OSCA of Cabianca-Roghi won the 1100cc class, and an Italian-crewed Dyna Panhard the 750cc class. In the "International Grand Touring" category, Fagioli's works Lancia B20 won the 2.0 liter class, while Porsche placed one-two-three in the 1500cc class, and a French-crewed Dyna Panhard won the 750cc class. Only the British were left to sulk, with just a 7th overall finish for the Nash-Healey of Johnson-McKenzie and a class victory for Wisdom's Aston Martin DB2 (12th overall).

Here was the kind of race Cameron Argetsinger had in mind when he started dreaming on the roads around Watkins Glen in 1946-1947. Much more than a merry-go-round for great cars and talented or celebrity drivers, this was extreme competition at the highest level of the sport. Even more important, intense rivalries between famous car manufacturers, national pride and dices between the best drivers in the world were part and parcel of the whole

TOP LEFT: May 30, 1952 - Indianapolis. Alberto Ascari in a Ferrari 4.5 liter Special. This was a weak attempt by the great European racing marque to test its mettle on the American brickyard. Ascari was doing well but then one of his wire wheels failed on lap 30 (of 200), while in the seventh place. He hit the wall, harmlessly for him, but fatally for his red car.

TOP RIGHT: Alec Ulmann (center) officiating at Sebring. To his right are Colonel Herrington (bowtie) and Fred Royston. To his left is Reginald Smith.

spectacle. No wonder an estimated two million spectators lined the Mille Miglia course during the race, and tens of millions of enthusiasts throughout Europe followed at least part of the saga on their radio.

The Great Controversy - Act 2

Alec Ulmann was a fighter. After his demotion from Activities Chairman of the SCCA early in 1951, then the unseemly "paper war" that ensued, he took great pleasure in preparing his trip to Le Mans and Paris in June of that year. This time, he would pursue his vision for Sebring without regard for the isolationists' point of view. Ulmann would be going to Le Mans first as team manager for Equipe Cunningham, so that he was responsible for securing the FIA inspection approval for the three C-2s before they left for France. Jim Clemenger was the AAA representative who had that approval authority in the United States. As both men were already friends, Clemenger was only too happy to give Ulmann an Official AAA Contest Board appointment and letters of introduction to the CSI officials. This would also make it possible for the wily American to achieve two important objectives. First, he could secure an official international date from the FIA for the next Sebring race, which he now planned as a twelve-hour event to be staged in the early part of 1952. Second, he could also con-

tact prospective European works teams and try to convince them to participate.

Though, as we have seen, the June trip to France was not a success for Equipe Cunningham at Le Mans, Ulmann's stay in Paris after the French classic turned out to be a coup. He was well received by the FIA authorities and secured positive answers from them. Then, to quote *The Sebring Story,* "I set out to do what I was told was impossible. In short order, I signed up the first post-World War II French team to come to the United States. With the able assistance of Hobart (Bill) Cook, the Grumman test pilot and great aficionado of the sport, I was able to arrange the necessary financial help to get to Sebring the winners of the Le Mans Index of Performance Cup, the Deutsch-Bonnet team of cars, with René Bonnet acting as *Chef d'Equipe.*"

By October, shortly after the fourth Watkins Glen Grand Prix, the FIA granted Ulmann March 15, 1952, as the official international date for the first "Twelve Hours of Sebring." Since D. Cameron Peck had just announced his resignation as President, a new SCCA Board would have to be elected early in the new year. The closing date for registering nominations was November 19, 1951. Why not, thought Ulmann and his principal compatriots, take advantage of this unexpected opportunity, rush into the breach immediately and, in *Blitzkrieg* fashion, win the war in short order?

As one of the earliest members of the SCCA and life-time member, Ulmann still held sway in the club. Miles Collier was also an early member with strong influence and a devoted internationalist. Cameron Argetsinger who had started what was now the biggest and most famous SCCA event of the year, was on their side. The *Blitzkrieg* approach was chosen in the form of a formal campaign within the club membership to elect Miles Collier, as the new President and Alec Ulmann, as the Vice President. Should they succeed, total victory would be theirs. In Ulmann's own words, this is what ensued:

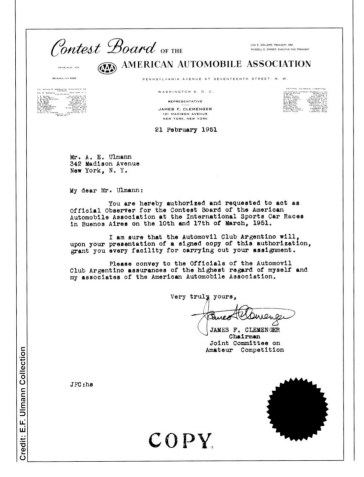

LEFT: Letter of J.F. Clemenger of AAA to Alec Ulmann, showing the closeness of the relationship and leading to American participation in the 1951 Juan Perón Sports Car Grand Prix.

"The 'powers that be' of SCCA saw a most sinis-ter danger in the slate that was being proposed to the membership, and took quick and violent action.

I was summoned to a Board Meeting of the club, held in a smoke-filled room at the St. Regis Hotel in New York and given the choice of either recanting all my oft-repeated opinions regarding the desirability of the inclusion of professional drivers from all over the world, and apoligizing for some of my more ebullient statements about the club's management, or resigning my life membership in SCCA. I could not compromise with the principles that were so lucidly clear to me and accepted the 'walking papers' that were presented by this ultimatum — resigning on the spot."

Actually, as he described himself in the mailing card prinited below, Ulmann first got a call from Fred Wacker on November 13, offering him either to recant publicly at the November 19 meeting, or to offer his res-ignation. Ulmann chose not to attend and the next thing he knew, a registered letter from the club's Secretary, Charles Moran, was handed to him on November 20, informing him of the cancella-tion of his life-time member-ship and includ-ing a $100 check as refund for his annual fee!

THIS CAN HAPPEN TO YOU

On November 13, 1951—six days prior to the closing of nominations for SCCA officers—I received a long distance telephone call from the Club's Vice President, Fred Wacker, requesting my resignation from life membership in the Club. No charges were preferred, but I was asked to appear at a Club Officers' Meeting three days later, which became impossible for me because of a prior en-gagement away from the city. I so notified Mr. Wacker by wire the next day and offered to meet the officers at their convenience at a later date.

Thereupon, I received on Tuesday, November 20, 1951, a registered letter from the Club's Secretary informing me that my life membership had been cancelled and that the Treasurer was refunding $100.00 direct to me.

Section V, Article 2 of the SCCA By-Laws states that "Any member may be expelled for infraction of Club rules or such other causes as may be determined by the majority of officers as being in the best interest of the Club. However, before such action is taken the member shall have an opportunity to submit in writing or in per-son his position on any charge of which he shall be noti-fied."

So far no charges have been preferred nor have I been notified by word, telegram or letter as to my transgression.

Under the circumstances, I deem it best not to run for the office of Vice-President to which, I understand, I have been nominated by friends. However, it is my sincere recommendation that you vote for new officers who will reintroduce judicious and impartial administration of club affairs.

Alec Ulmann

This card is printed and mailed at my expense.

Ulmann then decided to go ahead on his own, and "damn the torpedoes!" In the race program for the first Sebring Twelve-Hour race, he wrote an article claiming, "This is the first time that such an event is being run in the United States on a full-fledged international basis. ... The Sebring event and the Indianapolis Sweepstakes are the only International Competitions for automobiles in this country that are entered on the Auto-Sporting Calendar of the World." Ulmann commented further in *The Sebring Story*, "To cap this bomb ... was the statement that the race was open to drivers having current AAA credentials in good standing, with foreigners required to have International FIA licenses valid for 1952, and would be run in accordance with the rules as published in the 1950 International FIA sporting code and its Annex C. Not a word about the SCCA, not a word about the dreaded presence of so-called 'professionals' who would run our 'sporty boys' off the road."

In the tone of these paragraphs, one can sense a trimphal feeling not only of goals achieved, but also of revenge accomplished. The isolationists might have won the first battle, but now the internationalists had returned fire, with active support from the big guns in France. A large beachhead for the freedom fighters had been secured in Florida. The war, however, had just begun.

On January 19, the SCCA membership elected Fred Wacker as new President by a vote of 691 to 418. George Felton was re-elected Vice President, a victory he used to indulge in a verbal counter-attack on the defeated group, describing them with words such as "intent on disrupting the club," "disloyal" and even "evil!" Wrote Bill Callahan, editor of *Motorsport Magazine* and witness to the proceedings in his publication's April, 1952 issue, "Unfortunately, the victorious Vice President, Col. George Felton, indulged in an attack on the opposition group which was as inexcusable as it was inept. To us, Col. Felton's remarks confirmed in resounding detail the charges of adamancy, imperialism and incapability to accept criticism or suggestions from members that had been the basis for Miles Collier's candidacy in the first place." Despite this, the attempted *coup d'état* of the internationalists had back-fired badly. It was Pearl Harbor instead of Midway. The war was now lost for

Equipe Cunningham on its way to Le Mans. From left to right, "Mr. C.", Smith Hempstone Oliver, John Oliveau, Alec Ulmann and Bill Spear. This is the departure for the first attempt: 1950.

the foreseeable future. Only the beachhead at Sebring still stood, but the victors of the St. Regis were not going to let it stand for long if they could help it.

The Battle of Florida

The SCCA "powers that be" could not prevent the Sebring Twelve-Hour race from taking place, but they would do their best to sabotage it. The most effective option at their disposal to achieve that goal, they decided, was to stage their own SCCA-sanctioned Twelve-Hour race in Florida only a week before the Sebring race! Thus, drivers would be forced to choose and show their loyalty. An SCCA member available to enter the club's race but not participating would be considered a traitor. For those few who would try to enter both races, the likelihood of having their car re-tuned and race-ready for another twelve-hour marathon just six days later was seriously diminished. Part of the animosity between the two camps was reinforced by the intense personal and business rivalry that existed between Alec Ulmann and Max Hoffman, who had arrived in the United States in 1941.

Ulmann's family had emigrated from St. Petersburg, Russia, to Finland in 1919, then Switzerland, to escape the communist repression. Alec went to the United States in 1923 to study at M.I.T. and became an American citizen in 1925.

Max Hoffman emigrated from Vienna to Paris in the late 1930s to escape the Nazi menace. He eventually arrived in New York on a Portuguese ship in June of 1941. By 1950, both Ulmann and Hoffman were New York City residents but fierce competitors. They both were making a living by utilizing their in-depth knowledge of the European automobile industry and culture; they both had the same hobby related to imported sports cars; and finally some of their businesses overlapped, as, for instance, Alec Ulmann was also the American agent for Borrani wheels. Last but not least, Hoffman was a strong defender of the isolationist cause within the SCCA.

It is actually Hoffman who took the lead in organizing the sabotage. With the backing of the SCCA, he chose a small coastal East Florida resort about 150 miles north of Palm Beach Shores as the venue for the competing race. Its name was Vero Beach. Probably not coincidentally, Vero Beach was situated almost at the same latitude as Sebring, which lies in Central Florida about half way between Orlando to the north and Lake Okeechobee to the south. Probably not coincidentally either, the circuit would be traced on the local airport. So everything about the two competing events would be nearly identical, except for the sanctioning body. That would make the dilemma of would-be candidates even tougher. Everybody else would just be confused.

The presence of the official Jaguar team at Sebring, with at least one C-Type and Stirling Moss, became a major pawn in this battle. Sir William Lyons had expressed an interest in such participation because of the critical importance of the American market for Jaguar. As soon as Ulmann became aware of it, he sent a telegram to Coventry which read:

> *"Sebring internationally sanctioned 12 hour race definitely scheduled March 15 - You are cordially invited - Sports Car Club running internationally unsanctioned race undetermined length - Members-only probably March 8 - Believe your drivers and works cars subject to FIA disqualification if participating latter event - Alec Ulmann"*

Of course, Sir William Lyons heard a different song from Hoffman, who had the tacit support of a large group of Jaguar dealers on the east coast of America. Shortly thereafter, rumors spread in the SCCA membership that Jaguar owners who would participate in the Sebring race might run into real problems getting parts in the future... Lofty England, the Jaguar Racing Manager, finally said, "We're not going at all if they cannot decide when or where to have it." That, of course, was a major loss for Alec Ulmann, though he would not report it in *The Sebring Story*.

The SCCA directors also thought that communications would be an advantage for their side in this battle. All they had to do to secure an exciting field was mail invitations to the entire membership of the club, now numbering 2,240 people. How would Ulmann, without a huge P. R. budget, publicize his race in a country where road racing was still so minuscule a sport? That was underestimating Alec Ulmann's flair for public relations and the far-reaching influence of many of his friends. Hobart Cook — his full name was Hobart Amory Hare Cook — was able to get early publicity for two New York papers: *The Mirror* and *The News*.

The first event they were able to attract reporters to was the arrival and unloading of the French Deutsch-Bonnet team. The two little blue roadsters and their *équipe*, headed by René Bonnet himself, had sailed on the French liner *Ile de France* which was now docked at a pier jutting from Manhattan. Ulmann and Cook were there to greet the first overseas team to come race in America since 1937. Both newspapers ran a feature on the event and *The Mirror* even portrayed the Sebring race as "a great international society event." The French press was there too and the coverage in France was substantial.

There was another publicity hotspot for Sebring in New York: the El Morocco Club. John Perona was, of course, a good friend of Alec Ulmann. He was only too pleased to lend his famous club to his endeavor. One of the first things Perona did was to display the first poster for a Sebring race, which carried the "Noon to Midnight" theme, prominently in his club. He also spread the word to his patrons. This was no small favor as El Morocco, which featured a terrific Rhumba Band and seats covered in natural zebra skin, was a magnet for celebrities and society members. You could run as easily into Humphrey Bogart or Clark Gable or Bob Hope, as into Barbara Hutton in those days. By mid-February, entry forms were arriving in numbers and quality sufficient to guarantee a decent race.

Vero Beach, March 8, 1952

The SCCA had planned a three-race event, starting with a one-hour sprint, then a six-hour race, then the twelve-hour main race. The course was 3.25 miles long with haybales marking the circuit in most places. A little over thirty entrants were on hand to take the green flag on a clear and warm day. Most were the people and cars familiar to the Watkins Glen spectators: Cunningham, Fitch, Kimberly, Spear, Walters, Wacker, Koster, and so on. Almost all of the cars capable of contesting victory in the main race had been seen at the Glen the previous September, the main exceptions at Vero Beach being the Fitch-Whitmore Jaguar Special and Tom Cole's latest Allard, the J2X. The newest Allard version had Alfin drum brakes and a new, more rigid tubular chassis which allowed the engine to be placed almost eight inches further forward, improving handling significantly — the J2 was "tail-happy." There was one remarkable and novel presence in the 1500cc category: two Porsche 356 coupes. This was

Buenos Aires, March 1951 - Tom Cole in his new Allard J2 racing during trials on the Circuito Costanera Norte.

their second race on the east coast of America (the first was at Palm Beach Shores three months earlier).

The one-hour race was won by Paul O'Shea in an Allard J2X. John Fitch in the Fitch-Whitmore Jaguar Special established the fastest lap for the day in 2:34.0 before he had to retire the car due to clutch failure. The six-hour race was won by Byron King in a Jaguar XK-120, followed by George Rand in a similar car entered by Max Hoffman. When the time came to start the big event, the first race of that duration ever to be run in America, there were 12,000 spectators spread around the track. No crowd control problem existed here. Twenty-four cars took the green flag, nine of which with a single driver intending to go the whole twelve hours. The major contenders were Cole-O'Shea in the new Cadillac Allard J2X, Fred Wacker in his Hydramatic-equiped Allard J2, and Kimberly-Lewis in Spear's Ferrari 340 America.

The race was hard-fought and saw many upsets. Eventually, raw power and resiliency paid off, as the Kimberly-Lewis Ferrari 340 America won the race, six laps ahead of the Cole-O'Shea Allard. Three more Ferraris completed the "Top Five" list: third was the Walters-Spear 166 MM, followed by the Benett-Moran 212 Export then Cunningham's first Ferrari, the 166 SC, driven by "Mr. C." himself during the whole twelve hours. Both Porsches finished and the John Bentley-Karl Brocken entry won its class. Winner on the index of performance — another imitation of Sebring — was Briggs Cunningham's small Crosley Siata, prepared by Ernie McAfee and driven by George Huntoon and Bob Gegen.

The first Vero Beach race was a modest success, even though the racing itself had proved exciting and featured a lot of interesting machinery. Its usefulness would be decided exactly a week later, according to how the first Sebring Twelve Hours would fare. A first sign of trouble was the fact that a lot of the drivers, and even cars, which participated in the March 8 event were also entered in the March 15 event. Among them was a majority of the most important names: Cunningham, Spear, Fitch, Walters, Kimberly. Now was the time for the most conservative SCCA board members to apply some additional political pressure. There were only six days to go. The first major name to fold was

Jim Kimberly who never had been in favor of going the international route anyway. A few lesser names succumbed after that. But would it be enough to really hurt the Sebring race?

Sebring, March 15, 1952

Alec Ulmann and his wife Mary had long been famous for their organizational skills also. These included delegating key responsibilities to the best possible people. Forrest Howard, president of a very influential local organization, the Sebring Firemen's Association, was named General Race Chairman. The organization of the race itself was entrusted to Reggie Smith who would remain Race Secretary for two decades. Smith Hempstone Oliver was appointed Chief Scrutineer. Joseph J. Lane was made timing and scoring chief. Russell Boss became the starter nominated by the AAA since Nils Mickelson was an SCCA member who held back. The race course was lengthened to 5.2 miles with the addition of two corners and a few other changes. The single race of the day would start at 12:00 hour sharp and end at 00:00 hour, hence the catchy slogan "Noon to Midnight." The index of performance was maintained, but only as a special prize. The real race would be run according to the traditional criteria, "first on distance."

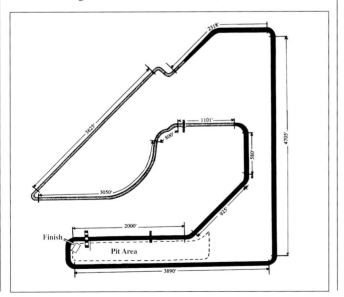

BOTTOM LEFT: The Sebring course in 1952. But for constant minor changes, it remains similar today.

BOTTOM RIGHT: The "North Americans" and two of their hosts in Buenos Aires, March 1951. From left to right, standing: Tony Pompeo, Fred Wacker, John Perona, Argentinean host, Bill Spear, George Rand, Jim Kimberly, host. Sitting: Alfred Momo, Jack Donaldson, John Fitch. Alfred Momo, a mechanical genius and great friend of Cunningham's, after seeing Fitch's performance, recommended him to "Mr. C." for Le Mans.

The morning of March 15, 1952, was a rainy one at Sebring, Florida. Alec Ulmann and his team, who had been so pleased to secure a good field of over thirty cars, began to worry. In those days in America, one never raced full-bore on a wet track. The yellow flags at Watkins Glen in 1950 — meaning "no passing" — were a perfect example of that policy. In Europe, road racing in all forms was considered to be a test of cars and drivers in real life conditions, including rain and snow. Winter events, especially the famous Monte Carlo Rally, were highly attended annual contests mostly held in treacherous snow and ice conditions. Fortunately for the Sebring organizers, the skies above them started to clear about noon. The start of the race was rescheduled for 1 pm and by then, a bright, warm Florida sun had almost completely dried up the entire course. The finish was pushed back to 1:00 am, the next day.

Thirty-two cars were lined up for the official start of the first Twelve-Hours of Sebring. They were angled at a forty-five degree angle relative to the axis of the start/finish

147

straight, for a Le Mans-type start. There should have been thirty-eight cars on the tarmac, but six did not show up for various reasons. Jim Kimberly's Ferrari 166 MM fell victim to political pressure. Ironically, Erwin Goldschmidt's new J2X Allard was also a no-show, but only because the car's transmission became irreparably damaged while its driver was on his way to Sebring. The Tom Cole-Paul O'Shea Allard J2X which had finished second at Vero Beach suffered from the same problem during practice. It could not race. Then there was the first newly-minted Cunningham racer designated for Phil Walters and John Fitch; it turned out not to be ready in time. Still, the field that day was a respectable one and a leap forward compared to the first Six-Hour race.

Drivers who finished would be expected to cover a distance of over 700 miles and therefore, contrary to the much shorter Watkins Glen Grand Prix, reliability would be as much a factor for overall victory as top speed or even, to a degree, driver ability. Among the leading contenders in this scenario were the now well-known Ferrari 340 America roadster owned by Bill Spear and to be co-driven by its owner and Briggs Cunningham; four XK-120 Jaguars; a Frazer-Nash LMR which Larry Kulok and Harry Gray would co-drive; then two Ferrari 166 MMs whose drivers would be Robert O'Brien-Richard Cicurel and James Simpson-George Colby. Last but not least, there was a particularly well-prepared Allard J2. Owned by Bob Grier of New York, the president of the Motorsport Club of America, it would be co-driven by its owner and friend Myke Collins. Powered by a 4.5 liter Ardun Ford V-8 and also fitted with a Hydramatic transmission, its preparation had been supervised by René Dreyfus. A former French champion of great renown, Dreyfus had amassed a large number of brilliant results in the 1930s, especially at the wheel of Bugattis, Alfa Romeos and Delahayes. He was now a New York resident and would soon open a second famous restaurant for motorsport enthusiasts, Le Chanteclair, in that city.

The équipe Deutsch-Bonnet, with its 745cc Panhard engines, could only reach for the Index victory. Their main rivals for that prize would be several Siatas, some Crosley-powered, some Fiat-powered; and an open-top Morris

Minor with a 980cc engine. Young Walt Hansgen was there too, his hopes placed on an MG TD which he would co-drive with a Randy Pearsall. In all, sixty drivers would participate in the race, and thirty-two of them were lined-up across the runway from their cars when the clock struck 1 pm, EST. At exactly 1:05 pm, starter Russell Boss lowered the green flag, and off the thirty-two sprinted towards their waiting machines.

Within less than twenty seconds, a roar not dissimilar to that of a squadron of B-17 bombers taking off filled the old airport runway. First to turn wheels was the Jaguar XK-120 of Charles Schott and Maurice Carroll, but by the end of the first lap, Bill Spear's potent Ferrari was in the lead, followed by the Gray-Kulok silver Frazer-Nash LMR. The Ferrari America roadster continued to hold a firm lead as attrition began to take its toll. After the first hour on the rough Sebring surface — mostly made-up of uneven concrete slabs — six cars were out, including the Simpson-Colby Ferrari 166 MM which was holding third when it retired. Next to go was the Aston Martin DB2; Bob Gegen was at the wheel when his rear suspension broke in the "esses" leading back to the hairpin turn. The British Coupe spun out of control, but the driver got out unhurt as there are no trees or berms around airfields. Commented Gegen afterwards, "The esses is where the Martin lost its Aston."

The third and fourth hours saw two dramatic developments. The Grier-Collins Allard J2 moved up from 7th to 3rd during the third hour, making a bid for eventual victory. Then shortly after 4 pm the Ferrari 340 America, which had built a two-lap lead over its nearest competitor, broke an axle. It was instantly out of the race, leaving the lead to the surprising Frazer-Nash, with the Allard J2 now in second position and the Schott-Carroll XK-120 third. By the sixth hour mark, or mid-point through the race, the lead Allard's automatic transmission seized, sidelining a second serious contender. René Dreyfus was as bitterly disappointed as the two drivers. The Frazer-Nash was still in the lead, but now the O'Bien-Cicurel Ferrari 166 MM had moved into second followed by the surprising Siata 1400 GS of Bob Fergus and Dick Irish. For those still in the race nothing seemed impossible.

The rest of the event, however, turned out mainly to be

a battle for position between the top six remaining contenders, and a battle for survival for everyone else. Though the Frazer-Nash ran into clutch problems at one point, the car recovered quickly and never lost its lead. It eventually finished at 1 am with a six-lap advantage over the second finisher. They achieved an overall average of 62.8 mph over a total of 145 laps. Most surprising was the fact that the winning British racer had been delivered by the factory to its American buyer, Stuart Donaldson of New York City, a mere four days before the start of the race! The O'Brien-Cicurel Ferrari held on to second until the eighth hour, when it dropped to fourth which is where it finished. The second spot was hotly disputed until the end between the Schott-Carroll Jaguar and the Fergus-Irish Siata GS. The Siata was second at midnight, but eventually fell prey to the more powerful Jaguar. Still, the little Italian roadster made the top three, which was a remarkable accomplishment.

Fifth was the Jaguar XK-120 of Chuck Wallace and Dick Yates. Sixth was an east coast MG Special, owned and co-driven by David Ash. The other driver was John Van Driel of Mount Vernon, New York. This car had a cigar-shaped aluminum body and highly modified mechanicals, including a Mercedes 170 swing rear axle. With a mere 1390cc engine, both its finish and placement were a real achievement. Not so lucky were a total of fifteen cars, practically fifty percent of the starting grid. The index of performance was won by the Deutsch-Bonnet co-driven by Steve Lansing, at Sebring on his honeymoon (!), and Wade Morehouse. René Bonnet himself drove the last hour of the race. The little blue car was 7th overall, also a commendable result. The award ceremony took place the next morning, with the flatbed of a humble truck serving as speaking platform. After a speech from James Lamb, secretary to the AAA Contest Board, Alec Ulmann took great joy in awarding the prizes to the deserving winners.

Who Lost Florida?

On the surface, the first Twelve Hours of Sebring was not a great success. The Watkins Glen field of the previous September was much more impressive both in terms of cars and participants, with the sole exception of the "foreign" works team presence of Deutsch-Bonnet in favor of Sebring. Deutsch-Bonnet, though, was hardly a major part of the dream of most European road racing enthusiasts, even the French. In addition, the crowd at Hendricks Field on March 15 numbered only 7,000 spectators according to the most optimistic estimates. This was almost fifty percent under the Vero Beach attendance and even less than the first Watkins Glen event in 1948. Alec Ulmann had predicted a field of 75 cars and an attendance of at least 50,000. He had fallen far short of both goals. His SCCA arch-enemies had staged a good event at Vero Beach and successfully siphoned off important participation and energy from his FIA-approved "Little Le Mans." This was probably the period Ulmann referred to when he dedicated his 1969 book, *The Sebring Story*, to his wife with these words:

> *"This book is dedicated to my wife, Beatrice Mary, née Foote, born in Surrey, England, who, by consecrated loyalty and tenacity, followed her husband in his oft unrewarding hobby to get European road racing back to the continent of North America.*
>
> *In the darkest hours, when defeat seemed inevitable, she gave her everything in perseverance and equanimity, thereby keeping the author of this story of the Sebring Races from going off the cliff and dragging with him the whole enterprise.*
> *There is no price for this sort of love."*

The surface of things was misleading. While the Vero Beach race had succeeded in lessening the quality of the field which took the start of the first Sebring Twelve Hours, it had added nothing whatsoever to the SCCA cause in America. In Europe, it proved to be a serious mistake later on. From a political point of view, British racing manufacturers were the wrong people to confuse. Since they were the main providers of road racing cars to Americans in those days, showing that American racing authorities had a clear strategy was the least the SCCA could do to promote the cause of its members. Instead, their actions backfired, as the Jaguar case illustrates. Even more important, since the French were still pretty much in charge of all

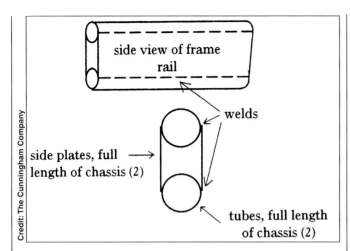

side view of frame rail

welds

side plates, full length of chassis (2)

tubes, full length of chassis (2)

TOP LEFT: Drawing of the Cunningham C-4R chassis frame element.

BOTTOM LEFT: Digitized shape of the Cunningham C-4R

international racing regulations and activities, keeping them at least neutral should have been a critical part of any long term strategy for the SCCA's ruling faction. Alec Ulmann had just dealt them a complete defeat on that score.

In fact, the French and Italian press ran major articles on the Deutsch-Bonnet victory. *L'Equipe* claimed, "René Bonnet and his D.B. Panhard are the best ambassadors for the French automobile industry." *Le Figaro*, with typical French exaggeration, wrote, "The whole American industry is bewildered by the triumph of a 745cc, two-cylinder, air-cooled, Panhard-engined sports car." René Bonnet became an instant hero in his country. The "battle of Florida" had been a marginal national victory for the isolationists, but it was a grave defeat at the international level. With the first Twelve Hours of Sebring, Alec Ulmann had gained full credibility with the FIA, even offering France the gift of a "great national victory" to celebrate. Now, the "powers that be" in Paris were on their side. Within less than a year it would prove the key to Ulmann's eventual success.

The second Cunningham Racer

The Cunningham workshop at 1402 Elizabeth in West Palm Beach got started on the C-2 successor much further ahead of the next Le Mans race than it did on the C-2. In fact, the original goal was to first break in the new car at Sebring in Mid-March, 1952, then at Bridgehampton at the

end of May, before sailing to France. This way, the new racer would arrive at Le Mans fully tested and with all the gremlins eliminated. The Cunningham team missed Sebring by ten days, but they would be ready for the Bridgehampton race.

The first goal for the new car's designers was to shed a lot of weight without reducing chassis rigidity. Accordingly, the wheelbase was decreased by 5″ to 100″, the track narrowed by 4″ and the new body was planned to be 6″ slimmer. G. Briggs Weaver, father of George Weaver of "Poison 'Lil" fame, had now joined the Cunningham enterprise. He and Phil Walters were the two men principally responsible for the second Cunningham racer. They gave it a new, lighter chassis, but with superior rigidity and capable of holding the heavy Chrysler V-8 without undue stress. Instead of a ladder frame, Weaver conceived frame rails employing two tubes per element, with side plates welded between them. This resulted in a chassis whose tortional rigidity was far superior to any ladder frame design. By the time the finished new car was weighed, the team had saved almost 500 lbs. compared to the C-2.

Briggs Weaver also had a major influence on the rear suspension. One of his major decisions was to drop the de Dion rear-axle unit and replace it with a more conventional live-axle borrowed from the Chrysler parts bin. His thinking was that he could save a little in absolute weight while

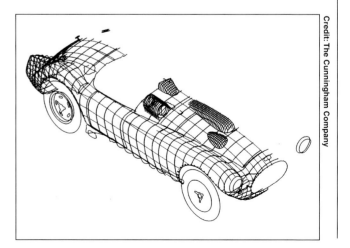

losing a bit in unsprung weight, thanks to the new Chrysler rear axle design. The trade-off in handling characteristics would not be material in the races the new car was primarily designed for. The Ford-based front suspension of the C-2 was kept almost unchanged. Weaver also switched from the C-2's wire wheels to Halibrand magnesium wheels, being fully aware of Ascari's trouble at Indy. These were designed to combine lighter weight with increased sturdiness.

Meanwhile, Bob Blake was developing the new car's shape and body. When he started, Blake was conscious that of the three cars Briggs Cunningham wanted for the 1952 season, one had to be a coupe. A German aerodynamicist who counseled with car makers in Stuttgart in the late 1930s, Professor Wunibald Kamm, was invited to provide advice during a number of weeks, concentrating primarily on the coupe. Cunningham was also involved.

The result of the team's work was an aggressive-looking roadster, with a big "jaws-like" oval radiator shape, an elegant fender line sloping gently from the top of the front wheel arch to the back of the cockpit, then rising elegantly over the rear wheel arch and ending in a fin-like shape behind the rear wheels. It was a big car with a very long hood, typically American, exuding strength, power and overwhelming force. At the minimum, it would be great for the spectacle! The car was called the C-4R, successor to the C-2 and the C-3 customer version. The new coupe had a back that descended nearly vertically from the lower

BOTTOM LEFT: Briggs Swift Cunningham aboard his C-4R at Le Mans, 1952.

BOTTOM RIGHT: The C-4RK, here driven by Phil Walters at Watkins Glen, September, 1952. The coupe had a theoretical 12-15 mph aerodynamic advantage over the roadster; however, the Chrysler Hemi, in its 1952 configuration, could not reach the rev limit in top gear.

roofline down to the rear hemline. This followed one of Professor Kamm's theories stating that a "chopped off" rear improved airflow. Taking the "K" from "Kamm," the coupe was designated C-4RK. Phil Walters was involved in the coupe's design, which is why he would most often drive it.

The Chrysler engine was also fine-tuned to produce even more power. This time, Chrysler engineers cooperated actively with the Cunningham team. K. T. Keller had realized that race victories would bring great publicity for his company while his own engineering department could learn a lot from the experience of "racing at the limit." Using various refinements, such as using a roller-tappet camshaft, it was determined that the Hemi could deliver up to 400 hp! Briggs Cunningham's goal, however, was to win endurance races, especially the Le Mans Twenty-Four Hours, and therefore reliability was a primary concern. As a result, the team agreed to a compromise between raw power and longevity. The final setting produced 325 hp at 5200 rpm. This was an increase of over 100 hp compared to the 1951 Le Mans version, with a car that was 500 lbs. lighter and judged to have better aerodynamics. Top speed went up to near 160 mph. The little West Palm Beach shop was making progress in giant leaps.

From Bridgehampton to Le Mans

After the first Twelve Hours of Sebring, the next two road races in America took place in California, at Palm Springs on March 23, then at Pebble Beach on April 20.

There was no time to drive the new cars back and forth between the two coasts. In those days, flying them, though not impossible, was extraordinarily expensive. The next big event on the east coast was the Bridgehampton race on May 24 and that is where the new C-4R would be race-tested. All three cars had to be put on a boat shortly after the Long Island event to arrive in France in time for Le Mans. As a result, the Cunningham team decided to enter only one car to lower its risk. There would be no time to fix any potential damage incurred at Bridgehampton, engine breakdown or otherwise. One of the two roadsters was chosen and Phil Walters was designated to drive it.

The Bridgehampton event turned out to be a bittersweet experience for the Le Mans-bound team. Phil Walters drew an unlucky number, finding himself in ninth place on the starting grid. By the second lap, however, Walters had seized the lead! His main competitors were the Allards of Tom Cole and Fred Wacker, Bill Spear's Ferrari 340 America and the Fitch-Whitmore Jaguar Special driven by John Fitch. Alas for Walters and the entire Cunningham team, an exhaust pipe broke on the C-4R and its driver was accordingly black-flagged. Bill Spear won the race in his now well-trained big Ferrari roadster, Fred Wacker finished second in his red "Eight Ball" and John Fitch was pleased to finish third in his Jaguar Special on its second time out. Tom Cole did not finish. Equipe Cunningham did not gain much from the experience. The three big American cars left for France with any possible outcome imaginable.

France, Early June, 1952

The 1952 edition of the Le Mans classic promised to be a full return, in modern endurance terms, to the great national Grand Prix battles of the late 1930s. There were many reasons for that. First and for the first time since 1940, the German juggernaut was back, in the form of an official three-car Mercedes-Benz team aiming squarely at overall victory. An official three-car Porsche works team would compete in the 1100cc class. Adding spice to this come-back, the performance of the amazingly slick 300 SL at the Mille Miglia, especially its top speed, had all the lead competitors in a near-panic. When a clear aerodynamic advantage had been gained, the long 3.7 mile Mulsanne

Le Mans, June 14, 1952. The Cunningham cars on the grid sporting the American colors. To the left is a private Talbot *barquette* and to the right (number 4) an Allard J2X Le Mans with stream-lined body.

straight at Le Mans offered the opportunity to gain a second or two every lap over the competition, horsepower being equal. That is because at top speeds of over 150 mph, a significant percent of an engine's power is used in overcoming air resistance. Stirling Moss, in fact, had been deeply shaken by the aerodynamic advantage of the new Mercedes.

Second, international endurance racing, though still not as popular as the Formula 1 championship, was beginning to draw audiences of a remarkable size. The 1951 Le Mans event had welcomed 300,000 on-site spectators and millions of radio listeners from all of western Europe. Accordingly, the FIA had paid attention and taken some important decisions which would take sports car racing into the modern era within a year. First, for FIA-sanctioned sports car events in 1952, "fully-enveloping bodies" would be required. This spelled the official end of the infamous "cycle-fenders" which by then were clearly past their time. Imagine the drag they would register in a wind tunnel test!

Third, from 1953 on, a "Manufacturer's World Championship" would be created for sports car racing teams participating in a select list of classic events, among which would be not only Le Mans, but also the Mille Miglia, the Twenty-Four Hours of Spa, a new One-Thousand Kilometer race at the Nürburgring plus ... the season-opener, Twelve Hours of Sebring and the Carrera Panamericana at season end. The sport was going intercontinental and the reputation of high-profile manufacturers, as well as their country's reputation as industrial leaders, would be at stake. The 1952 Twenty-Four Hours of Le Mans served as a grand rehearsal for this major increase in international importance for endurance racing. What a happy coincidence that the Mercedes-Benz team was coming back into the fray just at that juncture, along with a competitive American squadron led by Briggs Cunningham. What a great *mélange* this was!

On the British side, besides the expected three works Jaguar C-Types, Aston Martin would be present with its own works team and three of the company's latest DB3s — like Cunningham, two roadsters and a coupe. The DB3 was David Brown's next step in turning the company he acquired in 1947 into a top-rung race and sports car manufacturer. For Le Mans, his three cars would be powered by the 2.6 liter version of the six-cylinder which, with three Weber carburetors, produced 138 hp at 5500 rpm. Many observers had doubts about the DB3 as its power output was quite low, especially when asked to propel the car's relatively high dry weight of 2010 lbs. On the other hand, David Brown and racing director John Wyer had secured the services of talented drivers, particularly Reg Parnell, Dennis Poore and a promising young lad named Peter Collins. Finally, two private DB2s would back up the efforts of the works team.

Two works Allard J2Xs were entered, with lead drivers being Sydney Allard and Zora Arkus-Duntov. As Sydney Allard was striving to keep up with the big guys and new regulations, the J2X chassis was now clothed in a full-width body. This made it look less "agricultural," as one reporter put it, but it was still pretty crude. As to Donald Healey, he entered two Nash-Healeys. These cars were the result of a new joint venture between Healey and American

Le Mans, June 14, 1952. Briggs Cunningham leaves the grid ahead of three Ferraris and a Nash Healey (number 11). Number 15 is the Rosier/Trintignant 340 America of Equipe France; number 62, the Ascari/Villoresi 250 S Berlinetta; number 30, the Pagnibon/Tom Cole 225 S. Of these cars, only the C-4R would finish. Tom Cole would die at Le Mans the following year in a Chinetti-entered Ferrari 340 MM.

manufacturer Nash-Kelvinator aiming at selling a made-for-America British sports car in large numbers (for the category) in the United States. The engine was the 4135 cc six-cylinder Nash Ambassador unit; the chassis was a modified Silverstone; the body was a clumsily re-robed Silverstone too, while the driver pair of the two special Le Mans roadsters would be British and French: Les Johnson and Tommy Wisdom plus Pierre Veyron and Yves Giraud-Cabantous. This was the most international *"équipe"* of the entire field!

On the French side, Talbot would be fielding three T 26 GS *barquettes* and Gordini two cars, one being their new 2.3 liter six-cylinder rocket. The three Talbots were an evolution of the 1950 winner, with the well-known and reliable 4.5 liter six-cylinder in-line Lago engine. Now the light-blue cars sported an all-enveloping aluminum body, two being shaped and built by French *carrossier* Dugarreau and one by Talbot itself, though still much inspired by the *carrossier*. Aesthetically, those cars, though clumsily flat-sided and not shaped by wind tunnel testing, looked reasonably good by the standards of the day. More important, their basic mechanics, from engine to chassis to suspension, were all improved and well-proven. Hence they were potential winners and the driver teams, Levegh-Marchand, Mairesse-Meyrat and Pozzi-Chaboud, were of high caliber.

Conversely, Gordini's best hopes for overall victory were placed in only one car, the new 2.3 liter T22 *bar-*

153

quette. With a fantastic weight-to-horsepower ratio, it would be co-driven by two renowned French drivers: Jean Behra and Robert Manzon. Simca having officially pulled out of racing, Gordini was now an independent manufacturer. Capital financing, always the Achille's heel of Amédée Gordini, had therefore become even tighter, making intensive testing of any kind nearly impossible.

The Italian camp would be led by Ferrari, as had now been customary in international sports cars races for three years. The Maranello factory would have seven cars representing the Prancing Horse, two of its own, two fielded by Luigi Chinetti and three by different private teams. Four of those would be the marque's most potent model, the 340 America, and one would be the prototype 250 S of Mille Miglia fame. The latter, one of the two works cars, would be driven by Italian champions Alberto Ascari and Luigi Villoresi; the other works car, a 340 America, would be entrusted to two well-known French drivers: René Dreyfus and namesake though unrelated Pierre-Louis Dreyfus, racing under his *nom de course* "Heldé." This subterfuge helped separate his professional activities as a prominent Parisian banker from his true love, car racing. Chinetti would co-drive one of his 340s with French driver Jean Lucas and entrust another to the reliable Simon-Vincent French pair. Ecurie France entrusted a third 340 America, this one a *barchetta*, to French champions Louis Rosier and Maurice Trintignant. On the eve of the race, Ferrari looked like a steamroller. Finally, Lancia had entered two of its fast and lightweight B20s also with talented pairs of drivers, the star being Felice Bonetto.

Le Mans, June 14, 1952

The 1952 edition of the French classic became even more of a promising event in the week preceding the race. Not only was it going to be a *bataille royale* between major teams of five countries, including the returning Germans and a full-fledged American Equipe, but suddenly aerodynamics and brakes were the talk of the pitlane. The performance of the wind tunnel-tested Mercedes-Benz 300 SL at the Mille Miglia had made everyone else incredibly nervous. The Stuttgart company could not have chosen a better moment to come out with its new racer. Not only was

1952 the first year when full-width bodies were mandated (requiring a lot of old sheet metal to be scrapped and fresh one to be shaped) but Le Mans was *the* circuit where aerodynamics counted the most.

During the twenty-four hours of the race, the lead cars were expected to complete over 270 laps, meaning they would have to go down the 3.7 miles of the Mulsanne straight that many times. At speeds of over 150 mph, superior aerodynamics could translate into a substantial gain at every pass. So, of course, would engine reliability at maximum revs. At the end of the straight, where lurks the less-than-ninety degree Mulsanne corner, brakes capable of slowing the massive kinetic energy of one-ton racers from their top speed to less than 50 mph were needed. To quote John Fitch, "If the straight is an engine destroyer, the slow corner at the end of it is the prime cause for brake failure at Le Mans. The grinding punishment of slowing from top velocity down to about 40 mph for the Mulsanne Corner is simply too much for conventional brake design, and restraint must be used beginning with the first lap. The scarred bank testifies to countless cases of over-optimism."

Two major surprises resulting from these new calculations became quite visible during the practice week preceding the race. Jaguar showed up with its three C-Types wearing completely modified bodywork. Mercedes-Benz experimented with a spectacular roof-mounted air brake with a surface area of 7.64 sq. ft. Both companies were trying to gain a last-minute advantage to win the most prestigious endurance race in the world. Stirling Moss had been so shocked by the 300 SL's top speed in the Mille Miglia that he had sent a telegram to Sir William Lyons, the Head of Jaguar, before even flying back to London, saying; "must have more speed at Le Mans." With only three weeks to go before departure for France was scheduled, Sir Lyons had had to make a quick, critical decision in early May.

The fearful memory of the German dominance of pre-war years undoubtedly entered into his considerations. He decided to order a rush streamlining of the proven C-Type's shape, which his body designer Malcolm Sayer translated into a longer, lower sloping nose and a longer, wedge-shaped tail. The lower nose required a rearrangement of the

Credit: Briggs S. Cunningham III Collection

radiator and cooling system, all of which kept the Coventry team extraordinarily busy throughout the month of May. On the German side, Neubauer knew only too well that the 300 SL was really not as fast as Moss believed, a real 150 mph versus an imagined 160 plus. He also knew that Jaguar had accumulated tremendous racing experience in the previous years, whereas this would only be his 300 SL's second race and the first post-war Le Mans for the Stuttgart team. He was more worried about the weight of his cars and the added stress on the brakes at the end of the Mulsanne straight. The 300 SL weighed in at 1914 lbs., 150 lbs. higher than the target that had been set at the project's initiation, though still lighter than the Jaguar.

That is why the air brake solution was being tested. While it would add some drag when feathered, it would dramatically reduce brake and tire wear lap after lap when deployed — tilted upwards. This solution was not retained for the race as the two roof pylons on which the air brake was articulated could not sustain the tremendous aerodynamic force applied to them backwards by deployment. Still, the device achieved a useful purpose for Mercedes-Benz: the daring innovativeness and spectacular visual effect of the air brake during the practice sessions had everyone convinced the German dominance could very well be unbeatable right off the gate. Interestingly, Ferrari was not concerned much by aerodynamics, counting on the power and reliability of its famous V-12, plus the instinctu-

LEFT: Mexico, November 19, 1952. The 300 SL number 4 of Kling/Klenk is being serviced during the first stage of the Carrera Panamericana. As required by the Le Mans authorities, the doors are now longer, overlapping on the side of the car. They would become the trademark of that remarkable automobile.

RIGHT: Le Mans, June 14, 1952. Briggs Cunningham at speed in front of the grandstands. Nursing a weak clutch and fearing his friend and co-driver Bill "Hammer" Spear would kill said clutch, Cunningham drove 20 of the 24 hours.

al feel of Touring's and Vignale's body designs, to beat the wind. The wind, however, was changing fast.

The Toughest Test Of All

At 4 pm exactly, as tradition dictated, Charles Faroux lowered the French Tricolors — one did not use a green flag in France — and off sprinted fifty-seven men in white overalls towards their cars in front of a record crowd of over 350,000. Everybody expected a giant duel between the three Mercedes-Benz, the three Jaguars and the big Ferraris. It would turn out to be much more interesting. The Cunninghams were impressively strong at the start. Fitch led the first lap, followed by Walters in the C-4RK. Fitch then had to pit briefly to get an errant plug wire reattached so he could race on with all eight cylinders firing, while Walters increased his lead over Stirling Moss and the rest of the field. By the second hour, two of the works Jaguar were out and the third would retire two hours later. The rushed re-design triggered by Stirling Moss turned out to be a disaster: the re-arranged cooling system was flawed and the engines overheated so quickly, head gaskets failed on two Jaguars. Poor welding attachments broke on the third.

Several Ferraris also disappeared from the field early, including two of most hopeful 340 Americas, both due to clutch failure, and the very fast 250 S works car of Ascari-Villoresi. The pace imposed by increasing speeds was tak-

Credit: Briggs S. Cunningham III Collection

ing a heavy toll early. One of the three Cunninghams, the roadster driven by Fitch-Rice, had joined these cars in early retirement. Remembers Fitch, "The Cunningham started with a bang, one might say, but later retired with another bang, this one in the valve train." Meanwhile the other two were way back in the field. Briggs Cunningham influenced by former Midwest racer, Phil Walters, had taken a bet on two young American oval racers as teammates for two of three cars at Le Mans: Duane Carter for Phil Walters and George Rice for John Fitch. When Carter first took over from Walters at 6:30 pm, their car held a strong second spot. The veteran Indy driver, though, promptly plowed the big American roadster into the Tetre Rouge sandbank, eventually taking nearly three hours to dig it out. This was one of Briggs Cunningham's extremely rare unwise driver decisions.

After the British disaster became complete, and to everyone's surprise, the Mercedes team was not the one on top. Instead, as dusk turned into night, two French cars were pacing the race. The surprising leader was the Gordini 2.3 liter of Behra-Manzon, followed by the Talbot of Levegh-Marchand. The French public was in a nearly delirious state. Two Mercedes coupes came next, followed by the first Ferrari, the 340 America of Chinetti-Lucas. The night at Le Mans is always treacherous. It proved terminal to nearly twenty additional cars, including some of the remaining potential winners. Before the twelfth stroke of midnight, the Cunningham coupe of Walters-Carter (valves) and the Mercedes-Benz of Kling-Klenk (dynamo) had both retired. In the early hours, two more Ferraris, private entries, bit the dust. Next was the Talbot of Mairesse-Meyrat due to oil pump failure.

The little Gordini lost its front brakes just before 4 am, while still in the lead. It soon retired, ceding the prize position to the big Talbot driven almost constantly by Pierre Levegh. French racing blue was still in the lead, but the back up ranks were thinning quickly. In the darkest of the night, around 5:00 am, a *coup de théatre* took place in the Ferrari pits: the 340 America driven by Luigi Chinetti, then lying in fifth place and still with a shot at victory, was disqualified for refueling outside of the time limits dictated by the race regulations! As a result, there was only one Ferrari

left, the second Chinetti entry co-driven by Simon-Vincent. It was holding fourteenth place at that moment. The wind was turning fast indeed.

When dawn broke, blinding banks of fog were drifting slowly over most of the course. Pierre Levegh and his Talbot were still firmly in the lead, with a four-lap advantage over the next car, the Mercedes 300 SL driven by neophytes Helfrich-Niedermayr. Third was the other Mercedes still running, the car entrusted to the more experienced drivers, Lang-Riess. The Aston Martin DB3 of Macklin-Collins was a surprising fourth. The second Talbot *barquette* of Pozzi-Chaboud was fifth. The last remaining Cunningham (Cunningham-Spear) was holding seventh place and the last remaining Ferrari ninth. By 10 am on Sunday, only twenty cars out of the original fifty-seven were still racing. This was already an all-time record attrition rate for Le Mans and there were still six hours to go!

The race by now seemed Levegh's and Talbot for sure, as the French driver knew the course infinitely better than his German pursuers. Similar Talbots also had both won the 1950 edition and finished second to Jaguar in 1951. The French public, the hundreds of thousands strewn about the course and the millions glued to their radios, was transfixed. So were other millions of radio listeners in all of western Europe, especially in Germany, Italy and even still, Great Britain. Somehow, almost undetected, the homely-looking Nash-Healey co-driven by Les Johnson and Tommy Wisdom had moved up from eleventh to sixth place during the night. It seemed quite fresh compared to some of the remaining opposition.

As to Briggs Cunningham, he surely felt happy that he still had one car in the top ten given the extraordinarily severe attrition rate of the race. Especially, since it was the C-4R he was co-driving with Bill Spear. Barring a miracle, his car was too far back still to have a shot at overall victory. But "Mr. C." had a shot at a top three placement yet, a great accomplishment for such a fledgling racer. As he was rocketing down the Mulsanne straight about every five minutes on that Sunday morning, the American sportsman may have wished that millions of people in the United States were also following his quest on the radio. He knew only too well it was not the case.

The Hare and the Tortoise

At noon, Pierre Levegh was still in command of the race, though perhaps not himself. He had now been driving for almost eighteen hours, refusing to hand the big light blue car to his young co-driver. Though Pierre Levegh carried the hopes and pride of his whole country, it was his car after all. He had sensed there might be a problem with the engine and decided only he could nurse the Talbot to a successful finish. At each refueling stop, however, Pierre Levegh looked increasingly tired, as any 47-year-old man would look after half as much effort. In a Mercedes-Benz film documentary of the 1952 Le Mans race, at each successive refueling stop in the last hours, Levegh looks increasingly limp, to the point where he has to be lifted out of and back into the Talbot. Still, on he went, with two "Silver Arrows" behind him. His margin of safety looked good: four laps still.

Shortly before the clock struck 2 pm, two more cars within the top ten retired: the last of the three Aston Martin DB3s and the Talbot of Pozzi-Chaboud. With only one hundred and twenty minutes to go, and a steady four-lap lead, Levegh seemed to have it made. Behind him, the two turtle-shaped German 300 SLs were lying in wait, but without much hope. There were clear signs, though of erratic driving from the leading Talbot's driver. His lap times varied greatly and inconsistently, between 5:03 and 5:20. Such a difference would never be displayed by a fresh professional driver, who would be expected to operate within a bracket of no more than two or three seconds a lap. The lead Stuttgart pursuer was now the Lang-Riess car. Behind the two "Silver Arrows" were the amazing Nash Healey of Johnson-Wisdom, then Briggs Cunningham in his C-4R. He too was nursing his own car and not handing it over to co-driver Bill Spear.

The sun that had graced the start on Saturday was again shining bright when the big clock at the start/finish line began to get close the 3 pm mark, though the shadows were slowly beginning to get longer. The lead positions had been steady for the previous two hours. All of France was aware of the pending victory, anxious to see the end. Ten minutes before 3 pm, Pierre Levegh was racing ahead down the Mulsanne straight at over 140 mph. After driving

Le Mans, June 14, 1952. Early in the long race, two dazzling 300 SLs run in tandem. Number 20 is the Helfrich/Niedermayer car which would finish second. Number 22 is the Kling/Klenk car which would retire at the eighth hour. The winning car bore number 21. It was the first closed car ever to win Le Mans.

for more than twenty-two hours, he only had twelve more laps to complete. Fatigue, not Mercedes, was the enemy. He was now braking for the Mulsanne corner, shifting down into second gear, a hand maneuver Levegh had managed thousands of times in the preceding hours. Instead, the gear went into first, sending the engine screaming far above the red tach line. Moments later, a crankshaft bolt gave. Past the Arnage Corner, before the Maison Blanche right-hander leading back to the main straight, the Talbot came to an irretrievable standstill. Levegh was so weak, he had to be lifted out of his car by spectators. All was lost, including honor.

Even Alfred Neubauer could not believe his luck! From one minute to the next, he and the Mercedes-Benz team moved from a good finish to absolute victory at Le Mans, the first for the marque in its entire history! Indeed, when the checkered flag was waved at 4 pm, it was a Mercedes-Benz one-two, with the amazing Nash-Healey in third! Not only did this race turn into a nightmare for France, and a disaster for both Jaguar and Ferrari — only one Ferrari finished, in fifth place — it was an colossal triumph for Germany! Porsche added insult to injury by winning the 1100cc class with a 356/4 co-driven again by Veuillet-Mouche —eleventh overall. Cunningham scored big points by finishing fourth, though almost nobody in Europe worried about an American menace. The big threat

157

was always the guy just across the border, in whatever cardinal direction that border might have been drawn.

The French felt so insulted by this latest Teutonic victory, they refused to play the German national anthem — Deutschland Über Alles — at the award ceremonies. In turn, the German team felt quite insulted. Old European rivalries never die. In addition, the Second World War was still fresh in memories and emotions remained strong. These were naturally not helped, on the French side, by a stark reminder of another humiliating German victory which remained standing between Mulsanne and Arnage, in the form of a Nazi prison camp tower. For those who wished to remember, the infield at Le Mans had even served at one point as a major Luftwaffe airfield, until allied bombers turned it into a moonscape in 1944.

Revenge stirs the imagination. Though no woman driver even started the 1952 race, the *Coupe des Dames*, normally awarded to the best placed female crew, was award-

Watkins Glen, September, 1952 - The Nash Healey number 10 which finished third at Le Mans is showcased near the start/finish line by the importer.

ed "out of sympathy" to a teary Mrs. Levegh. The very evening of the race, French radio, in a tone appropriate for a national mourning, nearly claimed that France was "robbed" of a rightful victory. Said André Labarthe over the airwaves "Levegh and Marchand were victims of a mechanical failure. The Germans have won everything again! Millions of French citizens are going to be gripped by a deep sense shame and discomfort." The next day, these words would prove almost understandable, as both the German and international press proclaimed in major headlines, "The Mercedes-Benz 300 SL is the Best Sports Car in the World!"

When the hysteria is taken out of the reflective equation, one can find rational explanations for what happened at Le Mans in June, 1952. Clearly, the bar for international sports car racing had just been raised substantially. The winning Mercedes, though not the fastest car in the field in terms of top speed, still broke both the overall speed and distance records at the end of the twenty-four hours: 2,320 miles and 96.67 mph. That was 76 miles and 3.2 mph better than the preceding record established by the winning Jaguar the year earlier — admittedly in less favorable weather conditions. Before he was forced to retire due to clutch failure, Alberto Ascari and his Ferrari 250 S established a new overall fastest lap in 4:40.5 or 107.595 mph, 2.363 mph faster that Stirling Moss in the 1951 Jaguar C. This raised benchmark, in turn, made every aspect of the sport, from the men, the planning process and every key component of their cars, a critical link in the chain that could make the difference between victory or defeat.

That is how the various fates of Jaguar, Mercedes and Ferrari were almost pre-determined. Jaguar's one-month redesign rush job almost insured the marque's total failure. Neubauer and the Mercedes-Benz team had been training and testing systematically since April, with absolute German rigor. While luck played a factor in their sensational victory, as even Neubauer admitted, "luck comes to the prepared man." As to Enzo Ferrari, he should have taken the 1952 race as a serious warning: while Maranello's V-12 was still the fastest in the field, his cars' level of preparation had become insufficient. Losing six out of seven cars is a strong signal! They were also falling behind in key

technical areas, such as brakes and aerodynamics. In this overall context, the fourth place gained by Briggs Cunningham and Bill Spear in their C-4R was remarkable. The question now for the small West Palm Beach company was how to keep pace with this greatly accelerated rate of progress?

As to the French, they had now but two marques vying for possible overall victory, and the picture did not look promising. Amédée Gordini was a true engineering genius and a charistmatic leader of men. Unlike Enzo Ferrari, however, business acumen was not his forte. Now devoid of official Simca support, Gordini had gained more experimental freedom, as his brilliant V-8 demonstrated, but he also had lost a nearly guaranteed source of basic funds. The French goverment had little interest in him, since Gordini was indulging in "a rich man's sports," unlike René Bonnet who was building "little cars for everyday people." Gordini's ultimate fate appeared shaky. As to Talbot, Toni Lago was also a fabulous engineer. Unfortunately, he was dealing in large engines and luxury cars which the French state was quickly taxing out of existence.

Then there was Pierre Levegh. His real last name was Bouillon. He had held such a long-standing obsession with winning Le Mans that he had become known as "The Bishop" for his somber seniority. He had come close many times, but never succeeded. Once again in 1952, his personal Holy Grail had cruelly slipped from his grasp. He would race on and try again, only to become a central figure in the most tragic chapter of motor racing history.

Back to America

In the Spring and early Summer of 1952, the bulk of the American racing season took place on the west coast. Cal Club staged its third Palm Springs event on March 23. Chuck Manning won in his Mercury Special. The third Pebble Beach race was held on April 20 under the auspices of the SCCA. Bill Pollack won the big race in an 6.0 liter Carstens-Allard-Cadillac after a fierce battle with a Ferrari 212 Inter and several Jaguars. Next came Bridgehampton in the East, then a new venue and event back West: the Golden Gate Park race in San Francisco proper on May 31. First winner was Bill Pollack in his "invincible" Allard in

front of an estimated 90,000 spectators. The second race at Torrey Pines was held by the SCCA on July 20 and won brilliantly by Phil Hill in his new Ferrari 212 Export. When the checkered flag was waved at him, Hill had lapped the entire field! The Californian had switched to a Ferrari earlier in the year following his desire to start winning big races. He bought the 2.6 liter *barchetta* from Luigi Chinetti. This was the first step in a long and successful relationship between Phil Hill and Ferrari that would culminate to a World Championship in 1961, the first Formula 1 title for an American driver.

The SCCA show returned east on August 16 for the second race at Thompson, Connecticut. Briggs Cunningham finished first and John Fitch second, making it a first one-two for the C-4Rs. A car capable of finishing in the top five at Le Mans in 1952 could certainly be expected to dominate American races, especially with the top driving talent the team also enjoyed. It is unfortunate that the Cunninghams were not entered into west coast races until much later and only once, actually March Field (Riverside) in November of the following year. A week after Thompson, on August 24, it was back west again, this time in Stockton, California, a town situated in the San Joachin Valley about one hundred miles east of San Fransisco. The field was good but not top flight. The race was won by Sam Weiss in an Allard, followed by promising Jack McAfee in a John Edgar-owned 340 MM Ferrari. Now, until the fall, the American road racing circuit would move back east in two steps for the two biggest races of the calendar: Elkhart Lake on September 7 and Watkins Glen on September 21.

Wisconsin, September 7, 1952

This would be the third Elkhart Lake event, but truly the first "big" Elkhart Lake race. With few exceptions, all of the best and fastest American drivers of the day were there. With the sole exception of the Mercedes-Benz 300 SL, all the big cars that had competed at Le Mans were represented in Wisconsin, such as two Jaguar C-Types, one brought in by Charles Hornburg for Phil Hill and the other by Max Hoffman for George Weaver, or Bill Spear's Ferrari 340 America, or even cars that had actually raced at

© Julian Silverberg

© Julian Silverberg

Le Mans, such as the three Cunninghams. A crowd of near-ly 100,000 spectators had assembled in and around the vil-lage to see the two-day show. There would be three races as in 1951, the main event being once more the "200" endurance race, which would require drivers to complete thirty-one laps of the revised roller-coaster-like circuit, now expanded to 6.5 miles. Phil Hill won the Sheldon Cup (100-miler) on Saturday in Hornburg's C-Type Jaguar after an incredible start-to-finish battle with Phil Walters driving Alan Guiberson's Ferrari 212 Export. The two cars finished a mere second apart.

In the big race on Sunday, John Fitch was the defend-ing champion. With the C-4R, he certainly had a car with which he could repeat his success of the previous year. But Cunningham and Walters (in the coupe) would go for the top prize just as hard, while the two C-Type Jaguars and Spear's Ferrari would certainly not give Fitch any quarter either. In fact, Phil Walters took the early lead in the C-

TOP LEFT: Elkhart Lake, 1952 - Jim Kimberly testing his Ferrari 340 America. The number 5 was his dedicated racing number when-ever allowed.

TOP RIGHT: Elkhart Lake, 1952 - Phil Walters races across the Wisconsin countryside in a 2.6 liter Vignale-bodied berlinetta. Phil Hill would beat Walters for the first time with the Hornburg C-Type Jaguar.

4RK. After seven laps, however, John Fitch took it from him, never to relinquish it again. At one point, Phil Hill got his Jaguar past the two trailing Cunninghams and not far behind Fitch, but then he was slowed by a broken tailpipe. Fitch finished the race in 2 hours 16:13.4, for an overall average of 87.5 mph. His car reached top speeds of over 140 mph without the benefit of a very long straight. Phil Walters finished second and Cunningham third, for a com-plete "Mr. C." triumph. The two runners up were Phil Hill and George Weaver, in that order, in their respective C-Type Jaguars. The first Allard was sixth, showing that even in America, Sydney Allard's old design was reaching its sunset.

Watkins Glen, September 20, 1952

Since mid-week, the streets of Watkins Glen and the roads all around the village had been filled with people milling about and exotic race cars shrieking occasionally in various garages. In fact, streams of spectators, participants and crews had been descending upon the hilly landscape surrounding Watkins Glen every day since Monday. Even before dawn on Saturday, it seemed all of Schuyler County had been invaded and was occupied by an encamped for-eign army!

Wrote Joseph J. Lane in the December, 1952 of *Road & Track*, "On Friday night, the whole course was lined by campfires as the more rugged braved the cool air ... the hotels as far away as one hundred miles were crammed with people, there being more MGs around the course than Fords. At 3 am Saturday morning, the course was one six-mile traffic jam as people tried to find places to park and catch a few hours of sleep. All night long the main street of town was alive, with refreshment stands going full tilt. Cars from every state of the Union and Canada could be seen lining the streets and side roads. As the sky dawned clear and blue, campfires glowed up again, eggs and bacon filled the air..."

This was terrific for local commerce. It was estimated after the 1951 event that about a million dollars (1951 dollars) had been contributed to local merchants, hoteliers and restaurateurs. This was also great for residents with even a tiny patch of land to rent. To quote Henry Valent from his 1958 book *Road Racing at Watkins Glen*, "The parking of cars became a racket. In the village, practically all vacant lawns were hired out for parking. The farmers having land adjoining the circuit made excellent parking income. The parking rates or fees were not regular. It ranged from a quarter on up, yes to ten dollars for a choice spot." Ironically, since the local committee could not find a practical way to charge spectators an entry fee given the extent of the circuit, spectators did not pay for attending the races, resulting, in 1951, in a staggering loss for the local committee and the SCCA of $280,000.

A key reason for this renewed popular invasion, besides the great success of the previous year, was the quality of the field promised in the press for the 1952 event. Close to one hundred cars were indeed there, including four Cunninghams (the three C-4s, and a C-2) of Le Mans fame, two C-Type Jaguars, seven Allards, four Porsches, several OSCAs and Siatas, one Aston Martin, one Nash-Healey and a number of new American specials. The best drivers were top talent, such as Fitch, Walters, Cunningham, Phil Hill, and Kimberly were also present. If the 1951 event had been so great as told by thousands and amply reported in the fast growing specialized press, this one was going to be the best Watkins Glen Grand Prix ever. You had to be there!

Watkins Glen, September 1952 - The Kieft of Richard Irish and crowds enjoying the Fifth Grand Prix weekend.

The Program

The organization of the race had been entrusted to George Shannon who was named Grand Prix Chairman. He would work under the supervision of key SCCA officers including, of course, Fred Wacker and Col. George Felton. Cameron Argetsinger was completely out of the picture. In 1952 he and wife Jean chose to move their home from Youngstown, Ohio to a permanent residence in Burdett near Watkins Glen. Cameron, now equipped with a law degree, also needed to establish his practice in Watkins Glen on Franklin Street. He indeed had many mouths to feed. Seven children, soon to be nine, were now part of the Cameron Argetsinger family!

Since the 1951 program structure had been a success, it was wisely decided to keep the same formula, with minor modifications. Technical inspection would now take place from the Tuesday to Thursday preceding the race, 9 am to 6 pm at Smalley's Garage. This allowed more time for proper inspection of the large number of machines entered. Friday would see the Drivers' Meeting at the

© Harold Lance

Courthouse at 11 am, then the Concours d'Elégance at 3 pm. Race day would be inaugurated at 10:45 am with the eight-lap Seneca Cup race. The unrestricted event would be followed at 12:15 pm by the fifteen-lap Queen Catharine Cup for cars under 1500 cc. Finally, the Grand Prix would start at 3 pm over a distance of fifteen laps also. A formal presentation of prizes at the Watkins Glen High School Auditorium was added and would take place at 9 pm. Based on the previous year's experience, practice laps were not even planned for the day before the races. Instead, the organizers decided to allow three hot running laps before the official start of each of the three races.

Even Stronger Safety Measures, Even Bigger Crowds

To avoid a repeat of the crowd control problems experienced in 1951, the organizers took several new measures. Preparation for the race was begun much earlier than in previous years. More snow fencing was unfurled along key sections of the track, to the point that "all that was available in the county was used." More volunteers were recruited from Sampson Air Force Base. The circuit-wide

TOP: Watkins Glen, September 1952 - A Bugatti Type 30 A at the Concours d'Elégance.

BOTTOM: A Bugatti Type 57 SC at the Concours.

communications system set-up by Fred German was further improved. Finally, safety zones were established in many places. On Friday, chicanes made of haybales were even installed at the railroad crossing in an attempt to slow down the drivers at that high-speed straight with a speed bump.

The AAA Contest Board was directly involved in all the safety measures in cooperation with the SCCA Contest Board, of which John Fitch was now Chairman. Based on the experience of the previous year, the AAA had insisted that each approach of a corner for all three races be officially declared a no-passing zone. Against the protest of some people, the rule was adopted, and the drivers had been briefed accordingly on Saturday morning. This seemed an odd measure for a sport whose main purpose was passing. Generally speaking, rules that are well-intended but decreed by people who really don't have direct experience with the matter at hand almost always have unintended results. The AAA did not see things that way.

Still, these additional improvements on the strong security precautions already adopted in 1951 were thorough and complete. They were the state of the art in America, far ahead of anybody else. The problem was that

Credit: C.H.A. Davison; credit E. Davison Collection

the crowd of spectators grew substantially between 1951 and 1952. Again the estimates vary widely. The Chamber of Commerce says the most likely number was 35,000 — still a seventeen percent increase over their count of the previous year. At the other end, *Road & Track* said, "almost a quarter million people." By looking at photos of various parts of the course on race day, and comparing these to the size of a crowd filling a 50,000 capacity stadium, for example, it seems safe to say that over 150,000 people were present that day. The visual impression of just the people strung in huge clumps along the six blocks of Franklin Street that were part of the course appears to approach the total attendance estimate of the Chamber of Commerce.

The Field For The Seneca Cup

George Weaver had won the previous Cup in his famous 1936 Grand Prix Maserati, after one prior successful try. He was going to go for an encore. Therefore, he was the most serious contender. Phil Cade would also be back with his own Maserati V8RI, presumably fine-tuned since the year before. That also made him an automatic candidate for victory. A third Maserati Grand Prix racer, this an 8CTF, was entered by Bret Harte Hannaway. In the category of old machinery finely re-tuned were two cars also considered as potential winners due to their sheer power. First was the huge Lagonda Special entrusted Sherwood Johnston. The chassis, frame and sheet metal were that of a 1937 Le Mans Racer. The engine was a most modern Chrysler V-8 Hemi. Next was "Old Grey Mare," the Ladd Special entered by Fred White of Cahasset, Massachusetts, this time. True to its name, the car was now well into its twentieth year of racing, though its original Ford Model T engine had long since been replaced by the Ford Flathead V-8.

Then there was Bill Milliken. True to his own words about the importance of an "open formula," he was fielding an entirely original car with unique technology in the Seneca Cup. Built by a British amateur racer by the name of Archie J. Butterworth, it was a truly special Special. Shortly after World War II, Butterworth had combined a highly eclectic assemblage of components into a single-

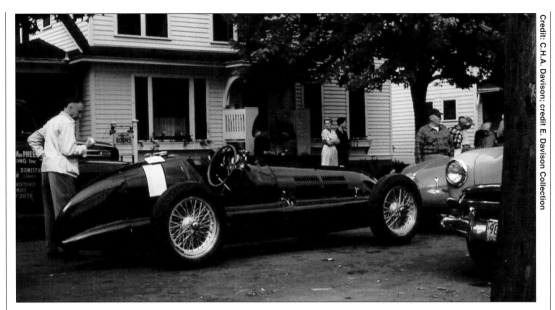

Watkins Glen, September 1952 - The Maserati 8CTF Bret Hannaway entered in the Seneca Cup. The 1939 Grand Prix racer had a straight-eight 3.0 liter supercharged engine. The car did not start.

seater racing car with tremendous power. The Willys chassis carried a four-wheel-drive Jeep transmission, a 4.4 liter (270 ci) air-cooled V-8 Steyr engine acquired from a captured German tank, and a *monoposto* body devoid of front sheet metal and looking like an American sprinter. The engine was said to deliver a amount of horsepower "in the hundreds," but a reliable figure would be around 250.

Bill Milliken had acquired what was called the "AJB," after the initals of its creator, a few months before and after Butterworth smashed his car and put it up for sale. When the Cornell Lab people opened the crate in which the racer had been shipped, they found it almost "crumpled into a ball." They eventually fixed it, but from then on, Milliken's Special would be known as the "Butterball." Though Milliken had never finished a race at the Glen, his new mount could not be discounted because of its tremendous power and four-wheel-drive.

The joker in that Seneca Cup would certainly be the beautiful silver Jaguar C-Type entered by Max Hoffman and entrusted to John Fitch. While its engine displaced as much as fifty percent less than some of the cars above, this was a Le Mans-proven European thoroughbred, with one of the top three American drivers of the moment at the

163

Credit: John Fitch Collection

wheel. Underlining the importance for the marque of the American market in general, and of racing in particular, both Sir William Lyons and Racing Director Lofty England were in attendance at Watkins Glen. This leaves little doubt that had the Argetsingar/Ulmann point of view prevailed within the SCCA, a Jaguar works team would have been present for the 1952 Grand Prix.

Other cars in the Seneca Cup would compete for class victories. Among these were six Formula 3 (500 cc) racers, four Coopers, a Kieft and an Effyh. Another class victory contender would be the familiar H.R.G. to be driven by Fritz Koster aiming for Class F (1100 cc to 1500 cc), along with Arthur Iselin, brother of Peter, in a Lea Francis. The field was diverse, full of happy surprises and promised a great race. Spectators were by now anxious to see a race. The sun was shining bright, stomachs were fed, let the show begin!

The 1952 Seneca Cup

By 10 am on Saturday, as organizers were touring the course to make sure that the masses of spectators were under control circuit-wide, one could feel tension building tangibly all around. The weather was gorgeous, but the air

TOP LEFT: Watkins Glen, September 1952 - John Fitch in the silver C-Type Jaguar with which he won the Seneca Cup.

BOTTOM RIGHT: Watkins Glen, September 1952 - Robert H. Fergus and crew push his MG towards the starting grid for the Queen Catharine Cup. Fergus, a former WW II fighter pilot, saw his first car race at the Glen in 1950. Shortly thereafter, he quit his job as Cadillac salesman in Columbus, Ohio, bought himself this MG and started racing.

of festivity that had reigned around Watkins Glen for three days was now turning to deep anticipation. For many, this emotion was a blend of intense joy and anticipation of terrific power about to be loudly unleashed. For others, the thrill was a sense of danger to be conquered by a firm resolve to keep watching the spectacle from up close without blinking. By 10:30 am, the sonic mayhem of twenty racers of all sorts coming to life all at once on Franklin Street in order to take up their assigned grid positions made this maelstrom of human emotions spin even faster.

The cars were now lined up in pairs down from the start/finish line. Drivers were constantly gunning their engine in a staccato of high shrieks rising from a flood of booming waves of deeper sounds. By 10:43, the visual aspect of the spectacle seemed nearly frozen, as the cars stood still on the grid and Nils Mickelson stepped onto the asphalt with his furled green flag. Everything looked fine to him, so he waved his standard and released the drivers for their three "open" practice laps. The decibels along Franklin Street rose by another quantum leap. Pair by pair, the howling herd passed by the Courthouse, then disappeared after taking the right turn leading to Old Corning Hill. Further uphill, near Seneca Lodge for instance, the sonic shock waves slightly muffled by distance and trees joyfully signaled the beginning of the festivities for which so many had come and waited.

Credit: Bob Fergus Collection

After completing three "practice laps," the drivers would reform the same grid they had just left behind, then be released again for the eight lap race. The thrill of being "free to race," even though this was just a brief practice session, was too much for some of the drivers, and some of the cars. First to drop out was the Maserati 8CTF of Bret Hannaway. Even before Stone Bridge, the Mount Vernon, New York, driver spun out and the Maserati engine stalled. It could not be restarted. Next to go was young Canadian Richard Mauron in an MG TD. The railroad straight leading to the crossing was too much of a thrill for him. He entered the haybale chicane too fast, which sent his car into a series of barrel rolls. Miraculously, Mauron was not seriously hurt, but the chicane was a mess.

Now the lead cars, still on their first lap, were heading down Big Bend. Milliken approached the corner he had unwittingly named four years before. Somehow, just like in 1948, he entered the ninety degree bend past the Steuben Building too fast. In the short stretch of Fourth Street leading back to Franklin Street, he spun, hit a light pole and broke a wheel of his "Butterball." Bill Milliken was a brilliant engineer, executive director and an effective booster of road racing. His driving skills were said to be quite good, but his luck at the Glen was terrible. A fourth car dropped out during the practice laps: the 500 cc Kieft of Richard Irish. When the grid reformed on the village's main street, only sixteen contenders were left.

Before giving the Seneca Cup its official start, the organizers made a wise decision. Based on the Richard Mauron accident at the railroad crossing, they decided to remove the haybale chicane, as it was clearly more a hazard than a safety device. They simply declared the railroad crossing a no-passing zone. Some time was lost in the decision making and the actual removal of the haybales. The grid of sixteen cars had now reformed. When all was clear, Nils Mickelson waved his green flag one more time, and off the racers went again.

George Weaver and his big Maserati shot ahead to take an early lead, with John Fitch and his silver Jaguar in hot pursuit. At the end of the first lap, Weaver crossed the start/finish line in the lead in 5:03, or 78 mph. Fitch was not far behind him and Fred White was riding "Old Grey

Watkins Glen, September 1952 - Otto Linton's Siata V-8 approaching School House Corner, shortly before Stone Bridge.

© Harold Lance

Mare" in third. One more car was sidelined during this first lap, Otto Linton's Siata. Fitch started putting the pressure on Weaver in the second lap and by the time the two lead cars reappeared on Franklin Street, only a few car lengths separated them. Meanwhile, the other Maserati V8RI was black-flagged, as it was pouring a generous amount of oil on the track. For the second year in a row, Phil Cade was out of luck.

First Pass at 'Lil

The third lap saw the battle between the old Maserati and the new Jaguar reach a peak of intensity. Fitch was now right behind Weaver, looking for the opportunity to pass. In that endeavor, he suffered some handicap from the large plumes of blue smoke the Italian racer would emit at each acceleration. Big Bend, that long fearsome plunge back into the village, was where Fitch made his move. The silver Jaguar was first to complete third lap, with the Maserati now in the chase. Amazingly, this was the first time in five years that Weaver's Maserati had ever been passed during a race at Watkins Glen! The crowds went into a wild cheer for both drivers. Behind them, it was Fred

White, then Sherwood Johnston in his enormous Lagonda pulled by its potent Chrysler Hemi.

This situation remained essentially unchanged during the fourth lap, except that John Fitch pulled away from Weaver. Wrote Lane in *Road & Track*, "The handling of the Jag by Fitch was a sight to see ... accelerating in a very straight line, never varying from the line through the corner, and swinging the steering from side to side to aid the braking in the very best continental manner." Shortly into the fifth lap, the pursuit became too much for old "Poison 'Lil." George Weaver was forced to retire due to plug problems. Fitch was now miles ahead of his next pursuer, Fred White and "Old Grey Mare." The rest of the race proceeded pretty much without major changes. John Fitch got the checkered flag in 41:31.6 for a 76.6 mph overall average. This broke the record established by Weaver in the 1951 Seneca Cup, though by a mere twelve seconds.

Two of the little Coopers and their drivers deserved great credit and were rewarded with commensurate applause. R. L. Moodie managed to place fourth, behind the Lagonda whose engine displacement was more than ten times bigger! Here was a sign that handling characteristics could have a great influence on results on tracks as difficult as Watkins Glen. The other Cooper which was wildly

TOP LEFT: John Fitch in his first MG TC flying over the railroad track in 1949. Three years later, he was driving a Jaguar C-Type, the model that won LeMans in 1951, with great talent and winning the Seneca Cup

BOTTOM RIGHT: Watkins Glen, September 1952 - Bill Spear racing his OSCA MT4 to overall victory in the Queen Catharine Cup. Here approaching School House Corner.

cheered was that of Alexis du Pont. His tiny Triumph engine gave up its soul just after the driver turned back on Franklin Street to face the last stretch. Alexis du Pont got out of his car and pushed it for several blocks to cross the finish line and therefore be classified. The final results were as follows:

End of Seneca Cup - 8 Laps - Overall Average Speed

1. John Fitch	Jaguar C-Type	76.6
2. Fred White	Ladd Ford Special	68.9
3. Sherwood Johnston	Lagonda Chrysler	67.9
4. R. L. Moodie	Cooper F3	67.8
5. Arthur Iselin	Lea Francis	67.5
6. Fritz Koster	H.R.G.	67.0

Delays and Opera Songs

The delays caused by the last-minute removal of the haybale chicane at the railroad crossing snowballed into further delays. Explained *Sports Car* magazine in their November-December 1952 edition, "Many who have visited Watkins Glen do not know that a definite schedule has to be worked out with the New York Central Railroad whose tracks and freight trains cross the roadway of the Grand Prix course. If for one reason or another the first

race does not get underway on time, a prompt start of the second race is jeopardized because of the pre-arranged schedule with the New York Central. Crowd control, together with this, again was accountable for the delay this year."

There was no Le Sabre this year to distract the crowd, but opera star James Melton was on hand, as he had been since 1948. This time, however, the organizers could take advantage of the circuit-wide loudspeaker system to regale the entire crowd with his inspired singing. Melton was game, of course, for such an opportunity. He was known to be a ham! So while train schedules were being worked out, crowds policed on various parts of the course, and expired racers removed from their temporary resting places on road sides, Melton sang a number of famous arias which were instantly broadcast over an area larger than six square miles! This might have been the first live opera performance heard in the outdoors by so many people over so big a patch of land. Whether this is correct or not, James Melton's voice had the intended effect: it helped keep spectators happily entertained.

The Field For The Queen Catharine Cup

Forty cars were to start the Queen Catharine Cup, underlining the popularity of the event. Almost half, nineteen to be exact, were MGs. Among these, three were of special note. Denver Cornett's number 7 MG, that of Stone Bridge fame in 1948, was back! Cornett had simply grown tired of giving old Indy-based machinery a try. He reverted to his first love. David Ash would drive the MG Special he had brought to sixth overall at Sebring in March. That car might prove a serious contender for the Cup. Finally, there was the MG-Offenhauser of William Lloyd. Its 1.5 liter classic racing engine could also help cause a surprise. Among the favorites to win, though, were the two OSCA MT4s of Bill Spear and Jim Kimberly. Bill Spear had won the Kimberly Cup Race with that car at Elkhart Lake earlier in the month. Kimberly's OSCA, lent him for this race by Allen Garthwaite, was of the same ilk. Both were powered by a 1342cc engine.

There was plenty of other Italian machinery in the field, including seven Siatas and a Cisitalia. These would

Watkins Glen, September 1952 - Max Goldman racing his Siata during the Queen Catharine Cup.

be vying for class wins, as would five Crosleys. One of these was entered by George Schrafft, scion of the famous restaurant family. Since the SCCA had barred professional racing for the foreseeable future, the sport would remain the domain of the wealthy until further notice. Then there were the first Porsches to be seen at the Glen on the racetrack. In fact, there were four of them, three coupes and a rare American Roadster with an aluminum body. With their new 1488 cc engines producing 70 hp at 5000 rpm (the roadster was fitted with a 55 hp power plant), they also had a shot at overall victory. Fritz Koster and Fred Proctor would drive their own. Briggs Cunningham's son, Briggs Jr., would drive his father's, as he had at Elkhart Lake. William Lloyd entrusted his roadster to LeRoy Thorpe, just as he had done at Bridgehampton.

Finally, there was a car with strong French genes improved with American savvy: Roger Barlow's Simca Special. Barlow, the Sunset Boulevard car dealer, driver and Cal Club founder, had a special liking for Simcas. Starting with the conventional convertible version of the Simca Huit, he replaced the body with a two-seater "cigar-with-cycle-fenders" design that actually looked quite pretty. Then he modified and lowered its rail frame chassis, fit wire wheels, and tuned up the original 1200 cc engine considerably. His final touch was to paint the car powder blue, the national French racing color. Barlow was a real fran-

TOP LEFT: Watkins Glen, September 1952 - Jim Kimberly racing his OSCA MT4 in which he would finish second in the Queen Catharine Cup.

BOTTOM RIGHT: Watkins Glen, September 1952 - "Le Mans Start" for the three "hot laps" of the Queen Catharine Cup. The first car, number 46, is the MG Special of David Ash, called "the Cigar." Bill Spear's OSCA can be seen on the left near the street light.

cophile, owning numerous French classic cars, including a Talbot drophead, Delahayes and Bugattis. His first showroom had opened in 1945 in Beverly Hills. Before arriving at the Glen the "Barlow Simca" had accumulated quite an outstanding record, including impressive class wins at both Pebble Beach and Elkhart Lake.

The 1952 Queen Catharine Cup

The participating cars lined up in herringbone-fashion along Franklin Street shortly after the end of the Seneca Cup. This time the western side of the street had been designated as the starting point to make the first right turn easier on drivers. Denver Cornett had drawn first spot. So his MG which he had raced in both the Junior Prix and Grand Prix in 1948 was at the head of this grid of thirty-eight cars. What a wonderful symbol this was. The men and their crews, however, had to wait quite a long time before the cars would be released for their planned three-lap practice. By the time the crowd control and train schedule problems were cleared, it was well past 2 pm. The field had shrunk to 38 cars in the interim, as two Siatas were withdrawn due to mechanical problems: Tony Pompeo's and Logan Hill's.

When Nils Mickelson stepped one more time onto the asphalt with flag in hand, it was 2:20 pm, more than two hours behind the original schedule. To recoup some of the lost time, the Race Committee decided to shorten the race from fifteen to ten laps, as they had done in 1951. The drivers also agreed to use the Le Mans start only for the practice laps, while reforming into a standard grid start with driver on board for the race itself. This way, they would not have to re-park their cars, walk across the street, wait for the green flag, then run back to their car again. It was exactly 2:21 pm when Nils Mickelson freed the thirty-eight men to run across the street, hurry into their cars and immediately reach for the ignition key while strapping their seatbelts.

For the third time since mid-morning, the staccato roar of a large pack of race-tuned engines sent sonic shockwaves all along Franklin Street and beyond. The thirty-eight colorful racers boomed past the Courthouse, turned right after the State Park entrance, and up the hill they went. Bill Spear proved a little slower than some at this procedure. When the wire wheels of his red OSCA began to turn from their sixth position, several more cars were already ahead of him, led by the MG Special of David Ash. The Stony Point, New York, resident was followed by a Siata and several MGs as the OSCA began the chase.

Several of the top drivers turned those three "practice"

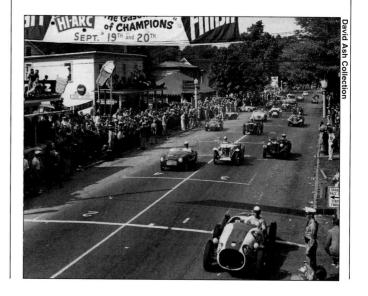

laps into "qualifying" laps, even though their lap time would not affect their placement on the grid, pre-determined by drawing the day before. Still, a fast time can turn into a psychological advantage in one's favor. Bill Spear must have been a believer in that theory. As the grid reformed for the official start, the loudspeakers around the course announced that twice-Le Mans veteran had achieved fastest lap in 72.8 mph. This was faster than the speed achieved by most Cadillac-powered Allards two years before!

Finally, the green flag was dropped for the official start. Within moments, the noise was overwhelming. Several MGs, including the Special driven by David Ash, were first to negotiate the right-hand corner past the State Park grounds. Spear, however, was in great form on this day. Up Old Corning Hill, he quickly made up his starting handicap, took the lead past the railroad bridge, then completed his first lap in 5:19.2, a stunning average of 74.5 mph! As the second lap proceeded, with Spear having already built an advantage measured in miles, Kimberly had moved his own OSCA in second place and Roger Barlow was third in his pretty Simca Special. Barlow was one of the favorites, but he was handicapped versus his main rivals in that this was his first time at the Glen. He was also occasionally taking pictures with his Leica!

Behind those three leaders, several sub-battles developed which kept spectators in a joyful state of high excitement. One such scrap was between Bill Lloyd's MG-Offenhauser, Hank Rudkin's blown Crosley Special, LeRoy Thorpe's Porsche, and Tom Scatchard's Siata. Once again, the Queen Catharine Cup was a great show! For some unlucky drivers, though, it turned out not to be a long show. The third lap saw two cars retire. First was Briggs Cunningham, Jr., whose throttle linkage came apart just as he completed his second lap down Franklin Street. He had to let his Porsche take this escape route further down, past the first corner. Soon thereafter, George Schrafft's F-S Crosley developed a leaky fuel line and the day was over for Palm Beach, Florida, resident. On lap 4, David Allen's standard MG broke an oil line, and that was it for the gentleman from Syracuse, New York. The sign he had attached to his dashboard, "Relax but Hurry," did not help him much.

Watkins Glen, September 1952 - Roger Barlow racing his Simca Special during the Queen Catharine Cup. He would finish third, a creditable achievement for someone unfamiliar with the circuit.

The lead positions remained unchanged for the rest of the race, though Bill Spear kept increasing his advantage over everyone else. There were a few more "unintended decelerations," however. On lap 7, Francis Dominiani spun the Pompeo-owned, Italian-made 750 cc Giaur Special at Big Bend and sheared off a front wheel. On lap 8, Robert Hitchcock spun his MG at Archie Smith Corner and had to retire. Finally, on lap 9, the penultimate of the race, two unfortunate drivers were sidelined by mechanical problems: James Pauley (Siata) and Hal Stetson (Crosley). These would be the last casualties. Total attrition was ten racers, leaving twenty-eight cars to be classified. The first of those to get the checkered flag was, of course, Bill Spear, in 54:03.0. Behind him, the classification was as follows:

End of Queen Catharine Cup - 10 Laps - Overall Average Speed

1. Bill Spear	OSCA MT4	72.3
2. Jim Kimberly	OSCA MT4	70.0
3. Roger Barlow	Barlow Simca	68.9
4. Thomas Hoan	MG TC superch.	66.5
5. William Lloyd	MG-Offenhauser	66.4
6. Fritz Koster	Porsche 356 coupe	66.3

Bill Spear's driving had been a terrific demonstration of the winning power of top talent combined with serious experience. His average speed for the race, with a small 1342 cc four-cylinder engine, was slightly faster than the average achieved by Erwin Goldschmidt's Cad-Allard in the 1950 Grand Prix. It was more than 5 mph faster than the average recorded by Phil Walters with the 6.4 liter Healey Cadillac in the 1950 Seneca Cup! Again, here was another clear signal that brute power could be bested by a combination of driving talent and a race car with superior handling characteristics, especially when the course was as challenging as the Watkins Glen circuit. Few in America's top racing circles would heed that signal for a long time.

On With The Grand Prix

It was well past 3:30 pm when the last Queen Catharine Cup contestants finished their race. Before starting the Grand Prix, which would feature the fastest cars and the SCCA's best drivers, the Race Committee had to

BOTTOM LEFT: Watkins Glen, September 1952 - Bob Fergus leading a Porsche Gmünd aluminum-bodied coupe at Milliken's Corner. Fergus would finish 9th overall and win the Robert O. Collins Memorial Trophy awarded the first owner-driven 1250 cc MG.

TOP RIGHT: Watkins Glen, September 1952 - The Cunningham C-4RK, assigned to Phil Walters, at Smalley's garage for inspection.

make sure one more time that spectators were under control in all places and that the race would be in accord with the mid-afternoon New York Railroad schedule. Quite a bit of time was spent taking care of those two tasks. Meanwhile, the grid assembled in pairs along Franklin Street, according to the positions drawn at the Saturday Driver Meeting. It was an impressive field, though not as diverse in machinery as it could have been. The "Great Controversy" kept exacting its toll.

The three stars of the show were of course the three Cunningham C-4Rs. As usual, Phil Walters would be driving the coupe, while both Fitch and Cunningham would drive the roadsters. The fourth Cunningham was a C-2 which had been bought by Irving Robbins. Given the C-2's weight and design inferiority compared to the C-4Rs, Robbins was not even considered a dark horse. The main threat for the Cunningham boys would come from a phalanx of Allards and one C-Type Jaguar. For reasons unknown, only two Ferraris were in the field, both small-engined machines with less than top talent at the wheel. None of the potent 340 Americas were entered.

Among the Allards, four were estimated to have a chance at overall victory against the Cunninghams. The first was Fred Wacker's "Eight Ball" — now re-fitted with a manual transmission. The other three were the V-8-powered J2s of Joe Sabal (Chrysler Hemi), Preston Gray and

George Harris. All three drivers knew the Glen circuit well. The main threat to the Cunninghams, however, was likely to come from the single Jaguar C-Type entered. It was the Hornburg-prepared car entrusted to Phil Hill. The young Californian's reputation had now spread east, and his mount was said to be even hotter than the Hoffman C-Type with which Fitch had won the Seneca Cup earlier in the day.

Another Jaguar entry had potential: the aluminum-bodied Jaguar XK-120 entrusted to Sherwood Johnston by Art Feuerbacher. Three of these special 1951 Jaguars had actually been built by the factory in the Spring of of that year in case the C-types should not be ready for Le Mans. When this eventuality did not happen, Charles Hornburg, who was in Coventry at the time, was only too happy to grab two. Phil Hill had already benefited from that snap decision. Finally, the former Nardi-Danese had become a Nardi-Cadillac since 1951. Still owned by Perry Fina, but to be driven by Harry Grey in the Grand Prix, it was considered a possible dark horse by some observers.

There were many other interesting cars in the field, even though, in all likelihood, their drivers could not vie for overall victory. The 1949 Grand Prix winner, "Ardent Alligator," recently acquired from Cameron Argetsinger by Bret Hannaway, was entered. The level of competition had

Watkins Glen, September 1952 - Harry Grey in the Perry Fina-entered Nardi-Cadillac the day before the Grand Prix.

changed so much since 1949, however, that the rudimentary Riley-Mercury was not given much of a chance. David Hirsch of New York City entered an Aston Martin DB2 and entrusted it to experienced Bob Gegen. That model had done quite well at Le Mans, but more out of sturdiness for the long haul than top speed for a short race.

Otto Linton entered a gorgeous white Siata coupe powered by a Fiat 2.0 liter V-8. It would vie for a class win. Two Nash-Healey roadsters, bodied by Pinin Farina, were also in the field, one owned by Frank O'Hare of Rochester, New York, and the other by Donald MacNaughton of Geneva, New York. A third though quite different-looking Nash-Healey was highly visible on Franklin Street, but only on the curb. It was the silver-blue racing number 10 Le Mans car which had finished third in France only three months earlier. Great publicity by which to sell a new Anglo-American sports car! E. J. Tobin of Yonkers, New York, entered a pretty BMW 328.

Finally, there was a very new American Special called the "Excalibur J." Product of the fertile mind of Brooks Stevens, this newest American Special was a relatively crude cycle-fendered aluminum body shaped around Henry J chassis provided by the Kaiser-Frazer company. The engine was a modified in-line six-cylinder Willys which only produced 100 hp. Ralph Knudson would drive the car at the Glen. Stevens' dream was to offer the American public the local equivalent of an MG, that is an affordable sports car based on production sedan components. He came into the game a little late, however, and his one-ton car riding on a 100″ wheelbase simply was not competitive.

The 1952 Grand Prix

By the time the Grand Prix grid began to assemble on Franklin Street, it was well past 4 pm. Once again, the Cunningham team had drawn unfavorable grid positions from the hat. Two Allards were in the front row: Fred Wacker's and Joe Sabal's. Next was a third Allard, with George Harris at the wheel, and the first Cunningham C-4R was right next to it, with Briggs Cunningham leading his team. John Fitch was in the third row, right behind Cunningham, in the second white roadster, and abreast of the Chrysler-Allard of John Negley. The last of the new

Cunninghams was the C-4-RK coupe of Phil Walters, sitting in fifth row next to Irving Robbins in the old C-2. Between Briggs Cunningham and Phil Walters, there were two more Allards — Preston Gray's and John Negley's (Chrysler Hemi), plus the competitive Nardi-Cadillac with Harry Grey at the wheel.

One wonders if at that tense moment, frayed feelings caused by the "Great Controversy" played any role. Even though Briggs Cunningham had mostly remained above the fray in that affair, there was his Le Mans-tested team of three cars bearing the American national colors mixed in with the epitome of isolationism, that is some of the lead drivers of the group who wished to maintain the amateur and nationalist status quo: Fred Wacker, George Harris and Preston Gray. All three drove Allards, a car now fairly outdated by international standards. The coordinated white livery of the Cunninghams, with the twin dark blue stripes dividing their silhouette longitudinally, emphasized the contrast between those state-of-the-art full-bodied racers, and the randomly colored, cycle-fendered Allards with their pre-war looks. Though the racers of the day always

TOP LEFT: Watkins Glen, September 1952 - The grid for the 1952 Grand Prix. Five Allard J2s surround the Cunningham trio.

BOTTOM RIGHT: Watkins Glen, September 1952 - Briggs Cunningham at work in his C-4R roadster during the Grand Prix's first lap.

said, "When the green flag drops, all the B.S. stops," would there be more than just a car race going on?

Indeed, after Honorary Starter Peter Helck released the forty cars for their three practice laps, "there seemed to develop a tremendous battle between the Allards and the Cunninghams, each one trying to feel out the other's strength," reported *Sports Car* magazine after the race. Their writer continued, "By the time the actual race got underway, spectator tension was almost uncontrollable." Undoubtedly, driver tension was even higher. During the practice laps, Phil Walters and the C-4RK had become the upper hand, with John Fitch's C-4R next, then Fred Wacker's Allard. Briggs Cunningham was fourth.

As the grid reformed with the Allards dominating the front rows, tensions were high indeed and the booming thunder rolling down Franklin Street was simply astounding. Even though he was there only as a non-participating member, Cameron Argetsinger was reveling at the incredible transformation he had wrought, in just five years, on the formerly quiet and little known village of his teenage summers. Now the clock was nearing the 4 pm mark. Though the sun was still bright, the shadows had become much longer than the organizers had planned originally. A chill was beginning to be felt. But was it the air, or was it the nerves?

One last time for the season, Nils Mickelson stepped onto the asphalt under the street-wide Grand Prix banner,

his white jumpsuit distinguishing him from the mass of officials and spectators overflowing the sidewalks on either sides of Franklin Street. With both feet on the white start/finish line, he waved the green flag. The rolling thunder of forty racing engines turning at low revs changed instantly into a violent, high-pitched scream of deafening proportions. The two Allards in the front row bolted ahead, followed by the next pairs of racers. As the lead machines braked for the first corner, the jostling for position began in earnest.

White Chasing Red

Fred Wacker and his red Allard were first rushing up Old Corning Hill, but the two Cunningham roadsters were soon behind him and giving chase, with "Mr. C." leading the charge. As the three lead racers zoomed under the railroad underpass at over 120 mph, the spectacle was as good as any in Europe's most famous venues. Successive safety stations reported the action over the loudspeaker system, so all spectators could follow the race as it developed. The first moment of drama took place on the open stretch of road just about where Sam Collier had met his fate. Pouring it on to near the limit, Briggs Cunningham took the lead from Wacker. The spectators standing by Stone Bridge saw the three lead cars rush past in that order: Cunningham, Wacker, Fitch. The snout of the latter's roadster seemed eager to swallow the red Allard's short, rounded tail.

Past Archie Smith Corner, there loomed Big Bend, that long descent back into the village, where the courage of drivers is tested as much as the maximum speed of their machines. John Fitch found it a good place to make his move. Soon it was Cunningham, Fitch, Wacker and not far behind, Phil Walters in the C-4RK. The fifth car was already far back as the four leaders negotiated Milliken's Corner. The crowds in the village were highly excited. All along Franklin Street, heads were craned towards the north end, the corner of Franklin and Fourth, where the leading machines were about to re-appear for the half-mile sprint to the course's first corner.

First to re-appear on Franklin Street was Briggs Cunningham, followed three car lengths behind by Fitch,

Watkins Glen, September 1952 - John Fitch in C-4R number 54 during the Grand Prix "hot laps" approaching School House Corner.

with the red Allard a few car lengths behind him. Cunningham rushed towards the start/finish line in the left lane (Courthouse side), while Fitch occupied the right lane (grandstand side) forty feet behind. Wacker saw an opportunity in this: the best place to be to take the first corner, the ninety-degree right-hander, was the left lane. Taking the lane, the Chicagoan and his red Allard began to gain on Fitch. By the time Cunningham crossed the start/finish line, still in the left lane, Fitch was two car lengths behind him, still in the right lane. Wacker was now less than a car length behind Fitch, but in the left lane behind Cunningham. Phil Walters was about three hundred feet behind Wacker, while no other car had yet re-entered Franklin Street. All four were going over 100 mph.

Now the three lead drivers had to downshift and slow down, then position their cars for the looming right-hander. Shortly after racing past the Courthouse, John Fitch moved over to the left lane. Unbeknownst to him, the red Allard had just begun to overtake his Cunningham on the outside, its front fenders beginning to move up the white side of the Cunningham. Just ahead to the left, overflowing the sidewalk right in front of the Watkins Glen souvenir shop, were hundreds of people with nothing between them and the asphalt but thin air. There were no haybales, no fence, just a simple limp rope strung along thin two-foot-high poles to mark the border between the "spectator zone" and the race track.

173

Start • Fifth Annual International Grand Prix • Finish
ATLANTIC HI-ARC "the Gasoline of CHAMPIONS"
SEPT. 19TH and 20TH

Watkins Glen, September 20th, 1952 - Briggs Cunningham is first to cross the start/finish line at the end of lap one. Three car lengths behind him is John Fitch, in the right lane, in the second C-4R. Fred Wacker's Allard is not far behind in the left lane. The three cars, probably going at over 120 mph, are preparing to brake for the ninety degree turn at the end of Franklin Street, just 0.2 miles away.

As Fitch moved further left, his peripheral vision suddenly caught a glimpse of the red shape moving up his left side. This was the first time he became aware of the attempted pass as he thought he could not be overtaken at that spot: the cars were now in the pre-turn "no-passing zone." The sudden red flash made him miss a heartbeat then immediately veer back right to give Wacker space. Wacker was in turn surprised as he thought Fitch was fully aware of his intentions. As the sitting president of the SCCA, Wacker should certainly have been aware of the "no-passing-before-corners" rule his organization had adopted only days earlier. It is very likely that in the heat of the action, and based on his experience in similar races where such a rule was never decreed, he forgot about it.

Red Flash, Red Flags

Wacker had no time to think. Reflexively, he moved his big Allard further to the left, putting his two outside wheels on the soft ground beyond the asphalt. The clump of spectators at that very point were further back by about a foot, but just ahead, several hundred people were packed ten-deep between the souvenir shop's storefront and the edge of the curb, only fifty feet ahead of the fast approaching one-ton racer. In the front row were mostly men and women sitting on camping chairs, their legs and knees jutting under the symbolic rope. There were also many children peering with their heads out better to catch the action. Among these people were Mike Fazzari, a young father who had brought his two boys to the race: James, 9, and Frank, 7. He had rejoiced in giving them the thrill of their young lives. The two kids wore checkered woolen shirts over a white undershirt. Manuel and Edna Repoza were a middle-aged couple from Corning who thought they simply could not miss the Grand Prix. Mrs. Ethel McAnn, a well-to-do young women from Rochester, New York, had come to witness the "spectacle of the year." So had Wilbur G. Pray, 39, of the same town.

Fred Wacker had no room left for any bold maneuver. Still going about 80 mph, breaking or swerving harshly would have only risked his completely loosing control of the car, with the worst possible consequences. Wacker did the best he could: he began to veer right ever so slightly, trying to distance the Allard from the files of spectators without losing control of his speeding racer. Alas, there was no margin left. The edge of his two outside wheels were still beyond the asphalt when the Allard passed by the souvenir shop. The blood-red fenders were about to become speeding scythes.

Wacker barely felt it. But as he began taking the right-hander, passing Fitch who had slowed down and turned his head sideways to check if something had happened to the crowd, his left door flew open; his rear left fender was creased. Behind him, it was mayhem. A a cloud of thin dust was rising along the tall, thick utility pole which stood right in front of the souvenir shop. At ground level, people lay screaming, crying, or shocked into stunned silence in the midst of trampled sandwiches, broken soda bottles, upturned camping stools, and blood.

The steward at the corner opposite the accident scene raised the red flag in less than two seconds. All his peers around the course did the same in quick succession and the entire Grand Prix was stopped by the time Walker reached the Stone Bridge. The spectators lined up behind the snow fences at Archie Smith Corner or along Big Bend were now wondering why the spectacular racers had gone silent. Everything was so suddenly quiet, even the loudspeakers. Nobody yet knew exactly what had happened, not even those next to the fateful souvenir shop. It would take a few minutes to take stock.

Fender of Fate

The Allard's rear fenders were not cycle fenders as those in the front. Rather, they were a rounded affair arching over the wheel and down, ending about a foot above ground as they became an integrated part of the car's short, curvaceous tail. They had a rounded edge where the fender's lowest curve turned sharply inside to form the rear hemline of the racer. The one-foot height of that rear edge corresponds to slightly above mid-calf for an average adult leg, and about face level for a squatting young child. That is exactly the part that scythed through the front row of spectators for about thirty feet in front of the souvenir shop.

175

In the split-second it took the Allard to pass by, it seriously injured twelve people and killed Frank Fazzari. The seven-year-old had the top of his skull crushed by the winged knock-off hub. His father, half conscious, and his brother, stunned and in pain, lay on the sidewalk, both with broken legs. Portly, Mrs. Repoza was still standing, uninjured, but she was stunned, looking at her husband lying unconscious on the ground. Mrs. McAnn was sitting on the sidewalk, leaning against her extended left arm, and staring in apparent disbelief at her broken left ankle. Wilbur Pray also had broken legs. By now, policemen and Army guards were rushing to the scene to help the injured. For Frank Fazzari, it was too late.

Once again at Watkins Glen, ambulances blared, then rushed to Montour Falls Hospital. After the damage was fully assessed, the Race Committee decided to re-start the Grand Prix. It would be better, some thought, if the race were completed and the historical record would look "normal," though a tragic accident had indeed happened. Tensions were high all around the course. James Melton was called in to try and soothe anxiety with his melodious voice. By the time the course had been cleared, a final decision had to be made about the continuation of the race. The late start of the Grand Prix and the latest delay dictated a cancellation. The sun was now slowly setting above the hills directly west of Seneca Lodge. The blazing ball would have stared the drivers coming up Old Corning Hill directly in the face. No additional risk could be taken. The race was cancelled.

Next, Fred Wacker was arrested by the State Police and taken to their station to make a statement. James Melton, who wielded great influence at Watkins Glen, was rushed to the rescue. He succeed in getting Wacker out of his pending trouble. By now, however, it was becoming clear to everyone involved in the decision making about racing on open roads that something had fundamentally changed. The sport itself might even be in grave danger.

The Aftermath

The press was not kind to this young sport. Henry Valent put it best, "Like dogs when their prey has been cornered, those in opposition to the races barked loud and long articles, pamphlets, editorials, magazines and other public media. They denounced the races, calling them 'nothing but Roman Holiday,' where thrill surfeited crowds press madly around the most dangerous areas, hoping to be eye witness of deathly spills and the flow of blood ... They even stretched their argument to the point that the local citizenry were so hungry for the dollar that they cared not from whose hide it came."

The *Life* magazine issue of October 6, 1952, offers a subtle but striking example of what Valent meant. The great national magazine devoted a two-page spread to the accident, featuring a short column and five large black and white photos with captions. The largest photo, in the middle of the spread, showed several of the casualties lying in shock on the ground, seconds after the accident. Another photo showed the dead boy in a pool of blood. The words in the feature titled "Quick Flick Of The Fender" were mildly xenophobic, not terribly harsh, and inacurate, "The gaudy and finely tuned cars, mostly foreign, had completed the first 15 laps ..." was the worst it got. But the photos were devastating.

Even *Motor Trend* was tough in its November, 1952 issue, "Since the very first races on the west coast, the solution to winning a race has not been to develop a greater skill with the car at hand, but rather to make the car at hand more powerful, and if this is not successful, to discard the car entirely and get a bigger one. ... A course as severe at Watkins Glen takes a driver of infinite skill. ... Yet men who drive perhaps four races a year think nothing of hurling themselves about this course with mad abandon, in machines that would make Nuvolari stop and think." There was an argument that the isolationist-amateur-only group, most of whom had rushed into ever-more-powerful cars, Fred Wacker included, perhaps had not considered as deeply as they should have.

Valent continued, "Thank God, we live in a land where people are free to express themselves. In our American way of life, we may not agree as to what others may say or write but we will defend their right to defend themselves." He would be proved correct in the long term, but the immediate future turned out to be a hard challenge. Already, the 1950 accident where a volunteer fireman and two spectators were injured had caused a lot of emotional and legal commotion. The victims sued, contending in court that, "The State of New York was liable on the ground of holding an affair which was designed to attract people and then not taking reasonable precautions for their safety." The judge ruled in their favor not long before the fifth Grand Prix.

This ruling and the latest accident caused the New York State Police to oppose any further racing on state highways, and a bill to be introduced in the New York State Legislature proposing to ban any racing on public roads. That bill was defeated at the committee level, but not without a political trick. Among the political powers that be in the state capital of Albany, when the bill was quashed, a tacit understanding had been reached that no more permits would be issued. Since new permits were needed every year, the politicians had found a way to ban racing on public roads effectively without saying so or legistating accordingly. In turn, insurance companies became unwilling to cover such risks and that was the last nail in the coffin.

The village of Watkins Glen had reached the end of the racing road; at least the end of the public racing road. Soon other similar venues, such as Elkhart Lake, reached the same dead end even before the start of the 1953 season. The legal risks had become too high; everywhere politicians were running for cover. The SCCA was thrown off balance, while Alec Ulmann, safe in his "private airport" in Florida, where no State highways were involved and crowd control was a lot easier to manage, was free to keep on inviting race drivers from around the world. History does have some ironic twists. This was not going to be the last one, though, of this extraordinary saga.

First, an American military figure bigger than life and a passionate enthusiast for the sport would step into the breach and provide a miraculous, though very real, series of extremely safe venues for two years. His name was General Curtis Le May. He was in charge of the Strategic Air Command and had authority over all the vast strategic Air Force bases and airfields around the nation. That was plenty of good racing tarmac!

Second, the citizenry and community leaders of those small American villages from which the Minutemen had sprung to beat the Redcoats, were not going to give up so easily on their newfound passion and commerce. In the two years or so Curtis Le May managed to get away with lending his airfields to the SCCA, the people of Watkins Glen, Elkhart Lake, Bridgehampton and other concerned villages, had found the energy and raised the money to plan and build enclosed permanent tracks. The sport goes on today. This was, indeed, America!

Watkins Glen, September 1952 - Just before disaster hit, Fitch has moved to the left lane to better negotiate the right-hand corner, unaware until the last moment that Wacker had caught up with him to his left. When the realization took place, Fitch instantaneously swerved right and braked. Wacker (here just behind the first Cunningham) swerved left and went on. Only yards ahead of the Allard, a large crowd overflows the sidewalk ...

ATLANTIC

Epilogue

The Strategic Air Command Scrambles to the Rescue

Once public roads became off limits for road racing, only two types of venues were left for SCCA members to practice their sport: private grounds such as the Del Monte estate at Pebble Beach, or de-activated airports such as Hendricks Field. Surely that was not enough for a sport undergoing rapid expansion. What was needed were more venues, not fewer. Crowd control, however, and the unacceptable liability of racing on public roads, had now become too big a problem. Unbeknownst to all, a solution to that nexus had been found earlier through a chance encounter at Elkhart Lake between two individuals. But even these individuals did not realize the importance of their first discussion in Wisconsin until much later.

In early September, 1952, Fred Wacker was at Elkhart Lake. He and his pit crew were preparing his Allard for the race. At one point he noticed a man in a fedora, Hawaiian shirt, and with a big cigar planted at the corner of his mouth. The tall, burly individual was milling about, asking constant questions from the crew about the red Allard. Wacker then walked to him, introduced himself and asked who he was. The answer came quickly, "Curt Le May." As Wacker remembered later, "I woke up to the fact that he was the head of the Strategic Air Command." This is a fairly casual description of the man who, at the time, was per-

"At the beginning of each season, the same feeling takes hold of my entire body and engulfs it: the crazed impatience again to find myself on the track, pushing my car to 200 kph in a battle of honor with my adversaries. Then, as always, the only vow I make is 'May Heaven help me and Fortune smile on me!'"

Alberto Ascari

haps the second most powerful person in America, after the country's President, Harry Truman.

In 1952, there were no intercontinental missiles. The Strategic Air Command (SAC) and its nuclear-armed B-47 bombers standing on twenty-four-hour alert were the shield and the sword defending the free world. SAC had large air bases all over the United States where those bombers were stationed. General Curtis Emerson Le May, who commanded the 20th Air Force in the Pacific theater in 1944-1945, was the man running SAC. He was also a racing car enthusiast, owned an Allard K2 and loved to attend races. Wacker and Le May became fast friends. They began planning a first race on a SAC airfield for late October in a sunny southern State.

Le May rationalized that the Air Force bases could be freed for racing without costing the government anything. Since his bomber crews had to do a number of routine flights every week for training, he would simply schedule those flights on weekends. No one at the Pentagon would challenge him! Better yet, SAC air bases had existing fences and gates all around, making collecting an admission from every single spectator a cinch. The bulk of the money would be returned to the base personnel (some of whom would undoubtedly be called upon to "volunteer" as security guards during the race weekends), in the form of a donation to a newly created "Living Improvement Fund." That fund would be used to build such things as gyms, bowling alleys or nurseries, improving the lot of servicemen and their families. Le May was also known for his brilliant political skills.

The first encounter between Wacker and Le May was followed by further discussions, then the date was set for October 26, 1952 at Turner Air Force base, situated near Albany, Georgia. The timing of that first planned SAC air base race could not have been luckier for the SCCA. By the time the Sowega Races (so named for the region in which Albany is situated: SOuth WEst GeorgiA) took place, the tragedy of Watkins Glen and its consequences for road racing were high on everyone's mind. The first road race ever to be run on a SAC base, won by George Huntoon in a Jaguar C-Type, was a big success. Wacker and his board soon got into serious discussions with Le May and his senior staff. Shortly after General Dwight Eisenhower was elected as the next President of the United States in early November, a long term contract was signed between the SCCA and SAC.

The air bases that defended the free world, from MacDill Air Force Base near Tampa, Florida, to March Field near Riverside, California, were about to become the main racing venues for sports car enthusiasts! While each base's main fleet of bombers would be flown out on exer-

The OSCA MT4 of James Simpson, a Chicago farmer. The racing circuit is traced within a Strategic Air Command base with nuclear-capable B-47 bombers clearly visible in the background.

cise during the weekend of the race, the B-47s that remained on the tarmac would each be guarded by a dozen MPs armed with machine guns, just in case.

Obviously, the perfectly flat concrete runways of SAC bases were not even close approximations of the great European road race venues. They were not what Cameron Argetsinger had in mind when he started the whole movement. Still, they allowed the fledgling sport to go on, grow and prosper. In fact, the share of revenues gained from those SAC air base races allowed SCCA to pay its debts and even finance additional races on other airfields. By the time a few United States Senators began inquiring into the matter, prodded by a group of constituents who did not think it was appropriate to run public races on SAC air bases, the SCCA had grown strong and closed circuits had been built so the sport could go on on its own. Late in 1954 the white flag was finally raised by General Le May who had to "stop lending taxpayer-financed public land to a private club." By then, however, the towns of Watkins Glen and Elkhart Lake had built permanent tracks. Sebring had become a major international event and venue, further reinforcing the appeal of road racing. The sport was safe.

Watkins Glen Against All Odds

When it became clear that the original circuit had to be abandoned, the Grand Prix Committee of Watkins Glen set out to find a new site where controlling and protecting crowds would no longer be a problem. After much deliberation, a broad rolling hilltop within the limits of the neighboring town of Dix was selected with the full cooperation of the Town Board. The site had existing dirt roads, but creating a racing circuit would require much construction work such as widening the roads, grading, ditching, surfacing, etc. The intended circuit would be 4.6 mile long. To finance the project, the Grand Prix Committee formed the Watkins Glen Grand Prix Corporation on July 15, 1953. The five Board Members and founders were Don Brubaker, Lester Smalley, Henry Valent, Liston Coon (an attorney) and Cameron Argetsinger. The latter's sharp organizational skills were deemed essential. Boldly, they set the race dates for September 18 and 19, 1953. Bill Milliken had an active role in designing the track and overseeing the project from

Map of the first permanent Watkins Glen circuit - 1953-56

a combined engineering and racing point of view.

Representatives of the SCCA were invited to see the prospective site early on, before any road work had commenced. With only dirt roads, meadows and brush, they immediately ruled out sanctioning the planned 1953 event, seeing it as impossible to have a safe circuit ready on time. Henry Valent explained what happened next, "Thus with fixed determination, when confronted with an outlawed circuit, and being vehemently denounced by the opponents of road racing, and having lost the goodwill and guidance of the State Department of Public Works and the State Police, and being told by the SCCA that they wouldn't sanction the race on another circuit, and there being only forty working days to construct a new 4.6 mile circuit, and with no money, the community proceeded to plan for the 1953 Grand Prix."

Those determined people of Schuyler County once again made the impossible happen. By September 17, the new circuit was race-ready, close to one hundred entries had been validated and the town of Watkins Glen and its environs were filling up with spectators. Snow fences surrounded the entire perimeter of the 4.6 mile course; parking areas and admission gates were clearly identified; non-spectator areas were clearly marked; and bleachers were put up at several vantage points. A control tower was even erected at the start/finish line. For the first time in the history of the Watkins Glen races, the drivers had a day of practice (Friday) before the actual day of the race. M. R. J.

"Doc" Wyllie won the Seneca Cup in a Jaguar XK-120; George Moffett won the Queen Catharine Cup in an OSCA; and Walt Hansgen won the Grand Prix in his own Jaguar Special. Tens of thousands of spectators were present. Watkins Glen had brilliantly succeeded in keeping itself a major center for motorsport.

The following year, the SCCA granted its sanction to the new circuit. The big cars returned and the number of races was increased to five. Phil Walters won the Grand Prix in a lightened Cunningham C-4R. By 1955, everything seemed back on course, with the Eighth Annual Grand Prix turning into another success with over two hundred entrants. There was more trouble ahead, however. The drivers did not like the circuit much, complaining, among other things, about the lack of escape routes and too many blind spots due to the rolling nature of the landscape. It was becoming clear to the Watkins Glen Grand Prix Corporation that it was left with only two options: bring major modifications to the existing circuit, or build an entirely new one somewhere else. Many community forums were held in late 1955 and early 1956. Then the SCCA added an entirely new and unwelcome twist to the situation.

The SCCA membership had grown tremendously and the Board had changed completely in the three preceding years. Jim Kimberly was now the club's President and Bill Lloyd the Vice President. Totally new policies had been enacted. The club now wanted to charge the Watkins Glen Grand Prix Corporation considerable amounts of money, such as a $2,000 sanctioning fee, the total pot constituted by the entry fees of the drivers and reimbursement for "the amount of assistance to be rendered." Between March and May, an angry exchange of letters, not unlike the Herrington-Peck duel of 1951, took place between the two parties. In the end, the Grand Prix Corporation decided to go it alone, then chose the option to build a new circuit.

The Grand Prix Corporation picked a site situated close to the first closed circuit and took options on 550 acres of land there. Then it set the date for the ninth Watkins Glen Grand Prix, once more on the third weekend of September, now a tradition, and therefore the 14th and 15th. Now all that had to be done was to build the new

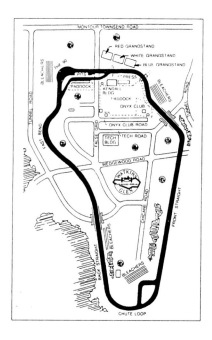

track and have everything ready on time. Once the contractor was selected, work proceeded immediately. Unfortunately, the summer of 1956 proved much wetter than normal; many days were lost. Though the crews tried to compensate by working overtime, the job was only completed on September 13, the eve of practice day. Despite some interference by the SCCA, an excellent field of drivers was on hand for the weekend, along with close to 30,000 spectators. The Watkins Glen Grand Prix Corporation had, it seemed, slain its second dragon. Then on Friday night, the beast started to stir and spew fire again.

The laying of the asphalt for the track having been completed only a few hours before the first race cars were to begin practice, the asphalt had not had enough time to cure. It was soft and, worse, the top spread of gravel had not been steamrolled enough, so it was loose in many parts of the course. Many of the road shoulders were still soft also. As practice began, "damages from flying pea stones amounted to some broken mirrors, cracked windshields and headlights, and spotted front ends" to quote Henry Valent again. But the asphalt did not break during the entire day and, in fact, the curing was accelerated by the nearly two hundred racing cars as they went round and round until dusk. Nonetheless, the situation had the three key SCCA representatives at the track quite perturbed. They met behind closed doors that very evening and called Jim Kimberly at his summer home in Neenah, Wisconsin.

Map of the second permanent Watkins Glen circuit, inaugurated in 1956. Though modified several times since, the track is operational and successful to this day.

Then, at about one o'clock on the morning of the races, a telegram "From SCCA" and signed by Jim Kimberly and Bill Lloyd arrived in their hotel. The sealed swatch of paper was delivered to them immediately. Only two-paragraph long, its key words were the following:

"In view of reports of serious and hazardous conditions, of Watkins Glen course, undersigned urgently recommend all SCCA members to withdraw from race. Members participating in event do so in recognition of hazard to safety and welfare of the sport."

The Corporation Board members were advised within minutes. All key officers were awakened and soon intense meetings and discussions were underway. In the early morning hours, the decision was made to go on with the races. When the drivers began arriving at the paddock, it became quickly obvious that a majority of them had heard of the telegram. After further deliberations, all 118 qualified drivers were asked to gather at the start/finish line fifteen minutes before the first race was scheduled to begin. The key issues on both sides were then summarized for them and the Kimberly telegram was read. The pros for getting on with the races were presented by the local committee, then the cons by two SCCA representatives. Finally, Doc Wyllie, winner of the 1953 Seneca Cup, asked a show of hands of those drivers wishing to withdraw from the pending events. Not one hand was raised. The Grand Prix races were on!

The rest is history. Though there was one more fiery clash with the SCCA shortly after the 1956 Grand Prix took place, things were smoothed out in a short time. Racing went on at Watkins Glen. By 1958, Cameron Argetsinger decided it was time to revisit his original dream: bring the best international factory teams and drivers to race to the southern shores of Seneca Lake. By then, Formula 1 had become the clear "top rung" of international motorsport, so Argetsinger set out to bring to the Glen the FIA and its pantheon of Formula 1 champions. His challenge was now quite different, though. Sebring and Alec Ulmann had become the preferred American track for the FIA and the relationship between the two sides was strong. Ulmann also wanted to bring Formula 1 to the

United States. Indeed, the international status of Sebring had grown tremendously between 1953 and 1958.

Sebring Blazes The International Trail

The FIA sanctioned the 1953 Twelve-Hours of Sebring as one of seven *Grandes Epreuves* counting toward the new World Championship for Sports Car Manufacturers. Sebring was thus instantly brought into a prestigious group. The other six championship races were the Mille Miglia, the Twenty-Four Hours of Le Mans, the Twenty-Four Hours of Spa-Francorchamps, the Nürburgring 1000 Km, the Tourist Trophy and the Carrera Panamericana. Sebring would be the season's first *Grandes Epreuve*, with the date set at March 8.

As a result, Alec Ulmann and his committee were able to attract a large field of entries including top caliber teams and drivers. First and foremost was an official Aston Martin works team of two DB3s entrusted to the driver pairs of Peter Collins/Geoff Duke and Reg Parnell/George Abecassis. The Deutsch-Bonnet *équipe* also returned for an encore with two cars. Then Equipe Cunningham fielded three different cars, a C-4R for John Fitch and Phil Walters, an OSCA MT4 (1342 cc) for "Mr. C." himself and Bill Lloyd, and a Frazer-Nash for Charles Moran and John Gordon Bennett. There were also three private C-Type Jaguars, several Ferraris, a slew of Allards and a half dozen XK-120s, including one entered by Cameron Argetsinger

CENTER LEFT: MacDill Air Force Base near Tampa, Florida - The second foil against Sebring after Vero Beach. The 4.5 liter Ferrari 375 of Jim Kimberly which won the 1954 race.

TOP RIGHT: MacDill Air Force Base, 1954 - Paul Farago with Siata and lots of vitamin Cs.

with Miles Collier as co-driver. In total, sixty cars were entered, a splendid accomplishment.

While the "powers that be" of the SCCA had again tried to sabotage Sebring by staging their own Florida race two weeks prior, this time it is they who suffered attrition from teams and drivers more eager to be part of a big international race. The SCCA's Six-Hour race was staged at MacDill Air Force Base near Tampa on February 21. Over fifty cars were entered but, aside from the three Cunningham C-4Rs and Bill Spear's potent Ferrari 340 America he shared with Phil Hill, the rest of the field was relatively unimpressive. The last two hours of the race saw a thrilling battle between Phil Hill and John Fitch, which the latter eventually won, though not by much, in a Cunningham C-4R roadster.

The second Twelve-Hours of Sebring on March 8 turned out to be a wonderful race. The two Aston Martins took the early lead, until Geoff Duke took over from Peter Collins at the three-hour mark. Duke was new to the team and probably did not have enough experience with the DB3. He made an early mistake, colliding with a Jaguar. Both cars had to retire. Then Reg Parnell hit a cement-filled marker barrel with the remaining Aston. It was not a big crash, but the front left fender was bashed, including the headlight. That would prove a severe handicap during the night hours. At the fourth hour, the lead car was the Fitch/Walters Cunningham C-4R, chased by the DB3 and two C-type Jaguars. But for its missing headlight, it is possible the Aston Martin could have won the race. The handicap was too much in the total darkness of Sebring's outside corners. Fitch/Walters won with a one lap lead over Parnell/Abecassis. This was the first victory for an American car in an international championship sports car event. René Bonnet and his team went back to France again with the Trophy for the Index of Performance. Sebring was on the world map.

By 1954, Hendricks Field was host to several top European works teams and drivers: Aston Martin, Healey, Lancia and Maserati entered a total of nine works cars. Scuderia Ferrari was fronted by Harry Schell, paired with Fons de Portago in a works-prepared 250 MM. Among the drivers of these factory teams were names like Juan Manuel Fangio, Peter Collins, Roy Salvadori, Alberto Ascari, Eugenio Castellotti and Luigi Musso, literally the cream of Europe. Briggs Cunningham entered three cars: a C-4R for himself and Sherwood Johnston, a big new Ferrari 375 for Walters/Fitch and a little OSCA MT4 (1452cc) for Stirling Moss and Bill Lloyd. The race was extraordinary, with attrition taking an enormous toll. With one hour to go, the only big-engined car left with a chance to win was the 3.3 liter Lancia D24 of Ascari/Villoresi. It had a big advantage over its first pursuer, the little OSCA of Stirling Moss. At the 11th hour, the lead Lancia blew its engine, leaving the victory to Stirling Moss and Equipe Cunningham.

From then on, Sebring had earned its mark as an major internationally recognized circuit. Scuderia Ferrari won its first victory there in 1956 with Fangio/Castellotti in a 860 Monza, while Maserati followed in 1957 with Fangio/Behra in a 450 S. Ferrari took the title back the following year with its newest world-beater, the 250 Testa Rossa. Phil Hill and Peter Collins, teamed up for the occasion, were the winning drivers. The 1958 Sebring race had a field of 65 entries with factory cars and drivers from Ferrari, Porsche, OSCA, Lotus, Aston Martin, A.C. Cars and Jaguar (represented by Ecurie Ecosse). Alfred Momo also had a strong private team of two Lister-Jaguars and one Jaguar D-Type. The best sports cars and road racing drivers in the world, with very few exceptions, were all at Sebring. So was the international motor racing press.

The Mercedes-Benz 300 SLR which won the 1955 Mille Miglia. Stirling Moss drove the car and renown British journalist Dennis Jenkinson navigated. The 300 SLR was a direct descendant of the 300 SL. Mercedes-Benz dominated the 1955 season but, because of the Le Mans catastrophe, withdrew from racing for over three decades after the last championship race that year.

Ulmann thought the time was right to bring Formula 1 to Sebring. In this new quest, he had to deal with the SCCA for great changes had taken place within the sanctioning bodies of American racing.

The Double Reversal

As the number of members and activities of the SCCA multiplied rapidly in 1953 and 1954, the AAA became increasingly uncomfortable dealing with such a volume of responsibilities. Insuring safety was also becoming an enormous task involving insurance companies and politicians as well. Then year 1955 turned into the darkest year in the history of motorsport. It started in France at the Grand Prix de Pau, on April 11. Italian driver Mario Alborghetti died in a crash in what was his first Formula 1 race. On May 27, the great Italian champion Alberto Ascari died at Monza while practicing in the new Ferrari 750. On May 30, it was America's turn. Bill Vukovich, while leading the Indy 500 race and going for his third victory in a row, became involved in a multiple-car crash and was killed.

Less than two weeks later loomed the greatest of all catastrophes. On the mid afternoon of June 11, before the start of the Twenty-Four Hours of Le Mans, millions of enthusiasts across Europe were looking forward to a titanic battle between Mercedes-Benz, Jaguar and Ferrari. In the late afternoon of that same day, the Mercedes-Benz 300

SLR driven by Pierre Levegh, and which John Fitch was soon to take over, ran at maximum speed into the sloping back of a much slower Austin Healey right where the grandstands begin.

The Mercedes was flung into the air, then bounced over the top of the earth wall dividing the road from the spectator area. The massive silver projectile was stopped dead by a concrete piling then exploded. Its heavy engine and front suspension broke loose and flew like rockets of death straight across the grandstands packed with spectators shoulder to shoulder. More than eighty five people died, including Levegh. Hundreds were wounded, most seriously. The race went on to avoid a panic, but the sport was changed for ever.

The biggest consequence in the United States was that the AAA chose to abandon any activities related to racing and handed over the job entirely to the SCCA. After drastic new safety measures were taken in Europe, the sport recovered. By 1958, the SCCA, led by Charles Moran, decided that it was time to give up its "amateur only" position. They reversed their 1951 statements and adopted the international rules. Commented Alec Ulmann, "This naturally was a great moral victory for me and for those who stuck by me in the difficult years of boycott and later inaction, after AAA withdrawal." At the award ceremonies following the Ninth annual Twelve Hours of Sebring, on March 22, 1959, Alec Ulmann made the announcement that he was applying for a date to run the first United States Formula 1 Grand Prix within the month of December, 1959.

The First and Second United States Grands Prix

Even though the procedures, rules and requirements for a Formula 1 event are totally different from those applying to a sports car event, Alec and Mary Ulmann and their friends managed once again to pull it off. They even got lucky. Sebring would be the last championship race of the 1959 season and the preceding event was the Grand Prix of Italy at Monza on September 13. Stirling Moss won the Monza race in a Cooper-Climax, and that left the championship undecided. Sebring would be the race where the world championship would be won or lost. Three drivers

Stirling Moss in 1955. One of the best and greatest racing drivers of all times. Journalist navigator, Dennis Jenkinson is on the left.

Credit: Mercedes-Benz

still had a shot at the prize: Stirling Moss, Tony Brooks (Ferrari) and Jack Brabham (Cooper-Climax). All the world motor racing press would be there.

The race itself was thrilling. Moss started strong until, early in the race, his transmission failed. The championship was now in play just between Brooks and Brabham. The latter took the lead, followed by two teammates, Bruce McLaren and Maurice Trintignant, Brooks trailing in fourth. This went on until the last lap when, 1200 feet before the finish line, Brabham ran out of fuel! Seconds later, McLaren took the checkered flag, followed by Trintignant and Brooks. Brabham was now pushing his car towards the finish line under the hot Florida sun. The crowd was cheering him with wild applause. Brabham finally made it to the line in just less than five minutes, in time to be classified fourth. Then he collapsed from exhaustion. Still, this finish gave him the points he needed to win the world championship, four points ahead of Tony Brooks.

Tough exciting, the race was not a popular success. Very few spectators witnessed it and the Automobile Racing Club of Florida (ARCF) Ulmann had incorporated to capitalize on Formula 1 lost money. The following year, he transported the Grand Prix to Riverside, California, where he hoped a broader interest in car racing would make a big difference. It did not. Most of the great teams and champions came, raced and gave a grand show, but almost nobody came to watch. Ulmann lost more money and the Formula 1 people were not happy. That is when Watkins Glen and Cameron Argetsinger became a desirable alternative.

Formula 1 at The Glen

After Ulmann's announcement at Sebring in March of 1959, it was obvious to Cameron Argestinger that he would have to bide his time before he would have a chance of bringing Formula 1 to the Glen. Even before that, however, Argetsinger and Watkins Glen had begun to establish a certain international reputation. The Watkins Glen Grand Prix Corporation staged a first Formule Libre race, a modernized version of the original Seneca Cup but now for professional drivers, in October of 1958. It was both a popular and participant success. Phil Hill and Dan Gurney were there, as well as some hot Ferrari prototypes which had raced at Le Mans. Jo Bonnier won in a 250F Grand Prix Maserati. Public attendance was high and the money was good for everyone.

The feat was repeated in 1959 (Stirling Moss being the star and winner in a Formula 1 Cooper), then in 1960, where world Champion Jack Brabham was on the grid. Over the span of those three years, public attendance quadrupled to highly profitable levels. The coffers were being filled, but the SCCA did not like it. No matter, Argetsinger and the Watkins Glen Grand Prix Corporation kept pushing ahead. When the second U. S. Grand Prix at Riverside proved a financial loser and an embarrassment for the FIA, the Watkins Glen officers moved in. They applied to become the official site of the United States Grand Prix. Though Alec Ulmann fought them through the summer (for which Argetsinger bears him no grudge), the Upper New York State people won.

The third United States Grand Prix was held at Watkins Glen on October 8, 1961. Though Phil Hill had already clinched the world championship title in a Ferrari at Monza one month earlier, all the top teams but Ferrari showed up. October 8 turned out to be a warm Indian summer day and public attendance was beyond expectations. For the record, Innes Ireland won the race in a Lotus-Climax, followed by Dan Gurney (Porsche) and Tony Brooks (BRM).

From then on and for two decades, Watkins Glen became the permanent stage of the United States Grand Prix, until 1980 when FIA politics changed markedly. From 1981 on, other venues were chosen such as Las Vegas, Long Beach, Phoenix, and even downtown Detroit, the latter two on the basis of dubious criteria. Those locales were quite inappropriate to the spirit of Formula 1 racing, and the lack of local popular support proved it. The last gasp was the Phoenix Grand Prix of 1991 which had an attendance of only 10,000 people (as opposed to, for instance, more than 250,000 at Monza). The United States Grand Prix for Formula 1 disappeared after that contract ran out.

Final Reflections

Cameron Argestinger, with almost fifty years of perspective over his whole intimate experience with road racing in America, reflects that, "The 'Great Controversy' and its aftermath in all likelihood postponed the development of international/professional road racing in America by up to ten years."

Perhaps, Cameron Argetsinger is too kind. Between 1965 and 1972 European and American road racing appeared fused, with both Daytona and Sebring being part of the world endurance manufacturer's championship, and Watkins Glen being host of the United States Formula 1 Grand Prix. By 1980, it all vanished. To this day, American motorsport, though very rich and growing fast in popularity, remains insular and dominated by oval track racing. The rest of the world, from Europe to Latin America and the Far East, is focused on Formula 1, sports car racing and rallying.

The chance to unite the two sides was an open option in the early days, when everything on either side was so young that merging or blending would have been simple and bonding for the long term would have been easy. Cameron Argetsinger, Alec Ulmann, Miles Collier and a few others saw that then. They were overuled by what can only be called a conservative old guard. That affected the world of international motorsport to the end of the millenium. May some lessons be learned from this by the powerful people who rule the most prestigious formula of motorsport today.

The Watkins Glen Pioneers - Still Involved

Cameron and Jean Argetsinger still live in Burdett, New York, a few miles north of Watkins Glen. Cameron has a busy law practice in Montour Falls. He and Jean are very active in their community. They were instrumental in the planning and organization of the Watkins Glen Motor Sport Research Library, the first of its kind in America. Its goal is to become a global source of information for all and every aspect of motorsport, from 1894 when the first car race ever was staged in France, onward.

William F. Milliken Jr. lives near Buffalo, New York, and is still occupied with the Cornell Aeronautical Laboratory's offshoot, named CALSPAN. In 1995, he and his son Douglas jointly wrote a book titled "Race Car Vehicle Dynamics," an exhaustive treatment of a subject about which relatively little had been written. The book, published by the Society of Automotive Engineers, has been a runaway success and is in its fifth printing. The Milliken and Argesinger families are very close and visit each other regularly.

Don Brubaker, one of the founding fathers and owner of Seneca Lodge, still paces the lounge, but his children now run the rustic establishment. The large bar room is crammed with racing memorabilia, from the early races to the Formula 1 days. Son Jim Brubaker has a collection of 8 mm films covering many of the races, from 1951 on. Copies of those films, made on video cassettes, are stocked behind the bar. Any friendly customer can ask for a specific videotape to be played and out comes the right cassette. In a minute, it goes into the nearby VCR and the historical footage soon shows on the large television screen.

Denver Cornett, the man of Stone Bridge fame, is alive and well in Kentucky, his home State. He still has the MG with which he raced at Watkins Glen starting in 1948. He maintains it in superb condition and returns to the Glen almost every year to participate in the September vintage race weekends. On a tour of the old course in that very car with Cornett at the wheel, said the veteran, as he was shifting gear like a champ up Old Corning Hill, "Man, I wish they'd stage another race on this course just one more time. I'd be the first to register!"

TOP RIGHT: Denver Cornett and the author at Seneca Lodge in September, 1997.

BOTTOM RIGHT: Larry Black, Director of The Cunningham Company, in the first continuation C4R (chassis number R-5219) at Watkins Glen in September, 1997.

Briggs Swift Cunningham II is retired in California. The Internal Revenue Service forced the closing of the West Palm Beach shop in 1954: as the C-3 was not selling well, the corporation's financial losses could no longer be written off. Shortly thereafter, "Mr. C." signed a deal with Jaguar Ltd. and went on racing D-Types, then E-types at Le Mans and in America. In 1958, he took some time off to participate in the world's most prestigious sailing competition: The America's Cup. This was the first challenge of the Cup since 1933. Briggs and his crew, sailing Columbia, first emerged victorious from the elimination races between American contestants, then won the Cup outright against the British yacht Sceptre.

Jaguar withdrew from racing in 1956 and by 1958, the D-Type was no longer competitive. Cunningham switched to Lister-Jaguars, then Corvettes and Maseratis. Briggs Cunningham was made Honorary Citizen by the city of Le Mans. Equipe Cunningham was finally disbanded in 1963. Briggs' last race was the 1966 Sebring Twelve Hours, where he entered and shared a Porsche 904 with John

Credit: Collection Edmond Perry

The Cunningham Maserati Tipo 63 (chassis number 63.001) raced at Spa by owner Edmond Pery in 1995. The car was originally bought by Cunningham in 1961. It was raced that same year at Road America and Riverside.

Fitch. They did not finish. After that race, Cunningham, then 59, and John realized they were not serious about winning but perhaps just wanted to see the race close-up. It was time to retire, and they did. The Cunningham legend, however, would go on. Son Briggs Cunningham III incorporated The Cunningham Company in Lime Rock, Connecticut in 1994. They are successfully building and selling a continuation C-4R and are branching out into other fields.

Briggs Cunningham was the spark that lit the international side of American road racing; he and his friends led the United States single-handedly into the international scene. His influence on the sport in America was monumental, and he was a friend to all who knew him then and now.

John Cooper Fitch went on racing for Mercedes-Benz, Porsche, then the Chevrolet Corvette team at both Sebring and Le Mans. He and co-driver Stirling Moss won the 1955 Tourist Trophy for Mercedes-Benz. After he retired from racing, John became the driving force behind the development and construction of the popular Lime Rock, Connecticut, race track. Throughout his racing career, Fitch only had one life-threatening crash (Reims Twelve-Hours, 1953, in Cunningham C-5R). Nonetheless, safety in road racing was always a primary concern with him.

John Fitch holds several patents for safety-related devices, including the yellow sand-filled barrels that have helped save countless lives at expressway junctions. Today,

he is still entrepreneurially developing more advanced safety-related devices in friendly cooperation with Bill Milliken. In January of 1998, John Fitch was awarded the Kenneth A. Stonex Roadside Safety Award in recognition and appreciation of his achievements in promoting highway safety.

The author started this book after seeing about thirty original color slides of the early Watkins Glen races while staying with friend Eric Davison in Manhattan Beach, California. Philippe Defechereux then was familiar with Watkins Glen's historical importance to a large degree, but he knew only the highlights of those early years. When he started his research, he was quickly swept by the enthusiasm of countless people who were excited that the magnificent story of which they were part was finally going to be told.

Between the day the first and last word of this book were written, the author had the extraordinary pleasure of talking to and meeting with many of the fascinating people "who were there." They had a lot to say that was never before recorded. The author was deluged with anecdotes, hundreds more original photos and received terrific support from a wide network of aficionados. Philippe Defechereux now believes there are still countless original documents, letters, photos, etc. out there, sleeping in attics, resting in dusty boxes, forgotten. Those are probably destined to be lost one day by a new generation unaware of the great feats a group of special heroes accomplished in the 1950's and 1960's. If you think you might have some of those, somewhere, please contact us.

TOP LEFT: Lester Smalley in an Indy two-man racer at Watkins Glen in 1997.

BOTTOM LEFT: The author and Bill Green (back), foremost historian for Watkins Glen, in the latter's study near his favorite race track.

TOP RIGHT: "Ardent Alligator," a.k.a. Riley-Mercury, winner of the 1949 Grand Prix as it stood in 1997 before getting back its original red paint job.

BOTTOM RIGHT: Early Internationalists. From left to right: Edward F. Ulmann, Arthur Richards, Alec Ulmann, Cameron Argetsinger and Mary Ulmann.

Watkins Glen 1948 Junior Prix — Entry List and Results — October 2, 1948

Place	Status	Laps	Driver	No.	Manufacturer	MY	Model	Color	C.	Engine	Type	Owner	Race Notes
1	✓	4	Griswold, Frank T., Jr.	3.5	Alfa Romeo	'38	8C 2900B	Blue	C	Alfa	L-8	F. Griswold	Winner Class C
2	✓	4	Cunningham, Briggs S	9	Special	'39	BuMerc	Blue	D	Buick	V-8	Cunningham	Winner Class D
3	✓	4	Ksayian, Haig	8	MG	'48	TC	D. Green	B	MG	L-4	Cunningham	Winner Class B
4	✓	4	Felton, Col. George E.	12	Vauxhall	27	OE 30/98	Silver	C	Vauxhall	L-4	G. Felton	Driver spun at "Thrill Curve," recovered
5	✓	4	Collier, Miles	25	MG	'47	TC	Black	B	MG	L-4	Collier Bros.	
6	✓	4	Collier, Samuel C.	24	MG	'46	TC	Beige	B	MG	L-4	Collier Bros.	
7	✓	4	Stiles, Phillip H.	29	MG	'48	TC	Black	A	MG	L-4	P. Stiles	Winner Class A
8	✓	4	Caswell, George C.	5	B.N.C.	'30	Type 527	Black	B	Ford	V-8	G. Caswell	
9	✓	4	Bedford, Dean, Jr.	3	MG	'47	TC	Black	A	MG	L-4	D. Bedford	
10	✓	4	Gallagher, William F.	14	MG	'48	TC	Green	A	MG	L-4	W. Gallagher	
11	✓	4	Addams, Charles S.	1	Mercedes	'29	S	Silver+	D	Mercedes	L-6	C. Addams	
12	✓	4	Vaughn, E. Mike	30	Lagonda	'38	Rapids	Silver	D	Lagonda	L-6	E. M. Vaughn	
13	✓	4	Boardman, George F.	4	Jaguar	'36	SS-1	Black	B	Jaguar	L-6	G. Boardman	
14	✓	4	Gegen, Robert B.	16	Bugatti	'32	T. 38	Blue	B	Bugatti	L-8	R. Gegen	
15	✓	4	Hendrie, George S.	17	Alfa Romeo	'28	6C 1750	Red	B	Alfa	L-6	G. Hendrie	Doors taken off to shed weight
16	✓	4	Brundage, J. J.	33	Duesenberg	'31	1930 Indy Racer	Black	C	Ford	V-8	J. Brudage	
17	✓	4	Wilson, Dud C.	32	Stutz	'28	BB Black Hawk	White	D	Stutz	L-8	D. Wilson	Last classified finisher
18	DNF	3	Milliken, William F, Jr.	21	Bugatti	'27	T. 35 A	Blue	B	Bugatti	L-8	W. Milliken	Flipped at "Thrill Curve," named corner
		1	Argetsinger, Cameron R.	2	MG	'48	TC	Red	A	MG	L-4	C. Argetsinger	
			Cornett, Denver B., Jr.	7	MG	'47	TC	Black	A	MG	L-4	D. Cornett	Went off into creek at Stone Bridge
			Hill, Kenneth	18	Special	'47	Merlin	Blue	C	Mercury	V-8	K. Hill	
			Linton, Irving Otto	20	MG	'33	J4	Black	A	MG	L-4	I. O. Linton	
			Weaver, George B.	31	Maserati	'36	V8RI	Red+	D	Maserati	V-8	G. Weaver	Brake failure
24	DNS		Ceresole, Paul	6	BMW	'38	327/80 MM	?	B	BMW	L-6	P. Ceresole	
			du Mont, John S.	10	Delahaye	'48	135 M	Black	C	Delahaye	L-6	du Mont	
			du Mont, William W.	11	Triumph	'47	1800	Black	B	Triumph	L-4	du Mont	
			Fitch, John C.	13	MG	'48	TC	?	A	MG	L-4	J. Fitch	
			Floria, James D.	34	Jaguar	'36	SS-1	?	B	Jaguar	L-6	J. Floria	
			Garthwaite, Albert, Jr.	15	Bugatti	'39	T. 57 C	?	C	Bugatti	L-8	A. Garthwaite	
			Hoe, Arthur James	19	Duesenberg	'34	J. Phaeton	?	D	Duesenberg	L-8	A. J. Hoe	
			Mueller, Carl E.	23	Bentley	'29	Van Den Plas	?	C	Bentley	L-4	C. Mueller	
			Sceli, Russell G.	26	Talbot Lago	'38	"Goutte d'Eau"	Silver+	C	Lago	L-6	R. Sceli	
			Shaw, Dr. Roger	27	MG	'48	TC	?	A	MG	L-4	R. Shaw	
			Stack, John Paul	28	Bentley	'25	Red Label	?	B	Bentley	L-4	J. P. Stack	

Watkins Glen 1948 Grand Prix — Entry List and Results — October 2, 1948

Place	Status	Laps	Driver	No.	Manufacturer	MY	Model	Color	C.	Engine	Type	Owner	Race Notes
1	✓	8	Griswold, Frank T., Jr.	35	Alfa Romeo	'38	8C 2900 B	Blue	C	Alfa	L-8	F. Griswold	Winner Class C
2	✓	8	Cunningham, Briggs S	9	Special	'39	BuMerc	Blue	D	Buick	V-8	Cunningham	Winner Class D
3	✓	8	Ksayian, Haig	8	MG	'48	TC	D. Green	B	MG	L-4	Cunningham	Winner Class B
4	✓	8	Collier, Samuel C.	24	MG	'46	TC	Beige	B	MG	L-4	Collier Bros	
5	✓	8	Collier, Miles	25	MG	'47	TC	Black	B	MG	L-4	Collier Bros.	
6	✓	8	Stiles, Phillip H.	29	MG	'48	TC	Black	A	MG	L-4	P. Stiles	Winner Class A
7	✓	8	Cornett, Denver B., Jr.	7	MG	'47	TC	Black	A	MG	L-4	D. Cornett	
8	✓	8	Gallagher, William F.	14	MG	'48	TC	Black	A	MG	L-4	W. Gallagher	
9	✓	8	Argetsinger, Cameron R.	2	MG	'48	TC	Red	A	MG	L-4	C. Argetsinger	
10	✓	8	Bedford, Dean, Jr.	3	MG	'47	TC	Black	A	MG	L-4	D. Bedford	
11	DSQ	7	Wilson, Dud C.	32	Stutz	'28	BB Black Hawk	White	D	Stutz	L-8	D. Wilson	Flagged off on lap 8
12	DNF	3	Boardman, George F.	18	Jaguar	'36	SS-1	Blue	C	Jaguar	L-6	G. Boardman	
		1	Felton, Col. George E.	12	Vauxhall	'27	OE 30/98	Silver	C	Vauxhall	L-4	G. Felton	
			Vaughn, E. Mike	12	Lagonda	'38	Rapide	Silver	C	Lagonda	L-6	E. M. Vaughn	
			Weaver, George B.	31	Maserati	'36	V8RI	Red+	C	Maserati	V-8	G. Weaver	

Watkins Glen 1949 Seneca Cup — Entry List and Results — September 17, 1949

Place	Status	Laps	Driver	No.	Manufacturer	MY	Model	Color	C.	Engine	Type	Owner	Race Notes
1	✓	4	Weaver, George B.	11	Maserati	'36	V8RI	Red+	D	Maserati	V-8	G. Weaver	
2	✓	4	Cunningham, Briggs S.	4	Ferrari	'48	166 SC	Red	D	Ferrari	V-12	Cunningham	Winner Class C
3	✓	4	Collier Samuel C.	5	MG	'48	TC	D. Green	C	MG	L-4	Cunningham	
4	✓	4	Roberts, George	6	Special	'39	BuMerc	Blue	D	Buick	V-8	Cunningham	Winner Class D
5	✓	4	Cole, Tommy L. H.	47	H.R.G.	'49	Sports	Green	B	Singer	L-4	T. Cole	Winner Class B
6	✓	4	Fitch, John C.	18	MG	'48	TC	?	C	MG	L-4	J. Fitch	
7	✓	4	Garroway, Dave	16	Jaguar	'39	SS-100	P. Yellow	D	Jaguar	L-6	D. Garroway	
8	✓	4	Felton, Col. George E.	12	Vauxhall	'27	OE 30/98	Silver	D	Vauxhall	L-4	G. Felton	
9	✓	4	Cornett, Denver B., Jr.	7	MG	'47	TC	Black+	B	MG	L-4	D. Cornett	
10	✓	4	Iselin, Peter	46	H.R.G.	'49	Sports	?	B	Singer	L-4	P. Iselin	
11	✓	4	Brocken, Karl	28	MG	'48	TC	?	B	MG	L-4	K. Brocken	
12	✓	4	Allen, Neal A.	43	MG	'49	TC	?	B	MG	L-4	N. Allen	
13	✓	4	Ehrman, Gus O.	60	MG	'49	TC	?	B	MG	L-4	G. Ehrman	
14	✓	4	Johnson, Alden P.	42	MG	'47	TC	Black	B	MG	L-4	A. Johnson	
15	✓	4	Hamill, Corwith	31	Allard	'47	K1	?	D	Ford	V-8	C. Hamill	
16	✓	4	Kotchan, Charles J. P.	61	MG	'49	TC	?	B	MG	L-4	MG Car Club	
17	✓	4	Torco, Louis	12	Alfa Romeo	'28	6C 1750	Red	C	Alfa	L-6	G. Hendrie	
18	✓	4	Wacker, Fred G., Jr.	8	MG	'48	TC	?	B	MG	L-4	F. Wacker	
19	✓	4	Hill, Kenneth F.	64	Special	'47	Merlin	Red	D	Mercury	V-8	K. Hill	
20	✓	4	Carson, James T.	62	MG	'48	TC	Red	B	MG	L-4	J. Carson	
21	✓	4	Ogilvie, E. Reg	38	MG	'48	TC	P. Yellow	B	MG	L-4	E. Ogilvie	
22	✓	4	Pfund, Ledyard H.	30	Special	'34	Ford	Silver	D	Ford	V-8	L. Pfund	
23	✓	4	Kouns, Charles	57	MG	'48	TC	?	B	MG	L-4	C. Kouns	
24	✓	4	Collier, Miles	39	Special	'39	Riley-Mercury	Red	D	Mercury	V-8	Collier Bros.	
25	✓	4	Pompeo, Antonio	24	Fiat	'49	1100 MM	D. Blue	A	Fiat	L-4	A. Pompeo	Winner Class A
26	✓	4	Whitcomb, David	19	MG	'49	TC	?	B	MG	L-4	D. Whitcomb	
27	✓	4	Fleming, George W.	45	MG	'49	TC	?	B	MG	L-4	G. Fleming	
28	✓	4	Vaughn, E. Mike	65	MG	'49	TC	?	B	MG	L-4	E. M. Vaughn	
29	DNF	3	Hill, Logan	21	Cisitalia	'49	1100 Coupe	Sil. Blue	A	Fiat	L-4	L. Hill	
		2	Boswell, Perry	51	Crosley	'49	Hot Shot	White	A	Crosley	L-4	A. Ulmann	
			Ferguson, Joseph B., Jr.	53	Cisitalia	'49	1100 Coupe	Sil. Blue	A	Fiat	L-4	J. Ferguson	
			Huntoon, George	23	Alfa Romeo	'35	8C 2600 Monza	Blue	D	Alfa	L-8	Sam Bird	
			Wilson, Dud C.	9	Mercedes	'30	S	Black	D	M-B	L-6	D. Wilson	
		1	Christy, William	15	MG	'47	TC	?	C	MG	L-4	W. Christy	
			Richard, Mark Gadd	58	MG	'48	TC	?	B	MG	L-4	M. G. Richard	
			Sceli, Russ G.	27	Bugatti	'37	T. 57	Blue	D	Buick	L-8	R. Sceli	
		0	Haynes, Richard	32	Fiat	'48	1100 S	Sil. Green	A	Fiat	L-4	Haynes/Keller	
38	DNS		Edwards, G. Sterling	54	Special	'49	Edwards	?	D	Ford	V-8	S. Edwards	
			Shaw, Dr. Roger	1	MG	'48	TC	?	B	MG	L-4	R. Shaw	
			Simpson, Davis	29	MG	'48	TC	?	B	MG	L-4	D. Simpson	

Watkins Glen 1949 Grand Prix — Entry List and Results — September 17, 1949

Place	Status	Laps	Driver	No.	Manufacturer	MY	Model	Color	C.	Engine	Type	Owner	Race Notes
1	✓	15	Collier, Miles	39	Special	'39	Riley-Mercury	Red	D	Mercury	V-8	Collier Bros.	Winner Class D
2	✓	15	Cunningham, Briggs S.	4	Ferrari	'48	166 SC	Red	D	Ferrari	V-12	Cunningham	
3	✓	15	Roberts, George	6	Special	'39	BuMerc	Blue	D	Buick	V-8	Cunningham	
4	✓	15	Cole, Tommy L. H.	48	H.R.G.	'49	Sports	Green	B	Singer	L-4	T. Cole	Winner Class B
5	✓	15	Fitch, John C.	18	MG	'48	TC	?	C	MG	L-4	J. Fitch	
6	✓	15	Wacker, Fred G., Jr.	8	MG	'48	TC	?	B	MG	L-4	F. Wacker	
7	✓	15	Brocken, Karl	28	MG	'48	TC	?	B	MG	L-4	K. Brocken	
8	✓	15	Hill, Logan	21	Cisitalia	'49	1100 Coupe	Sil. Blue	A	Fiat	L-4	L. Hill	Winner Class A
9	✓	15	Felton, Col. George E.	12	Vauxhall	'27	OE 30/98	Silver	D	Vauxhall	L-4	G. Felton	
10	✓	15	Pauley, James C.	36	Lea-Francis	'49	Type Sport	?	C	Lea-Fran.	L-4	J. Pauley	Winner Class C
11	✓	15	Ferguson, Joseph B., Jr.	53	Cisitalia	'49	1100 Coupe	Sil. Blue	A	Fiat	L-4	J. Ferguson	
12	✓	15	Ehrman, Gus O.	60	MG	'49	TC	?	B	MG	L-4	G. Ehrman	
13	✓	15	Eldridge, Arthur S.	17	MG	'48	TC	?	B	MG	L-4	A. Eldridge	
14	✓	15	Keith, Rowland O. H.	49	MG	'48	TC	?	B	MG	L-4	R. Keith	
15	✓	15	Collier, Samuel C.	5	MG	'48	TC	Black	C	MG	L-4	Cunningham	
16	✓	15	Kastrup, James S.	63	MG	'48	TC	?	B	MG	L-4	J. Kastrup	
17	✓	15	Kotchan, Charles J. P.	61	MG	'49	TC	?	A	MG	L-4	MG Car Club	
18	✓	14	Garroway, Dave	16	Jaguar	'39	SS-100	P. Yellow	D	Jaguar	L-6	D. Garroway	
19	✓	13	Carson, James T.	62	MG	'48	TC	D. Blue	B	MG	L-4	J. Carson	
20	✓	13	Bentley, John	14	MG	'49	TC	?	C	MG	L-4	J. Bentley	
21	✓	13	Johnson, Alden P.	42	MG	'47	TC	Black	B	MG	L-4	A. Johnson	
22	✓	13	Pompeo, Antonio	24	Fiat	'49	1100 MM	D. Blue	A	Fiat	L-4	A. Pompeo	
23	✓	13	Pfund, Ledyard H.	30	Special	'34	Ford	Silver	D	Ford	V-8	L. Pfund	
24	✓	13	Ogilvie, E. Reg	38	MG	'48	TC	P. Yellow	A	MG	L-4	E. Ogilvie	
25	✓	13	Hamill, Corwith	31	Allard	'48	K1	?	D	Ford	V-8	C. Hamill	
26	✓	13	Whitcomb, David	19	MG	'49	TC	?	B	MG	L-4	D. Whitcomb	
27	✓	13	Grier, Robert	25	BMW	'38	MM Coupe	Red	D	BMW	L-6	A. Pompeo	
28	✓	12	Cade, Phillip J.	10	Duesenberg	'34	J Sedan Conv.	?	D	Duesenberg	V-8	P. Cade	
29	✓	12	Fleming, George W.	45	MG	'49	TC	?	B	MG	L-4	G. Fleming	
30	DNF	11	Huntoon, George	23	Alfa Romeo	'35	8C 2600 Monza	Blue	D	Alfa	L-8	Sam Bird	
			Moran, Charles, Jr.	20	Bugatti	'29	T. 35 A	P. Yellow	C	Bugatti	L-8	C. Moran	
		10	Cornett, Denver B., Jr.	7	MG	'47	TC	Black+	B	MG	L-4	D. Cornett	
			Milliken, William F., Jr.	26	F.W.D.	'32	Miller	White+	D	Ford	L-4	F.W.D.	
		9	Keller, Robert	32	Fiat	'48	1100 S	Sil. Green	A	Fiat	L-4	Haynes/Keller	
		5	Allen, Neal A.	43	MG	'49	TC	?	B	MG	L-4	N. Allen	
			Iselin, Peter	46	H.R.G.	'49	Sports	?	B	Singer	L-4	P. Iselin	
		4	Arkus-Duntov, Zora	34	Allard	'49	J2 "Ardun"	?	D	Ford	V-8	Z. Arkus-Duntov	
			Kulok, Larry	56	Allard	'47	K1	?	D	Mercury	V-8	L. Kulok	
		3	Ord, Mel	40	Alfa Romeo	'38	8C 2900 B'S'	Yellow+	D	Alfa	L-8	T. Lee/W. Brown	
			Stevenson, Bruce J.	52	MG	'48	TC	?	B	MG	L-4	B. Stevenson	
			Timmins, Paul J.	55	Special	'49	Ardun Ford	Silver+	D	Ford	V-8	P. Timmins	
		1	Argetsinger, Cameron R.	3	Bugatti	'27	T. 35 A	Blue	C	Bugatti	L-8	W. Milliken	Fuel Pump Failure
		0	Christy, William	15	MG	'47	TC	Red	C	MG	L-4	W. Christy	
44	DNS		Boswell, Perry	37	Cisitalia	'47	Special	?	B	Offy	L-4	P. Boswell	
			Brundage, J. J.	44	Duesenberg	'30	Special	Black	D	Mercury	V-8	J. Brundage	
			Ceresole, Paul	35	BMW	'38	328 MM	?	C	BMW	L-6	P. Ceresole	
			Collier, Samuel C.	2	MG	'48	TC	?	C	MG	L-4	Collier Bros.	
			Grier, Robert	(25)	Alfa Romeo	'48	SC 6C 2500	?	D	Alfa	L-6	A. Pompeo	
			Hill, Logan	21	Alfa Romeo	'33	8C 2300	?	D	Alfa	L-8	L. Hill	
			N/A	33	Allard	'48	"Ardun" Special	?	D	Ford 100	V-8	Z. Arkus-Duntov	
			Simpson, Davis	29	MG	'48	TC	?	B	MG	L-4	D. Simpson	
			Stiles, James E., Jr.	22	MG	'48	TC	?	B	MG	L-4	J. Stiles	
			Weaver, George B.	11	Maserati	'36	V8RI	Red+	D	Maserati	V-8	G. Weaver	

Watkins Glen 1950 Seneca Cup — Entry List and Results — September 23, 1950

Place	Status	Laps	Driver	No.	Manufacturer	MY	Model	Color	C.	Engine	Type	Owner	Race Notes
1	✓	15	Walters, Phil	55	Healey	'50	Cad Special	?	B	Cadillac	V-8	Cunningham	Winner Class B
2	✓	15	Goldschmidt, Alfred E.	98	Allard	'50	J2	Red	B	Cadillac	V-8	A. Goldschmidt	
3	✓	15	Collier, Miles	1	Special	'39	Riley - Mercury	Red	C	Mercury	V-8	Collier Bros.	Winner Class C
4	✓	15	Ullrich, Hal	93	Bugatti	'31	T. 54	?	B	Bugatti	L-8	D. C. Peck	
5	✓	15	Boynton, Charles T., II	77	Frazer-Nash	'50	LM Replica	?	E	Bristol	L-6	C. Boynton	Winner Class E
6	✓	15	Wilder, Robert John	66	Special	'36	Ladd	?	C	Ford	V-8	R. Wilder	Nicknamed "Old Grey Mare"
7	✓	15	Stevens, Brooks	72	Jaguar	'50	XK-120	?	C	Jaguar	L-6	B. Stevens	
8	✓	15	Cook, Hobbart A. H.	102	MG	'49	TC	?	E	MG	L-4	H. Cook	
9	✓	15	Sabal, Joe B., Jr.	19	MG	'48	TC	?	E	MG	L-4	J. Sabal	
10	DNF	13	Grier, Robert S.	97	Allard	'50	J2	?	B	Cadillac	V-8	R. Grier	
		12	Knudson, Ralph W.	95	Veritas	'49	RS	?	E	BMW	L-6	R. Knudson	
		10	Abendroth, M.E.	52	Jaguar	'50	XK-120	?	C	Jaguar	L-6	M. Abendroth	
			Tours, Lt. Elliott C.	34	MG	'48	TC	?	E	MG	L-4	E. Tours	
		6	Dominianni, Frank J.	83	Special	'46	D&D Ford	?	C	Cadillac	V-8	F./D. Dominianni	
		4	Fitch, John C.	88	Special	'39	Merc-Lagonda	?	C	Lagonda	L-8	R. N. Sabourin	
			Hill, Kenneth F.	41	Special	'47	Merlin	Blue	C	Mercury	V-8	K. Hill	
			Hoe, Arthur J.	53	Duesenberg	'50	J Special	?	B	Duesenberg	L-8	A. J. Hoe	
		3	Weaver, George B.	3	Maserati	'36	V8RI	Red+	C	Maserati	V-8	G. Weaver	
		0	Cornett, Denver B., Jr.	7	Special	'32	Ford	Maroon	C	Ford	V-8	D. Cornett	
			Davidson, Jean	79	Allard	'50	J2	Black	B	Cadillac	V-8	J. Davison	Crashed against tree
			Huntoon, Goerge G.	44	Duesenberg	'30	Special	Black	B	Olds 88	V-8	J. Brundage	
22	DNS		Altemus, James D.	27	Special	'50	Altemus Stab.	?	C	?	V-8	J. Altemus	
			Davison, Charles H. A.	71	Jaguar	'39	SS-100	White	C	Jaguar	L-6	C. H. A. Davison	Ran rod bearing on way to Watkins Glen
			Felix, David H. H.	23	Alfa Romeo	'32	8C 2300 MM	?	C	Alfa	L-8	D. Felix	
			German, Arthur W.	10	Bugatti	'30	T. 35 B	?	C	Bugatti	L-8	A. German	
			Lansing, Steve	105	Fiat	'49	1100 MM	?	F	Fiat	L-4	A. Pompeo	
			Mashinter, William H.	16	Allard	'50	J2	?	B	Cadillac	V-8	W. Mashinter	
			Pompeo, Antoni	61	Alfa Romeo	'49	6C 2500 Coupe	?	D	Alfa	L-6	A. Pompeo	
			Vilardi, Dolph	58	Special	'50	Vilardi-Young	?	C	Ford	V-8	G. Vilardi	

Watkins Glen 1950 Queen Catharine Cup — Entry List and Results — September 23, 1950

Place	Status	Laps	Driver	No.	Manufacturer	MY	Model	Color	C.	Engine	Type	Owner	Race Notes
1	✓	8	Keith, Rowland O. H.	24	MG	'48	TC	?	F	MG	L-4	R. O. H. Keith	Winner Class F
2	✓	8	Koster, Fritz	101	H. R. G.	'48	Sports	?	F	Singer	L-4	F. Koster	
3	✓	8	Brocken, Carl	65	MG	'50	TD	?	F	MG	L-4	K. Brocken	
4	✓	8	Thomas, Marsh	63	MG	'47	TC	?	F	MG	L-4	M. Thomas	
5	✓	8	Ogilvie, E. Reg	51	MG	'48	TC	?	F	MG	L-4	E. R. Ogilvie	
6	✓	8	Beazell, Lester S.	109	MG	'50	TD	?	F	MG	L-4	L. Beazell	
7	✓	8	Magenheimer, Robert	78	MG	'48	TC	?	F	MG	L-4	R. Magenheimer	
8	✓	8	Whitcomb, David	15	MG	'49	TC	?	F	MG	L-4	D. Whitcomb	
9	✓	8	Farago, Paul	82	Fiat	'46	Farago Special	D. Blue	G	Fiat	L-4	P. Farago	Winner Class G
10	DNF	7	Ash, David	96	MG	'50	TD	?	F	MG	L-4	D. Dash	
			Babin, Arthur H.	12	Crosley	'50	TD	?	G	Crosley	L-4	A. Babin	
			Crocker, Peter J.	36	MG	'48	TC	?	F	MG	L-4	P. Crocker	
			Ehrman, Gus O.	47	MG	'50	TD	?	F	MG	L-4	G. Ehrman	
			Keller, Robert T.	22	Fiat	'48	1100 S	?	G	Fiat	L-4	Haynes/Keller	
			O'Hare, Frank B.	39	MG	'49	TC	?	F	MG	L-4	F. O'Hare	
			Wheeler, Jack W.	69	MG	'50	TD	?	F	MG	L-4	J. Wheeler	
		6	Dominianni, Francis J.	108	MG	'49	TC	?	F	MG	L-4	F. Dominianni	
			Fleming, George W.	18	MG	'49	TC	?	F	MG	L-4	G. Fleming	
			Hildebrand, Kurt	87	Special	'50	VW	Red	F	VW	L-4	K. Hildebrand	
			Lloyd, William B.	9	MG	'50	TD	?	F	MG	L-4	W. Lloyd	
			Meyer, Robert B., Jr.	91	MG	'50	TD	?	F	MG	L-4	R. Meyer	
			Stiles, Philip H.	46	H. R. G.	'47	Aero Special	?	F	Singer	L-4	P. Stiles	
		5	Toland, Richard H. R.	14	MG	'34	PA	?	G	MG	L-4	R. Toland	
		3	Whiting, Lawrence H., Jr.	67	Jowett	'50	Jupiter	?	F	Jowett	F-4	L. Whiting	
		2	Stevens, Brooks	73	MG	'48	TC	?	F	MG	L-4	B. Stevens	
		0	Barrett, George M.	74	MG	'50	TD	?	F	MG	L-4	G. Barrett	Accident
			Johnson, Alden P.	38	MG	'47	TC	?	F	MG	L-4	A. Johnson	Accident
			Stearns, Donald P.	25	MG	'50	TD	?	F	MG	L-4	D. Stearns	Accident
29	DNS		Boss, Russel	62	Cisitalia	'49	1100 Coupe	?	G	Fiat	L-4	R. Boss	
			Collins, Robert O.	106	MG	'48	TC	?	F	MG	L-4	R. Collins	
			Iselin, Peter	11	H. R. G.	'49	Sports	?	F	Singer	L-4	P. Iselin	
			Kemp, William S., Jr.	33	BMW	'37	315/40	?	F	BMW	L-6	W. Kemp	
			Linton, Irving Otto	5	Frazer-Nash	'34	TT Replica	?	F	?	L-6	Dr. S. L. Scher	
			Pauley, James E.	28	Cisitalia	'48	1100 Coupe	?	G	Fiat	L-4	J. Pauley	
			Pompeo, Antoni	29	Cisitalia	';49	1100 Coupe	?	G	Fiat	L-4	A. Pompeo	
			Rush, Richard H.	94	Cisitalia	'50	202 Coupe	?	F	Offy	L-4	R. Rush	
			Simpson, Davis	84	MG	'48	TC	?	F	MG	L-4	D. Simpson	
			Sterner, George	92	MG	'48	TC	?	F	MG	L-4	G. Sterner	

Watkins Glen 1950 Grand Prix — Entry List and Results — September 23, 1950

Place	Status	Laps	Driver	No.	Manufacturer	MY	Model	Color	C.	Engine	Type	Owner	Race Notes
1	✓	15	Goldschmidt, Alfred E.	98	Allard	'50	J2	?	B	Cadillac	V-8	A. Goldschmidt	Winner Class B
2	✓	15	Cunningham, Briggs S.	55	Healey	'50	Cad Special	?	B	Cadillac	V-8	Cunningham	
3	✓	15	Wacker, Fred J., Jr.	8	Allard	'50	J2	Red	B	Cadillac	V-8	F. Wacker	(Hydraulic transmission)
4	✓	15	Kimberly, James H.	26	Ferrari	'49	166 MM	Red	E	Ferrari	V-12	J. Kimberly	Winner Class E
5	✓	15	Huntoon, George G.	6	Alfa Romeo	'35	8C 2600	Blue	C	Alfa	L-8	Sam Bird	"Old Reliable" - Winner Class C
6	✓	15	Spear, William C.	111	Ferrari	'50	166 MM	Red	E	Ferrari	V-12	W. Spear	
7	✓	15	Pauly, Jim	48	Nardi-Danese	'48	Alfa Romeo	?	D	Alfa	L-6	Perry B. Fina	Winner Class D
8	✓	15	Fitch, John C.	85	Special	'50	Fitch B	?	D	Ford 60	V-8	J. Fitch	
9	DNF	14	Bentley, John	59	Healey	'50	Silverstone	?	D	Riley	L-4	J. Bentley	
			Floria, James D.	115	Talbot Lago	'38	'Goutte d'Eau'	Black	B	Lago	L-6	J. Floria	
			Hannaway, Brete H.	107	MG	'47	TC	?	E	MG	L-4	B. Hannaway	
			Keith, Rowland O. H.	24	MG	'48	TC	?	F	MG	L-4	R. O. H. Keith	
			Wilson, Dud C.	32	Jaguar	'50	XK-120	?	C	Jaguar	L-6	D. C. Wilson	
		13	Moran, Charles, Jr.	17	MG	'48	TC	?	E	MG	L-4	C. Moran	
		12	Brundage, H. L.	31	MG	'50	TD	?	E	MG	L-4	H. Brundage	
			Stearns, Benedict	37	Jaguar	'50	XK-120	?	C	Jaguar	L-6	B. Stearns	
		10	Reider, Robert W.	75	Jaguar	'50	XK-120	?	C	Jaguar	L-6	R. Reider	
		9	Stevenson, Bruce J.	89	Special	'50	Meyer Cad	?	E	Cadillac	V-8	J. V. Meyer	
		8	Argetsinger, Cameron R.	2	Healey	'50	Silverstone	?	B	Riley	L-4	C. Argetsinger	
			Farago, Paul	82	Fiat	'46	Farago Special	D. Blue	G	Fiat	L-4	P. Farago	
		6	Milliken, William F., Jr.	4	Bugatti	'33	T. 54	?	B	Bugatti	L-8	Dr. S. L. Scher	Rolled over near Seneca Lodge
		4	Garroway, Dave	103	Jaguar	'39	SS-100	P. Yellow	B	Jaguar	L-6	D. Garroway	
		2	Christy, Willard	81	MG	'48	TC	?	E	MG	L-4	W. Christy	
		1	Cole, Tommy L. H.	104	Allard	'50	J2	Silver	B	Cadillac	V-8	T. Cole	
			Collier, Samuel C.	54	Ferrari	'48	166 SC	Red	E	Ferrari	V-12	Cunningham	Crashed fatally past underpass on lap 2
			Griswold, Frank T.	35	Alfa Romeo	'48	SS 8C 1500	Red	D	Alfa	L-8	F. Griswold	Fuel starvation
27	DNS		Arkus-Duntov, Zora	114	Allard	'50	J2 "Ardun"	?	B	Ford	V-8	Z. Arkus-Duntov	
			Ceresole, Paul	112	Jaguar	'50	XK-120	?	C	Jaguar	L-6	P. Ceresole	
			Edwards, Sterling G.	42	Special	'49	Edwards	?	D	Ford 60	V-8	S. Edwards	
			Hill, Logan	21	Jaguar	'50	XK-120	?	B	Jaguar	L-6	L. Hill	Piston problem on race morning
			Kling, Karl	92	Veritas	'50	RS	?	E	BMW	L-6	I. O. Linton	
			Wharton, Richard T.	68	Healey	'50	Silverstone	?	D	Riley	L-4	F. Robinson	

Watkins Glen 1951 Seneca Cup — Entry List and Results — September 15, 1951

Place	Status	Laps	Driver	No.	Manufacturer	MY	Model	Color	C.	Engine	Type	Owner	Race Notes
1	✓	8	Weaver, Goerge B.	35	Maserati	'36	V8RI	Red+		Maserati	V-8	G. Weaver	
2	✓	8	Fitch, John C.	42	Ferrari		195 S	Blue		Ferrari	V-12	B. Cunningham	
3	✓	8	Cunningham, Briggs	42	Ferrari	'48	166 SC	Red		Ferrari	V-12	B. Cunningham	
4	✓	8	Harris, George R., III	3	Allard		J2	?		Cadillac	V-8	G. Harris	
5	✓	6	Bentley, John	41	Special		Meyer Cadillac	?		Cadillac	V-8	J. Meyer	
6	✓	6	Zeder, Fred	81	Allard		J2	?		Chrysler	V-8	F. Zeder	
7	✓	6	Hill, Kenneth F.	1	Jaguar		XK-120	?		Jaguar	L-6	K. Hill	
8	✓	6	O'Brien, Robert	77	Jaguar		XK-120	?		Jaguar	L-6	R. O'Brien	
9	✓	6	?	55	?		?	White+					Record lost; driver/owner unknown
10	✓	6	Ash, David	25	MG	'51	TC	?		MG	L-4	D. Ash	
11	✓	6	Saunders, W. H. III	44	MG		TC	?		MG	L-4	W. Saunders	
12	✓	6	Ramos, Paul P.	66	MG		TD	?		MG	L-4	P. Ramos	
13	✓	6	Byfield, Hugh W.	12	Jowett		Jupiter	Green		Jowett	F-4	H. Byfield	
14	✓	5	Marsh, Saxon	69	Special		Altemus Stab.	?				J. D. Altemus	
15	✓	5	Keith, Roland O. H.	59	Cooper		F3	?				R. O. H. Keith	
16	✓	5	Walters, Phil	56	Cooper		F3	?				B. Cunningham	
17	✓	5	Lipe, Gordon C.	5	Effyh		F3	?				G. Lipe	
18	✓	3	Cornett, Denver B.	7	Special		Ford	Silver		Ford		D. Cornett	
19	✓	3	Gent, Richard W.	26	Special		Bendini-Fiat	Red		Fiat		R. Gent	
20	✓	2	Iselin, Arthur, Jr.	31	Lea-Francis		Type Sport	L. Blue		Lea-Fran.	L-4	A. Iselin	
21	✓	2	Pearsall, F. Randolph	94	Healey		Silverstone ?	?				R. Pearsall	
22	DNS		Cade, Phillip J.	14	Maserati	'36	V8RI			Maserati	V-8	P. Cade	Car broke down on grid
	✓	8	Spear, William C.	34	Ferrari		166 MM	Red	nc	Ferrari	V-12	W. Spear	Allowed as non-official entry

Watkins Glen 1951 Queen Catharine Cup — Entry List and Results — September 15, 1951

Place	Status	Laps	Driver	No.	Manufacturer	MY	Model	Color	C.	Engine	Type	Owner	Race Notes
1	✓	11	Weaver, George B.	15	Jowett		Jupiter	White		Jowett	F-4	M. Hoffman	
2	✓	11	Viall, David C.	19	Special		Lester MG	Green		MG	L-4	D. Viall	
3	✓	11	Koster, Fred	93	H. R. G.		Sports			Singer	L-4	F. Koster	
4	✓	11	Scheffer, Hector S.	24	Siata		Sport	Red		Fiat	L-4	H. Scheffer	
5	✓	10	Ehrman, Gus O.	65	MG		TD			MG	L-4	G. Ehrman	
6	✓	10	O'Hare, Frank	20	MG		?			MG	L-4	F. O'Hare	
7	✓	10	Kinsley, Edward W., Jr.	63	MG		TC			MG	L-4	E. Kinsley	
8	✓	10	Hewitt, Geoffrey B.	58	MG		?			MG	L-4	G. Hewitt	
9	✓	10	Gordon Bennett, John	100	MG		?			MG	L-4	Gordon Bennett	
10	✓	10	Ash, David	25	MG	'51	TC			MG	L-4	D. Ash	
11	✓	10	Ferguson, James W.	68	Morris		F. M.	Green			L-4	J. Ferguson	
12	✓	10	Proctor, Fred, Jr.	91	Siata		Dains	Brown		Fiat	L-4	F. Proctor	
13	✓	10	Hawley, Chester C.	51	MG		?			MG	L-4	C. Hawley	
14	✓	10	Linton, I. Otto	33	Siata		Sport	Blue		Crosley	L-4	A. Pompeo	
15	✓	10	Iselin, Peter	37	H. R. G.	'49	Sports	Green		Singer	L-4	P. Iselin	
16	✓	10	Hildebrand, Kurt	92	Special	'50	VW Porsche	Red			F-4	K. Hildebrand	
17	✓	10	Crocker, Peter J.	43	MG		TC			MG	L-4	P. Crocker	
18	✓	10	Meyer, Robert, Jr.	90	MG		TD			MG	L-4	R. Meyer	
19	✓	10	Vilardi, Dr. Gandolph	4	MG		?			MG	L-4	G. Vilardi	
20	✓	9	Keller, Robert	60	Fiat	'48	1100 S	Sil. Green		Fiat	L-4	Haynes/Keller	
21	✓	8	Lloyd, William B.	30	MG		?			MG	L-4	W. Lloyd	
22	✓	8	Gent, Richard W.	26	Special		Bandini-Fiat	Red		Fiat	L-4	R. Gent	
23	✓	6	Peck, James R.	38	MG		TC	Beige		MG	L-4	J. Peck	
24	✓	5	Magenheimer, Robert	10	MG		TD	White +		MG	L-4	R. Magenheimer	
25	✓	4	Coppel, Alfred, Jr.	23	MG	'51	TD Special	Silver +		MG	L-4	A. Coppel	
26	✓	4	Morrill, S. Sheldon	22	MG		TC			MG	L-4	S. S. Morrill	
27	✓	4	Lansing, Steve	47	Crosley		Hot Shot			Crosley	L-4	D. Sauvigne	
28	✓	4	Ogilvie, Reginald	29	MG		TC			MG	L-4	R. Ogilvie	
29	✓	3	Byfield, Hugh W.	12	Jowett		Jupiter	Green		Jowett	F-4	H. Byfield	
30	✓	2	Schraft, George	49	Crosley		Hot Shot			Crosley	L-4	B. Hannaway	
31	✓	1	Grey, Harry	101	Connaught		L3			Lea-Fran.	F-4	H. Grey	
32	✓	1	Thomas, Marsh C.	82	MG		Special			MG	L-4	M. Thomas	

Watkins Glen 1951 Grand Prix — Entry List and Results — September 15, 1951

Place	Status	Laps	Driver	No.	Manufacturer	MY	Model	Color	C.	Engine	Type	Owner	Race Notes
1	✓	15	Walters, Phil	55	Cunningham	'51	C-2	White +		Chrysler	V-8	B. Cunningham	
2	✓	15	Fitch, John C.	54	Cunningham	'51	C-2	White +		Chrysler	V-8	B. Cunningham	
3	✓	15	Spear, William c.	86	Ferrari	'51	340 America	Whi./Blu.		Ferrari	V-12	W. Spear	
4	✓	15	Cunningham, Briggs	53	Cunningham	'51	C-2	White +		Chrysler	V-8	B. Cunningham	
5	✓	15	Sabal, Joseph B., Jr.	48	Allard		J2	Red		Chrysler	V-8	J. Sabal	
6	✓	15	Harris, George R., III	3	Allard		J2			Cadillac	V-8	G. Harris	
7	✓	14	Zeder, Fred	81	Allard		K2	White		Chrysler	V-8	F. Zeder	
8	✓	14	Johnston, Sherwood	74	Jaguar		XK-120	Black		Jaguar	L-6	S. Johnston	
9	✓	14	Hansgen, Walter E.	95	Jaguar		XK-120	Silver		Jaguar	L-6	W. Hansgen	
10	✓	14	Kimberly, James H.	42	Ferrari		166 SC	Red		Ferrari	V-12	B. Cunningham	
11	✓	6	Bentley, John	77	Jaguar		XK-120	?		Jaguar	L-6	R. O'Brien	
12	✓	13	Wacker, Fred G., Jr.	8	Allard		J2	Red		Cadillac	V-8	F. Wacker	
13	✓	13	Logan, Hill G.	34	Ferrari		166 MM	Red		Ferrari	V-12	W. Spear	
14	✓	13	Moran, Charles, Jr.	17	Ferrari		166 MM	Red		Ferrari	V-12	C. Moran	
15	✓	13	Merrill, Roger, Jr.	71	Jaguar		XK-120	D. Blue		Jaguar	L-6	R. Merrill	
16	✓	13	Stevens, Brooks	99	Jaguar		XK-120	?		Jaguar	L-6	B. Stevens	
17	✓	13	Tobin, E. J.	45	BMW		?	?				E. Tobin	
18	✓	13	Iselin, Arthur, Jr.	31	Lea-Francis		Type Sport	L. Blue		Lea-Fran.	L-4	A. Iselin	
19	✓	13	Grey, Harry	101	Connaught		L3	?		Lea-Fran.	L-4	H. Grey	
20	✓	13	Ramos, Paul P.	66	MG		TC	?		MG	L-4	P. Ramos	
21	✓	5	Hannaway, Brete H.	50	Allard		J2	?		Cadillac	V-8	B. Hannaway	
			Wilder, Robert J.	6	Allard		J2	?		?		R. Wilder	
23	✓	4	Christy, Willard	64	MG		Ford Special	?		Ford 60	V-8	W. Christy	
			Keith, Roland O. H.	5	MG		TC	?		MG	L-4	R. O. H. Keith	
25	DNS		?	40	Bugatti	'33	T. 54	Blue	B	Bugatti	L-8	Dr. S. L. Scher	Held at Cornell Lab as collateral

Watkins Glen 1952 Seneca Cup — Entry List and Results — September 20, 1952

Place	Status	Laps	Driver	No.	Manufacturer	MY	Model	Color	C.	Engine	Type	Owner	Race Notes
1	✓	8	Fitch, John	100	Jaguar	'51	C-Type	Silver	C	Jaguar	L-6	M. Hoffman	
2	✓	8	White, Fred	105	Special	'36	Ladd Ford	?	B	Ford	V-8	F. White	"Old Grey Mare"
3	✓	8	Johnston, Sherwood	106	Special	'51	Chrys. Lagonda	?	B	Chrysler	V-8	G. Fuller	
4	✓	8	Moodie, R. L.	96	Cooper	'51	F3	?	I	L-4		R. L. Moodie	Winner F3
5	✓	8	Iselin, Arthur, Jr.	117	Lea-Francis	'50	Type Sport	?	D	Lea-Fran.	L-4	A. Iselin	
6	✓	8	Koster, Alfons	36	H. R. G.	'50	Sport	?	F	Singer	L-4	A. Koster	
7	✓	7	Kotchan, Charles	128	BMW		328	?	F	BMW	L-4	C. Kotchan	
8	✓	7	Said, Boris, Jr.	126	Cisitalia	'52	GS	?	F	Fiat	L-4	B. Said	Substituted for intended Effyh
9	✓	7	Gray, J. Neal	126	MG	'52	TD	?	F	MG	L-4	J. N. Gray	
10	✓	6	Price, Joseph	108	Morris	'52	Minor	?	F	Morris	L-4	J. Price	
11	✓	6	Beck, Harry, Jr.	125	Siata		GS	?	H	Fiat	L-4	P. Hessler	
12	DNF	4	du Pont, Alexis	75	Cooper	'51	F3	?	I	Triumph		A. du Pont	Hand-pushed car to finish line
			Lipe, Gordon	32	Cooper	'51	F3	?	I			G. Lipe	Stalled at Archie Smith Corner
			Weaver, George	26	Maserati	'36	V8RI	Red +	B	Maserati	V-8	G. Weaver	"Poison'Lil"/Sparkplug failure
		2	Cade, Phillip	34	Maserati	'36	V8RI	?	B	Maserati	V-8	P. Cade	Not supercharged/Black-flagged: oil loss
		0	Linton, Otto	112	Siata		GS	?	G	Fiat	L-4	O. Linton	
17	DNS		Hannaway, Bret	91	Maserati	'39	8CTF	Purple	C	Maserati	L-8	B. Hannaway	Spun out and stalled in practice laps
			Irish, Richard	35	Kieft	'51	F3	?	I			R. Irish	
			Mauron, Richard	126	MG	'52	TD	?	F	MG	L-4	R. Mauron	Crashed in RR crossing haybale chicane
			Milliken, William F., Jr.	24	Special	'47	AJB 4WD	?	B	Steyr	V-8	W. Milliken	"Butterball" - Crashed in practice laps

Watkins Glen 1952 Queen Catharine Cup — Entry List and Results — September 20, 1952

Place	Status	Laps	Driver	No.	Manufacturer	MY	Model	Color	C.	Engine	Type	Owner	Race Notes
1	✓	10	Spear, William	82	OSCA	'52	MT4	Red	F	OSCA	L-4	W. Spear	
2	✓	10	Kimberly, Jim	57	OSCA	'52	MT4	Red	F	OSCA	L-4	J. Kimberly	
3	✓	10	Barlow, Roger	62	Simca	'52	Special	Blue	F	Simca	L-4	R. Barlow	
4	✓	10	Hoan, Thomas	59	MG	'50	TC	?	E	MG	L-4	T. Hoan	
5	✓	10	Lloyd, William	81	MG	'50	TC	?	F	Offy	L-4	W. Lloyd	
6	✓	10	Koster, Fritz	76	Porsche	'51	356 Coupe	Silver	F	Porsche	F-4	F. Koster	
7	✓	10	Procter, Fred	43	Porsche	'51	356 Coupe	Silver	F	Porsche	F-4	F. Procter	
8	✓	10	Magenheimer, Robert	41	MG	'50	TC	?	F	MG	L-4	R. Magenheimer	
9	✓	10	Fergus, Robert	38	MG	'50	TC	?	F	MG	L-4	R. Fergus	Winner of Collins Trophy for fastest MG
10	✓	10	Gent, Richard	58	Cisitalia		GS	?	F	Fiat	L-4	R. Gent	
11	✓	10	Allen, Fred	63	MG	'50	TC	?	F	MG	L-4	F. Allen	
12	✓	10	Thorpe, LeRoy	16	Porsche	'51	356 Roadster	?	F	Porsche	F-4	W. B. Lloyd	
13	✓	10	Thompson, Dr. Richard	84	MG	'52	TD	?	F	MG	L-4	R. Thompson	
14	✓	10	Cornett, Denver, Jr.	7	MG	'47	TC	Silver +	F	MG	L-4	D. Cornett	
15	✓	10	Devaney, Charles	45	MG	'51	TD	?	F	MG	L-4	C. Devaney	
16	✓	10	Plaisted, John	78	MG	'51	TD	?	F	MG	L-4	J. Plaisted	Winner Class G
17	✓	9	Vilardi, Gandolph	4	Crosley		Hotshot	?	H			C. Poole	Winner Class H
18	✓	9	Wessells, Henry, III	69	Siata		Roadster	?	H	Fiat	L-4	H. Wessels	
19	✓	9	Ash, David	46	MG	'51	Special	?	F	MG	L-4	D. Ash	
20	✓	9	McRae, Duncan	109	MG	'52	TD	?	F	MG	L-4	D. McRae	
21	✓	9	Ogilvie, Reg. R.	56	MG	'50	TC	?	F	MG	L-4	E. R. Ogilvie	
22	✓	9	Goldman, Max	37	Siata		Roadster	Red	F	Fiat	L-4	M. Goldman	
23	✓	9	Newcombe, John	47	MG	'50	TC	?	F	MG	L-4	J. Newcombe	
24	✓	9	Harris, Ben F.	51	MG	'52	TD	?	F	MG	L-4	B. F. Harris	
25	✓	9	Scatchard, Thomas	52	Siata		Roadster	?	H	Fiat	L-4	T. Scatchard	
26	✓	9	Puckett, James	42	MG	'50	TC	?	F	MG	L-4	J. Puckett	
27	✓	8	Rudkin, Henry	49	Crosley		Hotshot	?	G			H. Rudkin	
28	✓	8	Saunders, William, III	61	MG	'51	TC	?	F	MG	L-4	W. Saunders	
29	DNF	8	Pauley, James	39	Siata		Roadster	?	F	Fiat	L-4	J. Pauley	
			Stetson, Hal B.	64	Crosley		Hotshot	?	G			H. B. Stetson	
		7	Hitchcock, Robert	68	MG	'50	TC	?	F	MG	L-4	R. Hitchcock	Spun and quit at Archie Smith Corner
		6	Dominiani, Francis	79	Giaur	'52	Sport	?	H	Fiat	L-4	F. Dominiani	Spun at Big Bend and broke wheel
			Sanderson, George	65	Crosley		Hotshot	?	H			D. Sauvigne	
		5	Merrill, Roger	72	Siata		Roadster	?	F	Fiat	L-4	R. Merrill	
		4	Gillespie, Robert G.	98	MG	'52	Special	?	F	MG	L-4	R. G. Gillespie	
		3	Allen, David	83	MG	'51	TC	?	F	MG	L-4	D. Allen	Oil line broke
			Cunningham, B. S., III	73	Porsche	'51	356 Coupe	Silver	F	Porsche	F-4	Cunningham	Throttle linkage broke
		2	Schrafft, George	17	Crosley		F-S	?	H			G. Schrafft	Gas line broke
39	DNS		Hill, Logan	71	Siata		Roadster	?	F	Fiat	L-4	L. Hill	Mechanical breakdown before race
			Pompeo, Anthony	67	Siata		Roadster	?	F	Fiat	L-4	A. Pompeo	Withdrawn

Watkins Glen 1952 Grand Prix — Entry List and Results — September 20, 1952

Place	Status	Laps	Driver	No.	Manufacturer	MY	Model	Color	C.	Engine	Type	Owner	Race Notes
0	--	1	Atkins, Guy	18	MG		TC Superch.	?	E	MG	L-4	G. Atkins	
			Bentley, John	107	Jaguar	'51	XK-120	?	C	Jaguar	L-6	J. Bentley	
			Carson, James	97	MG		TC Superch.	?	E	MG	L-4	J. Carson	
			Cunningham, Briggs S.	53	Cunningham	'52	C-4R	White +	B	Chrysler	V-8	Cunningham	
			Dietrich, Charles	48	MG		TC Superch.	?	E	MG	L-4	C. Dietrich	
			Edmison, Robert	27	Jaguar	'52	XK-120	?	C	Jaguar	L-6	D. Witz	
			Felton, Col. George	101	Jaguar	'52	XK-120	?	C	Jaguar	L-6	G. Felton	
			Fitch, John	54	Cunningham	'52	C-4R	White +	B	Chrysler	V-8	Cunningham	
			Flynn, Chester	31	Jaguar	'52	XK-120	?	C	Jaguar	L-6	C. Flynn	
			Fuller, Erwin	117	Lea-Francis	'50	Type Sport	?	D	Lea-Fran.	L-4	A. Iselin, Jr.	
			Gegen, Bob	19	Aston Martin	'50	DB2	?	D	A-M	L-6	D. Hirsch	
			Gordon, Bennet, C.	13	MG		TC Superch.	?	E	MG	L-4	C. Gordon Bennett	
			Gray, Preston	14	Allard		J2	?	B	Cadillac	V-8	P. Gray	
			Grey, Harry	93	Nardi		Cadillac Special	?	B	Cadillac	V-8	P. Fina	
			Hannaway, Bret H.	92	Special	'39	Riley-Mercury	Blue	C	Mercury	V-8	B. Hannaway	Formerly "Ardent Alligator"
			Harris, George R., III	3	Allard		J2	?	B	Cadillac	V-8	G. R. Harris	
			Hill, Phil	2	Jaguar	'51	C-Type	Black	C	Jaguar	L-6	C. Hornburg	
			Johnson, Sherwood	31	Jaguar	'51	XK-120 LW	?	C	Jaguar	L-6	C. Hornburg	
			Knudson, Ralph	123	Excalibur	'51	J	?	C	Willys	L-6	B. Stevens	
			Linton, Otto	114	Siata	'52	Coupe V8	White	D	Fiat	V-8	O. Linton	
			Lunkin, Edmund	23	Ferrari	'49	166 MM	?	E	Ferrari	V-12	E. Lunkin	
			MacNaughton, Donald	116	Nash Healey	'52	Roadster	?	C	Nash	L-6	D. MacNaughton	
			McKenna, Trevor	12	Jaguar	'51	XK-120	?	C	Jaguar	L-6	T. McKenna	
			Moran, Charles, Jr.	89	Ferrari	'51	212 Export	?	D	Ferrari	V-12	C. Moran	
			Negley, John	94	Allard		J2	?	B	Chrysler	V-8	J. Negley	
			O'Hare, Frank	95	Nash Healey	'52	Roadster	?	C	Nash	L-6	F. O'Hare	
			Patterson, Allan	127	Jaguar	'52	XK-120	?	C	Jaguar	L-6	A. Patterson	
			Robbins, Irving	102	Cunningham	'51	C-2	Black	B	Chrysler	V-8	I. Robbins	
			Sabal, Joseph B.	7	Allard		J2	Red	B	Chrysler	V-8	J. B. Sabal	
			Schott, Charles	25	Jaguar	'52	XK-120	?	C	Jaguar	L-6	C. Schott	
			Soulas, Sr.	28	Maserati	'49	A6 GCS	?	E	Maserati	L-6	Sr. Soulas	
			Stiles, Phil	104	Jaguar	'52	XK-120	?	C	Jaguar	L-6	P. Stiles	
			Timmins, Paul	87	Jaguar	'50	XK-120	?	C	Jaguar	L-6	P. Timmins	
			Tobin, E. J.	21	BMW		328	?	D	?		J. Tobin	
			Wacker, Fred	8	Allard		J2	Red	B	Cadillac	V-8	F. Wacker	Car in accident
			Walters, Phil	1	Cunningham	'52	C-4RK	White +	B	Chrysler	V-8	Cunningham	
			Warner, Fred	9	Allard		J2	?	B	Cadillac	V-8	F. Warner	
			Wilder, Robert	6	Allard		J2 Ardun	?	B	Ford	V-8	R. Wilder	
			Wyllie, M. R. J.	124	Jaguar	'52	XK-120	?	C	Jaguar	L-6	M. R. J. Wyllie	